Listening for Echoes

FINDING HOPE IN THE DARKEST HOURS

PAM SAFFRAN

3Ducklings Publishing LLC.

No portion of this publication may be reproduced, distributed, or transmitted in any format without express written consent of the publisher, except for the use of brief quotations in book reviews as permitted by copyright law.

3Ducklings Publishing LLC
P.O. Box 2284
Winter Park, Florida 32790-2284

www.pamsaffran.com

Copyright ©2017

ISBN-10:0-9989262-0-5
ISBN-13:978-0-9989262-0-9

First Edition

Printed in the United States of America

Produced by Hannah Forman and Designed by Miki Hickel of Speed Banana Media. http://speedbananamedia.com

TABLE OF CONTENTS

AUTHOR'S NOTE

Everyone has a battle to fight. Some are more obvious than others. Often, they are battles we do not choose.

Mine was fighting to save my husband's life. He was diagnosed with cancer at the same time my mother was in a coma and near death. Suddenly, the tethers that had kept me grounded were cut loose. It was a cruel one-two punch.

The battles that choose us make us who we are and influence how we perceive the world. The challenges and obstacles they present can make us better or simply bitter. If we can find our inner strength, we can do things we never imagined.

My story is about how resilience and determination can keep you moving forward, regardless of the roadblocks that seem impossible to pass. What I have learned from my journey, and continue to learn, is to embrace the pain.

Learn from it, absorb it, and let it be a part of you. Let your pain motivate and fuel you to be a better, more compassionate, grateful, and sensitive person, parent, and friend. The ups and downs are part of life. We don't have a lot of time on this planet, so you shouldn't waste it. Time is precious.

Hopefully, my journey will inspire you to live a life of happiness with no regret. Loss happens to everyone. No one is immune.

*   *   *

The events in this book are factual, but some names have been changed.

Chapter One | Blindsided

It was a lovely spring day in Orlando, with sunny skies and temperatures in the low eighties.

But it was lost on me. I was inside, pacing another semicircle around the raised bed in the frigid ICU, wondering why it was so cold in there and staring at Mom's turbaned bandages. They made her head appear twice its size.

"It's a good thing Dorrie's in a coma, because the sounds of all these machines beeping and clicking to keep her alive would drive her crazy."

"That's terrible, Pam," said my sister Caroline, "but it's probably true."

It was a terrible thing to say, but I'd never been one to sit around holding my tongue. With death threatening my mother from the sidelines, I'd put my best game face on. I had to act as if the situation was under control, as if my mother's survival was a given, rather than an uncertainty. I didn't want to admit to anyone—not to my sisters, not to my husband or kids, not even to myself—how afraid I was of losing her. So, I kept my words and focus upbeat.

"She'd be even more upset about having her head shaved for the craniotomy—and about having to lie still," I said.

"That's definitely true," my ten-year-old daughter Ella spoke up from her homework. "Grandma's always busy."

Then, the call came. The call that would change not only my life, but the lives of my children. It was from my husband, Alan.

"Get the kids and come home, Pam. We need to have a family meeting."

This wasn't like him. My hand tightened around the phone. "Alan, what's wrong?"

"It's stage IV pancreatic cancer. I've got maybe six months. I'm a dead man walking."

I screamed. "What?" My heart jackhammered. "No! It can't be. This isn't right. It can't be!"

I must have handed the phone to Caroline—my hands were empty when she shrieked, echoing my denial. "No, it can't be! No!"

My knees hit the ground before I knew I'd fallen.

I crawled, like a baby, toward my mother, propelled by instinct. Crawled beneath the stainless steel of her hospital bed. Screamed, "Mom, wake up! Mom, I need your help. Wake up!"

I needed my mom. But under her bed, without a response, was as close as I could get. Of all the times I'd needed her, this day, April 8, 2013, was when I needed her the most. She'd never left my side in the fifteen years she'd lived with us. She'd been there when I was too ill with the Epstein-Barr virus to take care of myself. She'd been like a second mother to each of our babies. She'd eased me through debilitating panic attacks. But this...this was the most critical time.

And my mother, my rock, wasn't available.

I don't remember wailing, but Caroline later told me I did, over and over, "I can't lose them both!"

My heart skipped. Stopped.

The shock was basic. Elemental. I wasn't in my body while it slipped into survival mode, just to stay alive. I couldn't think about, or process, or feel what was going on. I wasn't there anymore.

I wasn't anywhere.

Chapter Two | Are You Single?

The day I met Alan, I was waiting for a flight to take me to New York for my five-year college reunion.

I had expected a crowd for the five o'clock flight to LaGuardia that Friday afternoon in June, but only a handful of passengers waited at the gate inside Orlando International Airport. I dropped my purse, carry-on, and tennis racket by a pair of isolated seats.

I smoothed a wrinkle in my silk pants. I'd asked a guy friend for a lift to the airport, so I'd gussied myself up for the trip. I wanted to look better than I usually appeared when I wasn't at work. My ride wasn't a boyfriend—I'd been too busy finishing my master's program and starting a new job for any serious relationships—but that didn't mean I didn't want to impress him.

I'd washed and brushed my hair. I'd even applied makeup and dressed in a cute little button-up, black silk, scoop-neck blouse.

I thought I'd be the only one dressed up at the end of the workweek, but not long after I arrived, a man in a jacket and khaki slacks approached.

He looked so nice, my first thought was, "Why is he dressed up for a Friday evening flight?"

My second thought on his approach was, "What the hell?"

The well-groomed man appeared not to notice the sparsity of passengers. He walked straight over to my row of chrome-connected chairs.

With all these empty seats, why is he sitting right beside me?

The waiting area was wide open; it was weird that he came over to these two little chairs paired with each other, where one was already occupied—by me.

He settled into place beside me. Instead of speaking or even making eye contact, though, he pulled out a thick, tan book and turned the pages with deliberation.

I didn't know what to think. I was put off by his choice of location. Didn't he respect the unwritten traveler's rule of giving fellow passengers as much space as possible?

I glanced at him from the corner of my eye as he read. Sure, his clean-cut good looks would have been impossible to ignore if I'd been in the market for romance, but I wasn't.

I wondered about the book he was reading. The enormous tome looked heavy, more like a textbook than the paperbacks most travelers prefer. Something about it seemed familiar. I tipped my head to better examine the faded brown, scholarly-looking cover.

"Oh, my gosh. You're reading that. I thought I'd never see it again. I can't believe you're reading that book."

He turned toward me, one eyebrow raised. "You've read *The Evolution of Consciousness?*"

"I just finished it for my master's program at Rollins. Are you reading it for a class?"

"Oh, no. This—" he held up the volume "—is for pure enjoyment. It's my second read."

I snickered, certain he was joking.

"I can't imagine anyone reading Robert Ornstein for pleasure," I said. "I thought it was grueling. I only read it because I had to, and I didn't understand a word of what he was trying to say. I was elated to be done with it."

He closed the book and smiled as he extended his hand.

"Hi. I'm Alan."

"Pam."

Right then and there my palm tingled, even after he released it, as if an invisible charge like a thread of electrical current stretched between us.

He chuckled, then asked, "Where are you flying today?"

"My five-year college reunion. I'm getting together with the people from my class and my...with various friends."

I didn't want to explain further.

"What about you?"

"I'm going to visit my dad. He's having some health problems after his hip replacement, so I want to check in with him. And it's my brother's birthday."

Whoa—this guy has great values.

I wasn't looking to start a relationship with anyone, but in spite of that, I couldn't stop myself from thinking, "This guy is really...he's just too smart for me."

But he was so engaging, I didn't care.

"Do you play tennis?"

His question surprised me—it wasn't the sort of thing a person randomly asks fellow travelers—until I noticed his examination of my racket cover. Its shape was a giveaway.

I nodded and smiled. "Mm-hmm. Yes, I do."

But that's all I said on the matter.

"I don't think I've ever met anyone who took a tennis racket to their college reunion."

"Some of my..."

I started to say teammates, but caught myself. I had been the first tennis All-American at Skidmore College in Saratoga Springs, New York.

"Some of my friends like to play when we get together."

I didn't want to think about, much less reveal, how much—or how well—I played. This man, as interesting as he was, didn't need to know whenever I returned to New York my coach at Skidmore had me play someone for fun.

The loudspeaker interrupted my thoughts with a call to start boarding. This was 1992, when airlines would take a handful of people on an otherwise empty plane. Fewer than a dozen of us rose to board; we probably formed the world's shortest boarding queue ever to fly on a commercial Boeing. Alan followed as I handed my ticket to the woman guarding the doorway to the boarding ramp.

Our footsteps thumped down the long, accordion-walled corridor to the plane. From behind me, he asked, "Hey, are you single?"

Chapter Three | Too Much to Process

Caroline's frantic voice came to me somewhere in a distant blur. She was talking to our sister Maryann.

"What the hell am I going to do? Alan's going to die, and Mom's in a coma, and Pam's under the bed, and you're in Boston. What are we going to do? ...OK, Maryann. A few hours. Thank you."

My body slid across the slick, stone-cold floor as someone pulled it—me—out from under our mother's bed.

After my initial outburst, I couldn't say anything. My thoughts were trapped, locked in a single loop.

This can't be happening. My mom's dying, and now my husband's dying. This can't be happening.

Strong hands lifted me into a wheelchair and pushed me to the front of the hospital. I don't remember getting into my car. Thank god Caroline was there to drive us home. Somehow, with Ella's help, she figured out the turns while I breathed into a paper bag. I was in no shape to help them navigate. I couldn't think (let alone say) as much as "go left" or "turn right."

*   *   *

As I boarded the plane for my reunion, Alan's question, straight out of the blue, kept bouncing around in my head. "Are you single?"

My heart galloped. This was after all of five minutes of conversation. Ten, at most.

Hadn't this handsome, professionally-dressed man at the gate just been making polite conversation? Or had he been flirting with me?

As I neared the door of the plane, I looked over my shoulder at him and said, "You know what? I am single, but I really don't have time for a relationship. I have a lot going on right now. I'm applying to PhD programs. I'm just incredibly busy."

He nodded and smiled.

I faced forward and squeezed my way through the narrow aisle, wondering as I passed row after row of open seats whether I should have answered him that way. I'd already been thinking (in the back of my mind, before he asked) that I'd like a relationship—with someone like him.

My answer, I realized, had been more my mother's words than my own. Dorrie had ground into me—and into each of my three sisters—that we had to prioritize training for our chosen careers, occupations she'd guided us into. She used to fight about it with Dad.

"I want Renaissance children," my dad argued. "I want them to be good at many different things."

"No," Dorrie insisted. "That's not what we're doing. Our girls are going to specialize. They're going to be exceptionally skilled at one thing. It's too hard to be good at many things— they won't be. But our daughters are going to be *good* so they can be self-sufficient. I don't want them to ever have to rely on a man, the way the women of my generation had to."

Over and over, she'd drilled that message into us.

"You have to focus," I remember her saying, "and really excel at one thing, whether it's basket weaving, tennis, or becoming an architect."

I sighed as I stowed my racket and bags, both deeply grateful and slightly resentful of my mother for being so ahead of her time. Nobody else thought that way back when we were kids, but she'd pushed us in that direction all our lives.

There were so few passengers that we could sit anywhere, and we chose to be as far apart as possible.

All of us but one.

There was Alan, bypassing empty rows, relocating in my direction. For the second time that day, he sat in the seat beside mine, this time grinning right at me.

"Tell me about your master's program, Pam."

Too surprised to say or do anything else, I told him of my studies in psychology, how my mother had always acknowledged my empathetic nature and told me I'd make a good therapist.

When I finally stopped talking, he asked about my work. I told him about my contract with Orange County Public Schools.

"I hope the funding never runs out. I love counseling the kids and their families."

"What ages?"

"Middle through high school. And it's from a really diverse part of the county. We've got families speaking eighty languages in the high school alone."

"Whew." He shook his head. "What kind of counseling do you do?"

"Just about everything."

I laughed as I thought of the pile of files sitting on my desk over the weekend.

"But what do you do, Alan? You haven't told me anything about yourself—except that you read indecipherable textbooks for pleasure."

As he laughed, his eyes lit up as bright as his smile. "I finished my otolaryngology residency at the University of Virginia not long ago."

"Oto-what?"

"Otolaryngology—most people call it ENT for ear, nose, and throat medicine."

"Oh, yeah. So, you're a doctor here..." I paused, realizing we were somewhere midway between Florida and New York. "I mean, back in Orlando?"

He nodded.

"That's right. I just bought a partnership in a Central Florida practice that's been around about nine years."

He was easier to talk to than I would have guessed by the weighty book that first broke the ice between us. We talked through the entire two-and-a-half-hour flight.

He really wasn't my type at all. Most of the men I'd socialized with were sun-bleached, sports-sculpted athletes, rather than academics. Although Alan was fit and trim, and his dark hair and unlined face were attractive enough, it was his intellect that placed him miles above anyone I'd ever known.

When the flight attendant delivered our landing instructions, my mind wandered.

Too bad this wasn't an international flight.

It was time to part ways. Alan pulled a card from his wallet and held it out to me; it displayed the logo of his medical practice.

"Do you have a business card with you, Pam?"

"Why yes, I do," I tried to sound nonchalant as I dug into my bag, grinning. I was proud of the shiny new business cards I'd tucked into my purse, largely in anticipation of sharing them with my college teammates. I had a great job in my field and couldn't wait to tell them about it.

There were moments I still had to remind myself what I'd accomplished.

"You have a master's in counseling, Pam. You're actually a therapist," I'd tell myself in the mirror.

Of course, there were no cell phones back then, so I said, "Here's my work number," as I gave him my embossed card.

Pulling my bags behind me on my way out of the terminal, I felt a ridiculous clash between professional pride and girlish elation. On the one hand, as a newly licensed psychologist, I'd traded business cards with an up-and-coming local physician. On the other hand, I'd exchanged phone numbers with an attractive, eligible man who'd expressed interest in my availability.

I knew I wouldn't call him; I was too busy. And although I thought the guy was great, I was sure I'd never see him again.

Chapter Four | She Has to Get Better

With my mother comatose in the hospital bed, it was hard to imagine that, only a few days earlier, she had driven herself down from her vacation house in Sea Island, Georgia. Our eighty-year-old mother had worked all day alongside our handyman, making repairs and preparing the place for renting to summer tourists.

"I don't feel so well," Mom said to me. "I just had a thunderclap headache."

I didn't know what the hell that meant, but it didn't sound good.

"Maybe you should try to get some rest."

"Nonsense. I'm not missing Grandparent's Day at the boys' school. I'll be there."

There was no talking her out of it. While Miles and Nat attended Trinity Preparatory School in Winter Park, Dorrie seldom missed the huge annual event. This year the boys' forensics speeches would be among the showcases.

True to her nature, she'd worked through the next day too—before making the more than three-hour drive to our home in Winter Park, near Orlando. She was so tired when she arrived, she'd gone straight to bed.

In the morning, Alan saw the pain in her face as he prepared to drive her and the boys to Grandparent's Day on his way to the office.

"I don't think your mom's ready to go," he said.

Never one to take a day off work over the inconvenience of the mysterious stomachaches he had been experiencing, Alan insisted his patients take better care of themselves.

"Go back to bed, Dorrie," he urged her. "You should rest."

She did, sleeping through most of Wednesday. And Thursday. When I couldn't awaken her, I'd taken her to the nearest emergency room, where they found nothing wrong.

Nothing, that is, until her jumbled words set off alarms that led them to discover bleeding in her brain.

They'd rushed her to the bigger, more comprehensive Florida Hospital main campus north of downtown Orlando.

Early Saturday morning, a neurosurgery team opened her skull and repaired the ruptured blood vessel—but in the course of the six-hour operation, they found another six aneurysms that could burst at any time.

Now, two days into the critical ten-day post-op wait-and-watch window, we stayed with her night and day, making sure she got the best care possible.

She had to get better. The kids needed their grandmother, who'd lived with us most of their lives. I needed her, because she'd always been there for me, and I couldn't imagine anything worse than managing my hectic life without her support.

She had to get better.

That's when my phone buzzed inside my purse, and I crossed the room to retrieve it, grateful my steps had a purpose. I glanced at the caller ID as I answered. "Hi, honey. Do you want me to go to the store and get some Pepto-Bismol? What did the doctor say?"

*　　*　　*

The boys reached home for our family meeting before we did. A friend—I don't know who—went and got them, because Miles wasn't driving yet. I sat, curled into myself, trying to regain composure.

Then Alan walked through the door.

We hugged and cried, Alan and I, clinging to one another. The kids joined us in a fierce family hug. Hugging and crying, crying and hugging. We held onto each other as if letting go would be the worst thing in the world. As if nothing else could hurt us as much.

When I regained the ability to speak, it came out as a protest.

"There has to be some kind of mistake. You're healthy. You can't be dying of cancer."

"I saw the CT scan myself, Pam. There are thirty-four tumors in my liver alone, and a five-centimeter mass—bigger than a golf ball—in my pancreas."

I didn't want to believe him, but my husband never exaggerated.

"We have to sit down and talk. We need a family meeting."

Caroline gave Alan a quick, brief greeting and then left to busy herself elsewhere in the house, giving us privacy.

Alan directed us into the family room—Alan, our three kids, and me. We settled around him on the sofa, and Alan wasted no time bullshitting us with false hope, opting instead to be as up-front with the kids as he was with me from the get-go.

"I know this is hard," he said, "but I'm not going to be here in six months."

We couldn't let that harsh pronouncement stand unchallenged. Our words tumbled over each other.

"No, don't say that!"

"It can't be that bad, Dad. It just can't."

"People can fight this and win, can't they, Alan? It happens, right?"

He shook his head 'no,' even while he acceded, the first word drawn out much longer than necessary.

"Yes...some patients last three years..." When he saw the look of hope on my face, he interrupted himself. "...But some only make it another five weeks or less. I've got six months."

Alan patiently, but firmly, shushed our cries of disbelief.

"I've been thinking about it ever since I saw the scan. There are three things I really want you to do when I am gone."

I couldn't stop myself.

"You shouldn't be talking like that, Alan. We're going to fight this."

"This is important to me, Pam. Please. I need to say it. One: I want you kids to stay Jewish." He looked at each of our children, holding their eyes until they nodded.

"Two: I want to make sure you and the kids are taken care of, Pam, that you're going to be able to support them." Again, he looked around our circle, this time including me. "With all of their educational expenses, the same way we've always planned, even though I won't be here to help."

"Three: I want you to be happy again, Pam." Alan took both my hands in his. "You have to promise me you'll be OK."

I shook my head, even as my words agreed.

"I promise, Alan, but we're not gonna deal with any of those things for a long time." Alan thought he knew his immediate future, but I had to hope, had to believe he was wrong. He was *not* going to die.

Chapter Five | Dumb Luck?

It was my college reunion. I couldn't help regaling friends and teammates with my story of the handsome stranger on the plane.

Privately, I thought, "Wouldn't it be nice if..."

But I doubted anything would come of it. I was sure I'd never see him again.

Meanwhile, my friends and I partied at the reunion; everybody got drunk—it was our first time together in five years. As a result, my friend who was driving me to the airport the next morning overslept, and showed up an hour and a half late. I threw my bags in the trunk and slammed the door as I thundered into the car.

"I can't believe it's this late," I said. "There's no way we're going to make it on time."

"Don't worry about it, Pam. You'll get there OK."

"I'm going to miss my flight."

"You can always catch the next one."

"Easy for you to say," I grumbled.

I shuffled my luggage through the reservations line at LaGuardia. As I feared, I missed my flight. Now I hoped the airline had a seat available on the next one.

There were significantly more people at the gate leaving New York than there were on my way there—everybody comes to Orlando in the summer.

"The flight is pretty full," the ticket agent said, "so you'll have to take whatever seat I can scrounge up for you."

"I don't care where I sit. You can put me in the baggage compartment or let me hang from a wing, as long as I can get on the next plane."

"Pam? Is that you?"

I turned at the man's voice.

"Alan! Is this your flight back?"

He stepped up beside me as the woman across the counter said, "You're in luck, Ms. Thompson. I've got you confirmed for this flight in seat 13F."

"That is lucky," said Alan, showing me his seat assignment. "I'm in 13G."

We talked all the way to the baggage claim area in Orlando.

Back then, airport security wouldn't chase drivers away for parking curbside at the baggage claim area; I'd arranged for my mother to pick me up there. I asked Alan to watch my luggage while I went to see whether she'd arrived ahead of me.

There she was. "Mom, I'm glad you're here. I'll be right back. Let me just go run to get my luggage. I met this nice guy on the plane, and he's watching it for me."

Dorrie craned her neck back and forth looking around me. As I turned to go back inside, her eyes all but shouted, "Hmm...I wonder who she met?"

I thanked Alan for watching my bags.

"It was great talking with you," I said. "That was one of the best flights I've ever had."

I extended my hand to say goodbye, again feeling a connection to this man—a stronger, more tangible thread than the first time we'd parted. Even so, and although we'd exchanged business cards and work numbers, I knew this was it.

He's leagues beyond you, Pam.

I dragged my luggage and footsteps away from Alan. Still, I couldn't help smiling at Dorrie. She was beaming at me through the car and airport windows.

I slid my suitcase and tennis racket into the back of her car, and heard her say something.

"What did you say, Mom?"

"Get in the car, Pam. What I said was, 'That's the man you're gonna marry.'"

*   *   *

Mom had arrived from Sea Island a few days earlier, and I decided to get my hair done after dropping Ella off at Park Maitland School. It had been six months—way too long! By ten o'clock, I was fully coiffed and walking into the house.

"I'm home, Mom."

She'd been up and moving around a bit when Ella and I left, but Dorrie didn't reply to my call. It didn't take long to figure out why—she was sound asleep on the family room sofa.

"Mom. Dorrie, what are you doing sleeping in here?"

She didn't budge.

I set my things down, got a drink of water, and tried again, this time nudging her shoulder. When I finally succeeded in rousing her, she covered her eyes with her arm.

"Wha-what's going on?" She was so groggy, she sounded almost drugged.

"Mom, are you OK?"

"I have a terrible headache. I drove over to the walk-in clinic..."

"You did what? You could hardly walk all week, and you *drove* somewhere?"

"I went to that place down the street."

For the first time, I noticed the prescription bottles spread out on the coffee table.

"Why didn't you wait for me to take you?"

"You're busy. I didn't want to bother you."

"Mom..."

"So, I went to the clinic." Her words were mumbled, but she persisted, though at a maddening, plodding pace. "They said I have a bad sinus infection, and I have to take these antibiotics, but I do think...I need to...see Alan..."

She fell asleep while talking.

I called Alan's office and got his nurse to put me through to him, even though he was seeing a patient.

"Honey, Dorrie wants to come see you. She's mumbling and telling me she thinks she has a sinus infection. Now I can't wake her up again."

"For God's sake, listen, Pam. She doesn't have a sinus infection. If she did, don't you think I'd have seen signs of it over the past few days?"

"You weren't around her very much this week."

"Forget about earlier. If she's that out of it, don't bring her to me. She's eighty years old. Take her straight to the emergency room. I'll call and talk to the triage team, and I'll speak to the doctor on call. But you need to take her over there now, and I mean NOW."

I coaxed Dorrie upright and to her feet, but she moved barely beyond crawling. Even her speech seemed in slow motion.

And that wasn't my fiery mother's way at all.

"My head," she said over and over, holding it in her hands the whole way. "My head is killing me."

As ill as she acted, she was still as independent as ever. She inched her way to the car on her own, not letting me hold or steady her.

We got Dorrie inside the car, and I stepped from the garage into the house for her bag. My cell phone rang as I put my leg in the car. It was Ligia Bottinelli, one of my tennis teammates, checking up on the roster I was putting together for the area's USTA's 5.0 pros summer league. I'd spent weeks setting it up, and had finally persuaded Elissa DeCampio, the number one singles player from

Rollins, to complete our team.

"Ligia, I can't talk right now. I'm taking my mom to the emergency room. I'll have to get back with you, but Elissa signed on, so we'll have a team for the summer."

My summer league would have to wait—longer than I could have imagined.

I floored the accelerator past the posted speed limits, leaving all thoughts of tennis behind.

Chapter Six | One at a Time

After our heart-wrenching family meeting with Alan, we took a walk through the neighborhood, something we never did at four o'clock in the afternoon. It was eighty degrees, but with a cool breeze. I picked flowers along the way; tiny purple tea roses, miniature white lilies, and fragrant jasmine.

As I walked alongside Alan and the kids, I couldn't help thinking, "God, what a beautiful day—for such a shitty time like this. How can we live? And how can my husband believe he's going to be dead in six months?"

While wandering the neighborhood, we ran into a neighbor, Joanne Miller, whose four kids' ages overlapped ours in school. We'd been to their house for dinner parties. She and her children were also Alan's patients.

"Saffrans!" she called out. "My gosh, what a pleasant surprise to see everyone, even Dr. Saffran, out here together in the middle of the day."

Little did she know.

As if nothing were wrong, I said, "Oh, it's great to see you," but I didn't stop. My feet kept going. I could not, would not let them slow, not letting myself admit our first daytime stroll together might be the beginning of the end.

We all walked on.

Alan took our kids by the hand, one at a time, and advanced a few feet ahead of the rest of us, speaking privately to each for a few minutes. I watched them holding hands with their dad as they ambled side by side.

With every footfall I thought, "This can't be happening."

Then father and child allowed the rest of us to catch up to them. We stepped together before Alan released that child's hand and took another, again walking several feet ahead of us.

It was my turn, just the two of us side by side. Alan didn't say much. When he broke the silence, he said, "I have six months. I think I should just do palliative care. With hospice, I can..."

"You can't, Alan." I was born a fighter, and I'd been trained never to give up. I didn't care if I sounded more fierce than supportive. "You've got to fight, we've got to fight."

"It's not gonna happen, Pam. I'm not gonna live."

Impossible. I would battle to keep him living and breathing.

"Don't think that way. There's got to be a solution. I'm not losing you."

"You're right." He sighed. "I've got to fight this. We're gonna fight this, Pam."

His hand tightened around mine, and he never spoke of settling for palliative care again.

But he was a doctor. He knew. He knew what a long shot it would be. How hard it would be.

"I'm not going back to work."

"I think that sounds like a good idea." I didn't yet realize all it would take to fight his cancer, but I understood we had a battle in front of us, and it would demand every waking hour.

*　*　*

Two days after my chance flight back from New York with Alan, my work phone rang.

"Pam, this is Alan. Alan Saffran. We met in the airport and flew together over the weekend?"

I grinned at the absurdity of his reminder, as if I could have forgotten all about him since Sunday.

"Would you like to have dinner at Jordan's Grove with me this Friday?"

I couldn't fully believe he'd actually called me. I stammered into the phone, "Yes, OK, that'd be nice." Nice? I chastised myself, as I heard him chuckle.

Can't you think up something more clever than that?

"You know, it wasn't easy calling you today."

"Why not?"

He seemed so confident and self-assured. I couldn't imagine what might have been difficult about it.

"Because I wanted to call you yesterday. I forced myself to wait a whole day so I wouldn't come across as pushy, but I was afraid to wait any longer than that."

I laughed loud enough to evoke a raised eyebrow from the work partner sharing my office. That Alan wanted to call even sooner sent warmth into my cheeks. I couldn't get through the week fast enough.

As Alan opened the car door for me that night, the butterflies in my stomach told me how important this date was. It felt like beginning the third set of a championship match with one unlaced shoe and a half-strung racket.

On the plane, our conversations felt natural. But flying alongside a new, temporary acquaintance wasn't the same as interacting in real day-to-day life. I wondered whether that effortless flow would carry into the closer confines of his car and then within the restaurant.

I needn't have worried. From the moment he picked me up, he was as attentive and complimentary as before. He kept telling me how pretty I was, how nice I was, how much he enjoyed talking with me. From anyone else, it might have come across as too much, but Alan exuded sincerity. He focused on me as if nobody else existed.

And yet, inside the restaurant it wasn't just me. As the old restaurant's 1920s plank floors creaked under our feet, Alan remained attentive to me while also acting in tune with the people around us. He treated the restaurant staff with genuine respect.

This guy is a catch. He's smart and sensitive. He's almost unbelievable.

After the waitress took our orders, Alan turned his full attention back to me.

"I want to know more about you, Pam. Who you really are on the inside. Tell me about where you grew up."

"We lived in Cincinnati. The best way to describe my childhood is idyllic. My sisters and I were privileged. Our parents gave us every opportunity we needed to help us reach our potential, but they made us work hard for it, too."

"Tell me about your sisters."

I chuckled. "There are four of us. We used to get into so much trouble."

"This sounds good."

"I'm the youngest, and we were all born about thirteen months apart within five years. By the time I was a teenager, our parents had four adolescent daughters in the house."

"That sounds chaotic."

Chapter Seven | 'Come Down, Come Now'

The frantic car ride with Dorrie seemed to take forever, even though Winter Park hospital was nearby. When we arrived, Dorrie's head hurt too much to fill out all the intake paperwork, so I rushed it through for her and she signed. Not long after, they ran an EKG and then a battery of other tests.

Between pokings and proddings, my mother wasn't her usual conversational self. Every time they woke her up for one more exam, she protested. "I'm just so tired."

We'd been there a while, waiting for test results, when Ligia called me back about the tennis tournament.

"Pam, when can we schedule our matches? We've got to get them in soon if we want to qualify for nationals again."

"Ligia, it looks like my mom is really sick. I think I'm gonna have to put this on hold. You guys go on and schedule without me for now."

I texted my sisters Maryann and Caroline, attaching pictures of Mom lying down. They both asked whether I thought they should come down, but I didn't have any answers for them.

At first the staff couldn't find anything wrong with Mom.

After at least two hours of testing and waiting, the doctor who'd first examined Dorrie pushed aside the curtain defining our waiting area.

"Your mother does have a UTI," she said, glancing through her notes, "and her blood pressure is a little high, but it's not bad. She'll need a prescription for antibiotics to fight the infection. Everything else is clear. After you sign the paperwork, we'll get you out of here so you can get this filled for her."

I reached for the printed prescription she offered, but before I could take it from her hand, Dorrie sat upright.

"Now, Pam," she said in a slurred voice, "have you been swimming? Nine-nine-nine, five-five-five-five-five, four-four-four-four-four..."

"Get the mobile CT scanner in here, stat!" the doctor yelled.

They wheeled in a huge machine. It made an ominous, deafening *ch-ching* sound as they took pictures of her head—of her brain—and then wheeled it back out. Sixty seconds later, six people in scrubs and lab coats filled the tiny room.

"She's got bleeding in her brain," her doctor said, "and she needs to be transported to Florida South, our main hospital, where the neurologists operate. Does she have an advanced directive?"

"A what?"

"Like a living will. Something to designate who makes decisions for her if she's unable to."

"I-I don't think so, but I don't know. I'm her daughter. I brought her here."

Before I knew how to continue, the doctor returned to Dorrie's bedside.

Bleeding in her brain.

I'd been concerned before, maybe even worried. But now I was scared.

"Yes," I texted my sisters. "Come down. Come now."

*   *   *

At dinner with Alan on our first date, I began to tell him about growing up on our estate in Cincinnati with four girls in the house.

"You have no idea, Alan."

I hesitated, not wanting to sound like I was bragging as I considered the size of the estate I grew up on. I came from a well-to-do family. It seemed too early in our relationship—if that's what this was becoming—to tell him about the horses and orchards and tennis court on the ten acres surrounding my 12,000-square-foot childhood home at Fairlea Farms.

"One night I was sound asleep when Mom slammed open my bedroom door at two o'clock in the morning," I told him. "I woke up and blinked against the light streaming in behind her, then more light as she hit the switch on the wall. I yelled, 'Mom, what is it?' as she rushed into the room and looked under my bed. She said, 'I heard something going on in here. It was an odd shuffling noise.'

"I pulled the covers up around me, freaked out that I hadn't heard something loud enough in my own room to rouse her from elsewhere in the house. Come to think of it, she must have been awake late in the TV room, just one room over from mine, or she'd never have heard it...Our house was..."

I grappled with the simplest way to understate the forty-five rooms she'd have to had searched before finding the source of the undefined sound.

"Our house was a big two-story."

Alan leaned forward, listening intently. "What was the noise?"

"The next place she looked was inside the bathroom, where she saw nothing. She crossed the room, threw open the closet door, turned on the light, and found one of my sister's boyfriends."

"Wait. Your sister's boyfriend was in your closet?"

"He was so scared. He kept saying, 'I'm sorry, Mrs. Thompson. I didn't know it was Pam's room. I thought it was Caroline's room,' as if that were any better. He'd climbed up the outside of our house and mistakenly crawled into my window. He kept repeating, 'I didn't mean to be in Pam's room, honest, Mrs. Thompson.'"

By now Alan was laughing with me.

"What did your mother do?"

"We all had to go downstairs and have a family meeting. With Scott—Caroline's boyfriend—and his parents. At two in the morning. To this day, I still defend myself to Dorrie. I still remind her it wasn't my fault. 'He's not my boyfriend,' I told her. 'He's Caroline's boyfriend!' After that incident, my parents installed a complicated alarm system that included the upstairs windows."

Alan laughed.

"I don't blame them. So, I assume that ended that kind of shenanigans?"

"Oh, no. Not too long after, probably before word of the alarm got around, another night my dad was out of town again, and my mother was packing for us to go on a skiing trip the next morning, around midnight the alarm shrieked, and Dorrie ..."

"Dorrie. Is that one of your sisters?"

"No. That's our mom. She always had us call her by her name."

"Sorry. Please go on."

"Anyway, Dorrie ran to the door of her bedroom and saw three boys running down the hallway. She called out, and between the bellowing alarm and her even louder yell, they skidded to a stop, too terrified of her not to do what she said."

"What happened?"

"She marched all three boys into the den downstairs and made them sit there, while one by one she called their parents—in front of them—to come pick them up."

"Was she furious?"

"She wasn't happy, mostly because she knew we had to get up early for our trip, but she never got really mad at any of us. She later told me she thought raising four pretty girls—and keeping the boys away from them—was like living a Broadway show. Most of it was funny to her."

"She sounds like an amazing mother. I'd like to meet her."

"You almost did. She saw you at the airport." I stopped myself.

No need to tell him what Dorrie said, Pam.

"You said one of your sisters is Caroline?"

"She's the one just older than me. And then there's Maryann, the oldest, and Cynthia, the one I was closest to growing up."

Alan wasn't letting me get away with any superficial answers.

"Tell me about them. Please."

"My sisters are all bright, intelligent women. I'm the only one of us who didn't go to Princeton. Maryann was drawing all the time as she grew up, so Dorrie nudged her toward architecture. She and her husband have a firm in Boston. Cinny—that's what we call Cynthia—and Caroline went to law school. We were as close as we could be when we were growing up."

"And now?"

Alan was such a good listener; all evening he'd asked leading questions that required I give more than brief answers.

"I've talked through most of dinner. Why am I rambling on and on about myself? Can't I hear something about you?"

Alan spent so much time listening that I had to coax him to tell me about himself. When he did, he committed the ultimate first date faux pas—talking about past relationships.

Chapter Eight | A Fighting Chance

Was it just hours ago that doctors had determined Dorrie's condition was life-threatening?

I couldn't believe she had been walking around with a ruptured aneurysm for nearly four days. Most people don't make it as far as stepping to the doorknob for help. How did my eighty-year-old mother put in a day's work, drive over three hours, and do who-knew-what-else for that long? And why hadn't I realized she needed medical treatment?

And why hadn't Alan? As soon as he finished with his late afternoon patients, he came to the hospital to wait with me. It felt like I'd been waiting all day.

Before Dorrie's doctors could stop the bleeding in her brain, they had to pinpoint its source. A neurosurgeon and an interventional radiologist examined her, but they needed a more invasive view than CT scans alone could provide. They had to insert a catheter through a blood vessel in her leg, then thread it all the way to her brain.

I was grateful to have Alan there with me during the procedure, but he kept excusing himself to the bathroom. In spite of his lingering stomachache, he'd put in a full day at work–so like him–and he was fatigued, which was so unlike him.

I looked around the stark waiting area, barely noticing the flat-screen TV on the wall.

"What am I gonna do if she doesn't make it through this?" I asked Alan when he returned from another bathroom break. "I still need my mom. The kids need their grandma."

"Don't give up, Pam. You know Dorrie." He chuckled and squeezed my hand. "If anyone can beat the odds, she can."

We sat in silence, me leaning against him for comfort. Then, as if there had been no pause, he said, "And her doctors are among the best. They'll give her more than a fighting chance. She'll come out swinging."

His confidence in his colleagues reassured me, but I tensed when the neurosurgeon, Dr. Chris Baker, approached us.

"Hey Alan, come out in the hallway a minute. I want to talk to you."

I followed them into the hall as Alan held onto his side. Poor Alan. His stomach must really be bothering him, I thought, but dismissed the idea as Dr. Baker relayed his findings.

"There's too much blood—we couldn't stop the bleeding—so we're going to have to open her up and see what we've got in there. I would do it without any more delay tonight, but this brain surgery is going to be a very lengthy, high-risk procedure. I need a fresh surgical team because this is such a long operation. We'll start at seven in the morning."

On the way home that night, all I could focus on was one terrifying fact: In the morning, they were going to cut open my mother's brain.

*   *   *

In spite of Alan breaking the unwritten rule not to discuss an ex on a first date, the way he brought it up, with utter sincerity, felt like the topic was a natural evolution of our conversation.

"I want to be honest and up-front with you, Pam." He glanced at the polished surface of the table between us, then raised his eyes to mine. "I was married for five years. She was my college sweetheart. I hope you're OK with that."

My stomach tightened. By the way he paused, as if waiting for me to tell him yea or nay, and by the reluctance in his eyes, I could tell he'd been badly hurt. I held my tongue, nodding for him to go on.

"When I was in medical residency at the University of Virginia, sometimes I worked gosh-awful hours. I was gone all the time. I would be on call at the hospital for seventy-two, eighty hours at a time. Anyway, I knew things were strained between us. I'd walk in the door and ask myself, 'Is this what married life is supposed to be like?' I would never, ever have acted on how unhappy I was."

"One day, I came home and my wife had taken the train from Charlottesville into New York. She'd been cheating on me with..."

The suspense was killing me.

"Who?" I leaned halfway across the table, expecting him to whisper.

"She was having an affair with one of my two best friends from back home."

My fingers covered my mouth, but couldn't fully conceal my gasp.

"When I went to med school, he went to law school, but we kept in close contact. Too close, I guess. The divorce was...rough. Thank god we didn't have kids together."

I took the warmth in his eyes as an invitation to probe deeper. I may have been new to practicing family therapy, but I knew enough to be leery of rebound relationships.

"How long have you been divorced?"

"Years. It's long over." Then, as if he'd read my thoughts, he added, "It's been long enough. I'm not on the rebound. I'm really sorry, Pam. It's not like me to go on and on like this about myself. I want to know more about you. Have you...do you...is there anyone else in your life?"

"No, not at all."

Why am I admitting that to him?

I mean, sure, I had a lot of boyfriends when I was a kid, but nothing serious. And I meant it when I told him I had been too busy, finishing my master's program and then working for the school district, to invest time in a relationship. I noticed (even as I said it) that this time I didn't say I *am* too busy.

"I mean, sure, I've had a few boyfriends, but nothing serious."

Alan's smile grew even brighter, and while waiting for the check, we made plans to meet again.

In spite of my assertion that I didn't have time for dating anyone seriously, Alan and I became nearly inseparable after that night.

Chapter Nine | Touch and Go

My sister, Maryann Thompson, and some of her kids flew down the night before Dorrie's brain surgery and stayed at the house. She insisted we get everyone up at 5:30, even though it was a Saturday, because she wanted us out the door early enough to have a Reiki and prayer ritual over Mom before the surgery.

Before we left the house, Alan reassured everyone again that Dorrie was in the best of hands. He knew, respected, and trusted Dr. Baker and Dr. Tom Arcario, the anesthesiologist with whom Alan had operated on countless patients. Alan knew Tom so well, we'd attended his children's weddings; Alan even mentioned they had nine surgeries scheduled together the following Monday.

Alan himself, however, stayed home. His stomach had been hurting him badly the night before, and someone needed to stay with our kids.

We entered the hospital at six in the morning. Maryann led us all in some kind of Reiki spiritual ritual as we stood around our mother's bed. I was willing to try anything in hopes that Dorrie stay with us.

Our family soon crowded the neurosurgery waiting area. Our sister Caroline Springer, her husband, Stephen, and their kids flew into town later that morning; they came straight from the airport to the hospital.

While Dorrie was still in surgery, my dad, Jay Thompson, also arrived with his girlfriend, whom we loved like family. Even though our parents were long divorced, they'd remained amicable, and I was glad he'd come.

I was grateful for everyone waiting with me. Six hours, even with company, seems interminable while your mother is undergoing brain surgery.

When Dr. Baker entered the waiting area, you could have heard a syringe needle land on the carpet. I held my breath.

"Dorrie made it through the surgery."

The din we made could have covered even the sound of another portable CT scanner, but Dr. Baker quickly shushed us.

"She made it, but the next few days will be critical. She didn't have one aneurysm."

"But isn't that what it means, that her brain was bleeding?"

"She had one aneurysm that burst, but she has another six that could burst at any time. We wrapped the one that looked closest to rupturing, but the others looked like they were nearly ready to blow."

Silence again. Then a blur of questions from everyone.

"I'm going to be blunt. The next ten days will be critical," Dr. Baker explained, "so she's not out of the woods yet. It's going to be touch-and-go. Your mother has only a 50-50 chance of living through this."

One of my sisters squeezed my hand. It was all I could do to squeeze it back, as Mom's neurosurgeon told us more.

"We are going to have to keep a very, very close watch on her blood pressure. I think that uncontrolled high blood pressure is what led to the aneurysm."

Dorrie had already beaten phenomenal odds. She'd been walking around— driving around—with an aneurysm bleeding inside her brain for a week, and another six waiting to burst.

But for now, at least, she was still with us.

*　　*　　*

I wanted our first real kiss to never end. It happened on a hot July night when we were walking along the beautiful grounds of Interlachen Country Club.

I'd always grown up in and around country clubs, and I wanted to show Alan how lovely Interlachen was. I'd joined it as the club's youngest single female almost as soon as I moved to the area, thinking it would be a great place to play tennis—until I learned they didn't have a high-enough ranked women's league.

The grounds, however, were as gorgeous as the late July air was hot. Hand in hand we walked, talking about nothing in particular in the growing dusk.

"We've been walking a while. Would you like to sit for a few minutes?" Alan gestured at the manicured green.

I lowered myself onto the cool, close-cropped ground. I felt like I could talk to Alan about anything, but silence with him was fine too.

This guy is so thoughtful. So fabulous.

Without segue, he said, "This reminds me of a baseball field."

"Really?" I looked around, not seeing it.

"Sure. The greens, how beautiful and serene it is."

"I guess." I'd learned early on how much he loved the sport.

"Remember when we met and I asked if you were single and you told me you didn't want to date anyone?"

I nodded, not knowing why we were talking about that now.

"It was refreshing, intriguing, having a woman not throw herself at me."

I looked over, and even in the dim light I saw the twinkle in his eyes, and couldn't help smiling back. As we looked into each other's eyes, his expression changed, sending my heart into a flurry of anticipation.

And then he kissed me.

Even though it was late when I got in that night, I called my mom.

"I was starting to think it was never going to happen," I told her. She'd sounded almost as excited as I was. "I hadn't wanted to rush anything between us, but I'd started wondering if he liked me as much as I like him."

"I told you, you just had to let him figure out the timing on his own," she said.

"After tonight, I think this—whatever we have—is moving forward."

Chapter Ten | Dorrie's Bedroom

While Dorrie was fighting for her life at Florida Hospital, my sisters and I realized we needed to take over managing her finances and properties. It should have been as easy as stepping into her bedroom and finding her checkbook and bills.

But our mother was incredibly eccentric, so nothing was that easy.

The first night Maryann stayed at the house, she meant to sleep in Dorrie's room—but couldn't get past the locked door.

"Pam, I need the key to Mom's room," she called out.

Beside me, a harumphing cough-chuckle escaped Alan. As I stood to retrieve mom's purse, the glare I shot Alan was lost to his grinning face. He purposely kept twinkling eyes pointed at the article on his iPad.

Dorrie had lived with us either full- or part-time for the past fifteen years, and Alan had always appreciated and respected her presence, but for one thing. Dorrie was a hoarder of the highest order, and kept people out of her bedroom by locking it.

When my sisters and I finally unearthed the bedroom key inside Mom's packed purse, we still couldn't open the door far enough to step into the room.

"How has she been squeezing through here?"

That I couldn't say, but my sisters shouldn't have been as surprised by the cluttered chaos as they were.

My sisters and I grew up living in huge homes, so all through our childhood, our mother had plenty of places to pile her accumulated acquisitions. Our estate in Cincinnati, for example, had forty-five rooms and a garage large enough to house our father's fourteen cars.

One of our household staff's ongoing duties was discretely cleaning up after our mother's nonstop "collecting," as everyone called it then. She would go shopping and find bargains to bring home, then stow them in random rooms of the house, or never take them out of whichever car she'd taken that day. Unopened mail, unworn clothing, uncomfortable furniture. It took our dozen full-time employees to keep up with her excessive, often secretive purchases, constantly cleaning up after her.

After our parents divorced, Dorrie never bought her own car. Instead, she rented one, sometimes for as long as ten years. When she had the aneurysm, she had not one, but two rental cars: the one she'd left at our house, and another she'd driven from Sea Island, now also parked in our driveway.

That wasn't the crazy part, though. When we started going through the mail in her floor-to-ceiling-packed bedroom, we learned she also had items crammed into storage units. Here in town...and *all over* the country. It was awful. For years, she'd been paying for places to house items she hadn't seen, didn't need, and couldn't use.

My sisters, bless their hearts, took on the task of cleaning Dorrie's room while they could. We didn't know how long she would be hospitalized after her surgery, and we suspected she might need a hospital bed when she got out—which would require access to the floor.

The cleanup was insane, not just because of all the random items she'd piled up—pantyhose, cookery, old makeup, swimming suits. It wasn't the stuff itself (although that was enough to manage). It was that when someone leaves you like that—has an aneurysm or dies or whatever—you're left to deal with all this physical and emotional baggage. And that was every bit as hard to manage as dealing with Mom's medical issues.

*   *   *

One of my dates with Alan ended up at the hospital. He wasn't on call, but his pager went off, and he stepped to the phone to call. When he returned to the table, he said, "We've got to go to the car now."

"Alan, what's wrong?" I asked.

"A nurse at the hospital said one of my surgical patients has bleeding coming through his bandages. I've got to go check him."

"Isn't one of your partners on call tonight? Isn't this why you rotate?"

"Yes, but this is my patient, and I need to do this."

It wasn't the first time (and I suspected it wouldn't be the last) that our night was cut short, but on each of the previous occasions Alan had me wait in the lobby while he tended to medical business. That night, for reasons I didn't understand and were never explained, he invited me back to see what he was doing.

We stepped into his patient's room, and Alan introduced me as his girlfriend, then asked if the boy minded if I remained with him—as we were on a date. I'm not sure whose grin was goofier, the adult-size football player who needed post-op care, or the woman who'd just been called *girlfriend*.

The young man had broken his nose playing football and required surgery to repair his damaged sinuses. Before Alan could figure out why the site was bleeding again, he had to remove the surgical gauze. As he began working, he spoke in soothing tones.

"We need to pull this out because we need to change your bandages, or else you'll get an infection. I want you to just sit very still, but please tell me if this hurts. If it does, I will stop, but only if I hear it from you."

Even I could tell the kid was squeamish from all the blood. His face paled and he wobbled to stay upright.

Calmly but firmly, Alan said, "I can see you're feeling uncomfortable. I want you to lean back and I'm going to lower you."

As he spoke, the bed's motor whined. Over it, he said, "We're going to stop for a moment, and then I need you to lie still and stay down while I do this."

It was incredible to watch Alan with this young man who was the same age as many of the students I counseled. I already knew I was in love with Alan, but watching the way he talked to his patient made me love him even more.

On our way back to the car, I told him what I thought.

"You were amazing, so soft and so gentle with that kid. You handled his anxiety so well in there."

"I did? That's just who I am."

His eyebrows lifted; he had no idea that's how he came across.

Chapter Eleven | Appointment at 3

I shivered through the warm spring days after Dorrie's craniotomy, wondering why Florida Hospital kept the air in her ICU room so frigid. I worried whether Mom felt the chill like I did—unconscious though she was.

Do people in comas know when they're cold? Is that why the nurses put those mitts on her hands?

It was easier to let myself focus on her immediate comfort than her long-term prognosis.

Normally, she was as much the center of attention at eighty as when she was a Ford Model at eighteen. Now, with Dorrie still and quiet in the beeping, whirring heart of medical machinery, her gauze-wrapped head looked out of proportion to her shrunken body. I knew they'd shaved her hair before the surgery.

Won't she be furious if—when—she wakes up?

Yesterday, Maryann apologized before flying back to Boston.

"I've got to get back to Mort, and the kids have school tomorrow, but call me if you need anything. Anything."

She'd made our sister Caroline and me promise, then hugged us goodbye.

I was so grateful Caroline could stay to wait with us through the critical period of Mom's post-operative recovery. Caroline's presence and assistance—with the kids and with any decisions Dorrie's medical team might demand—eased my overwhelming sense of responsibility.

I glanced at the time when my phone rang. *Yep, must be Alan.* Even when we didn't have a family member in critical condition, he always called during his short lunch break. No matter how backed up he might be with patients, he phoned halfway through every workday, anxious to check in and be reassured the kids and I were OK.

I answered him as I usually did. "Honey, how are you? What's going on?" Then I listened, waiting for him to tell me about his day so far.

"I only have a couple of minutes, but I wanted to check in. How's Dorrie been this morning?"

"Still on life support, but I think she's doing better," I said. "She's not awake, but earlier, even though the rest of her was completely inert, she flailed one of her arms a few inches into the air for a second, and then another time her leg jerked. Caroline and I were so excited, we cried."

"Purposeful movements," he mused. "That sounds promising for only forty-eight hours post-op. Let me know if anything changes."

"Is your stomach feeling any better?"

"No. It's a good thing I only had nine surgeries this morning. I canceled my afternoon appointments."

"You did?" I hardly knew how to respond. In twenty years he'd only taken two, maybe three sick days.

His pain must be worse than he's been letting on.

"I'm seeing a gastroenterologist at three to get this ulcer—or whatever it is—under control."

"Glad you're finally getting it checked. It's been...what, two weeks?"

His life-changing diagnosis was only a few hours away.

*   *   *

As our relationship became more serious, I took a chance and asked Alan if he would like to come to Maine and meet my sisters.

He raised one eyebrow at me, looking surprised but pleased.

"I thought it might be kind of fun for you to meet them," I told him. "One of my brothers-in-law has a family house on this island there."

"Sounds nice."

"The island's so small you have to get to it by ferry, and I think everyone rides bikes to get from one end to the other."

"I'll have to see if I can get the time off."

"That's the great thing—we're doing it over Labor Day weekend."

"Maybe. I think the office is still open that day. Or I might be on call."

Up until the week before, I still wasn't sure whether Alan could come. He'd seemed distracted and noncommittal every time I brought it up. I second-guessed myself at every turn.

Was this too soon for us to take a trip together? Should I back off?

When he finally told me he was coming, I couldn't wait to show him off to my sisters.

As we left the ferry station, Maryann (who'd come in from Boston with her husband and their son) pulled me aside and whispered in my ear, "In that London Fog trench coat and hoisting that big black bag, he looks like a hot, younger version of Marcus Welby."

I grinned in agreement.

When we arrived, everyone swarmed around Alan, who quickly met and remembered the names of all my sisters, their husbands, and my first nephew.

Gesturing down the hallway, Caroline said, "Let us give you two a quick tour of the house."

"This place is lovely," I said. "So simple and modern."

As they walked us through the floors, Maryann opened one door and said, "This is your room, but let's go back upstairs and talk a while before you unpack."

I glanced into the room and saw a pair of twin beds, but didn't think too much of it as we hurried to rejoin the others.

After about an hour of everyone getting acquainted with Alan in the living room, Maryann and Caroline excused themselves and disappeared together.

What the hell are they up to?

Later, when Alan and I took our bags downstairs, I realized exactly what they'd been doing. The two of them had found a not-so-subtle way to express their approval of my new boyfriend: The twin beds in our room were now moved together, made up as one.

Chapter Twelve | False Alarm

The day Maryann had to fly home, a friend brought Ella to the hospital to sit with Caroline and me. Miles and Nat were OK, because they had tennis and debate practice after school.

It was about 2:30, so I promised Ella if she did her homework right away she could spend the rest of the day however she wanted.

I was starting to get a little stir-crazy from staying in one place all day, watching Mom in her coma. Tennis taught me to keep looking ahead to my next move, but here in the ICU I felt trapped behind a net of waiting.

I'd paced around the room, burning off nervous energy, but now I perched on the narrow ledge at the back, trying not to talk to Caroline while Ella concentrated on homework. Whiteboard signs beside me identified, "Your doctors today are..." and "Your nurse today is..."

"Pam, look at her!"

I jumped to my feet and joined Caroline beside Dorrie. Her eyes fluttered open and one shoulder made a jerking shrug.

"Mom!" we both shouted.

I waved through the window at her nurse and shouted, "She's waking up!" but when I turned back to Dorrie, she lay as motionless as before.

The nurse rushed in and checked all the monitors and drains attached to our mother as Caroline, Ella, and I stood together crying and looking from one another to Dorrie.

"What's wrong?" I asked. "Why did she close her eyes already?"

At last, the nurse turned to us. Her eyes showed compassion, but her words sounded as if she'd said them to so many loved ones, she no longer had to think about them.

"She wasn't really awake. It's a good sign that she's showing these movements, but she's a long way from becoming responsive. In the meantime, random movements are a good thing, but it's been only a couple of days since her surgery. We'll have to see how she fares after the next eight."

"But she looked like she was waking up."

"No, she wasn't. There's a big difference in having a patient's eyelids flutter open a bit and having them see or be aware of anything. Try not to get your hopes up too much from this."

*　*　*

In the open air, on the glorious green course at Interlachen Country Club, I married the perfect man for me. It was December 1994.

I agreed with Alan that we would raise our children in the Jewish faith and tradition, so we were married by our rabbi. We had joined the Congregation of Reform Judaism, but Alan assured me he would never ask me to convert from my Christian faith.

On our wedding day, Rabbi Cohen's motorcycle roared into the parking lot, and he enjoyed a few cigarettes with Mom and one of Alan's cousins outside the pristine white canopy tent while guests filtered in. When more than 300 friends, family members, and business associates settled into their seats, the ceremony began.

Our families seemed as happy as we were.

Almost.

Alan's father, Murray, had died of a heart attack a few months before our wedding. When I met him only a year or so earlier, I'd seen him as a good soul, as soft and welcoming as a teddy bear. I'd loved him right away for his kindness and larger-than-life personality, and it saddened us both that he wouldn't be there to share in our celebration.

When we returned to Florida after the funeral, I admired Alan's deep concern for his widowed mother. He called her often on his way home from work, to see if she was OK.

At the wedding party, Alan spent a great deal of time tending to her. I was conflicted. On the one hand, I realized her husband had died only recently. Married less than a day to Alan, I couldn't imagine what that must have been like for her, seeing her son marry without her husband there.

On the other hand, I wanted to dance with my husband. But he was so attentive to his mother that we didn't dance together at all. I complained, but only inwardly. I loved the fact that he loved his mother so much.

But really? Can't he even dance once with me? It's our wedding.

Somehow, I kept my disapproval inside. I never told him.

My own parents were legally separated, but amicably so. Soon thereafter, they got divorced.

It was sad to think that Alan's father died so young and my parents stayed together only until their youngest child was married.

We'll make it longer than either of our parents. I just know we will.

Chapter Thirteen | Unexplained Pain

Standing in Dorrie's hospital room and talking on the phone with Alan about his upcoming appointment with a gastroenterologist, I started to wonder if his worsening stomach problems might have been related to something he had eaten.

For about two weeks, since we had returned from spring break at Dorrie's vacation home on Sea Island, Alan had been downing Prilosec and Tums while sloughing off weight he didn't need to lose.

I thought maybe he'd gotten a rare bit of bad seafood the night we'd eaten dinner at a famous dive on nearby St. Simon's Island. At the time, I wondered whether he had put too much butter on the king crab legs he ordered—we'd all sat around the table waiting for him to finish—but then I remembered he'd had as little as usual.

He always watched what he ate; as a doctor, he was very disciplined that way. But on our way to the parking lot he'd clutched his hands over his middle.

"Gosh," he said, "that really upset my stomach. Must have had something spicy in it."

"Honey, I've never had anything there that was too spicy."

"Yeah, well, it's just not sitting right with me. I don't know, Pam. My stomach really hurts."

It hadn't gotten better after we came home, though, so I wondered if he'd also picked up a stomach bug in the meantime.

I remembered one morning when Alan said, "Gosh, I've lost five pounds, and I've been so busy with all of my patients, I haven't been running as much. I wonder if I have an ulcer."

By then he'd covered his side of the bathroom vanity with too many brands of over-the-counter antacids to number.

*   *   *

The days that followed Alan's diagnosis and Dorrie's surgery were chaotic.

My tennis mentor Nick Bollettieri had always told me, "Life is like a tennis match."

With three young children, it sometimes felt like Alan and I were playing the doubles game of parenting under the onslaught of an untiring, randomly accelerating ball machine.

I hadn't yet realized the chaos was only beginning.

Each new crisis felt like a flaming projectile hurled straight at us. Someone had reset the machine from "oscillate" to "incinerate," and with Alan so sick, I was putting out flames right and left.

That first week, every day was like a fire drill. I scurried from one life-and-death crisis in my mother's ICU room to another life-or-death decision over my husband's tests and treatments.

Every day was divided by something or someone different. We had people in our house and airport runs back and forth at all hours, as family and friends came and went, and we played musical beds all over the house.

The morning of Dorrie's surgery, when Caroline arrived from Washington, she willingly camped on our fold-out sofa, committed to staying for the week beginning our mother's critical first ten days. Then, after Alan called Monday afternoon to tell me the CT scan revealed stage IV pancreatic cancer, Caroline said on the spot that she would leave her job—she loved Alan that much.

Of course, I couldn't let her quit her job at Georgetown Law. Still, I didn't know what I'd have done without her in the hospital that day, or in the days that followed. (She never left Dorrie's or my side).

The night of Alan's diagnosis, we researched pancreatic cancer treatments, and Maryann flew back to us for the second time in four days. As with her first trip, she had to return shortly thereafter, but in that brief overlapping window of time I leaned on having two sisters in person for practical support, to lift my spirits.

One night, Maryann fell asleep fully clothed, boots and all, on the sofa in my family room. Sticking out from inside her chic boots were the puffy little balls sewn into the backs of my tennis socks she'd borrowed. Caroline and I took one look at her, and burst out laughing at our sophisticated oldest sister. Her absurd footwear combination kept us cackling when we so badly needed something to laugh about.

The day after Alan was diagnosed, his best friend Jeff Zeitz flew in from New York City. The sofa downstairs in the family room became Jeff's makeshift bedroom whenever he was with us.

That same week, Dolores and Bruce, Alan's mother and brother, made the three-hour drive north from Boca Raton and visited for about a week. They slept in my mother's room—the logical choice, since the hospital would keep Dorrie in the ICU at least another six days.

A day or so before Dolores and Bruce left, my best friend, Cia Allf, moved in from Amelia Island to help me. We'd been all but inseparable since elementary school in Cincinnati.

"As soon as I have everything lined up, I'm coming to stay for as many months as you need me," she said.

Cia slept in my bed whenever Alan was in the hospital. When he was home, she stayed in Ella's bedroom, and Ella spent the night on the sofa in our room.

It might have been like watching a circus...if we hadn't been the ones living it.

Chapter Fourteen | You Can't Psyche Out Cancer

I knew what it took to do battle on the tennis court. Learning to master the sport was the hardest thing I'd ever had to work at. It wasn't just about the physical workouts, although they were grueling.

Yes, muscle and sinew moved and shaped the outcome of every match, but winning required another essential element. Tennis is a mentally tough sport. Not only did I have to be in good shape physically, but mentally as well. It has always been much more of a mental game than many people realize. It's a hard sport, a strategy-oriented, psychological game.

Winning took determination. I always decided I'd already beaten my opponents before I ever swung my racket. It took studying their moves and strategies until I knew where they would send the ball before they did. It took getting inside their minds to know I was winning—even if the score wasn't yet reflective of that. I knew it soon would be.

There were myriad pathways into other player's heads I learned through years of training and playing countless matches.

When they hit the ball outside the line, I yelled, "OUT!" as loud as I could, because I knew that would rattle them. Or if they were fast players who wanted to get in there and score quick, quick, quick, I slowed it down and dawdled between points to upset their rhythm of play. I did the exact opposite of what they wanted.

The minute I got them throwing a racket, or cursing, or radiating frustration with other body language, I knew I'd penetrated their thinking. I'd won the battle. I had them.

And I had them often. Never losing a match meant knowing my opponents well enough to get inside their heads.

I'd been battling tennis opponents for so long, getting inside their heads became as natural as walking.

But this fight—with cancer—was unnatural.

I mean, I'd always heard about "The Big C." I'd never thought it was going to affect me. Or anybody I loved. Yet here we were, about to battle Alan's cancer, and there was no other mind to get into, no opponent to look in the eyes and psyche out. It was frightening. It was unknown. I didn't know a lot about cancer.

I knew less about pancreatic cells. I knew nothing, in fact. Nothing.

I'd never experienced that.

Up until Alan's phone call, I'd never heard of a pancreas. I knew about the liver, the lungs, every other organ, but not the pancreas. I didn't even know we had a goddamned pancreas. I didn't know what the hell it did. Of course, Alan knew what it did and why we needed it, and in the months that followed, our kids and I became near-authorities on it.

*　　*　　*

The night of Alan's diagnosis, we lay in bed, our minds too preoccupied to sleep. Alan was on his iPad. True to his word from earlier in the day, he was researching pancreatic cancer treatments; but he also cautioned me not to get my hopes up.

I wasn't having it.

"Honey, I don't understand this. You've been telling me this is a death sentence. If we can put frickin' men on the moon, how come we can't find a cure for you, or at least some sort of remission?"

He only looked at me and shrugged. After a while, though, he sat up in bed and said, "I need dendrites, Pam."

"What the hell are dendrites?"

"Listen to this. Look."

I didn't know what he was getting at, but the excitement in his voice spread through me as he showed me an article on Dr. Ralph Steinman, a researcher at Rockefeller University in the 1970s, who'd identified and named dendritic immune cells.

"He figured out their role in the body's immune system, and he found ways dendritic cells aid the body in fighting tumors. It's breakthrough immunology, Pam."

My heart leapt at the excitement in his voice.

"You mean they can use it to treat cancer? Pancreatic cancer?"

"Yes—he applied his discoveries working with tumorous cells. Hmm ..." Alan lifted an eyebrow as he read on. "Doctor Steinman developed pancreatic cancer while working as a cancer researcher. So, he created—founded—dendritic cell therapy and used it on himself."

"Did it work?"

"He injected himself with his own dendritic cells, and yes, he prolonged his life because of it." Alan radiated excitement. "Pam, it says here he was able to live an extra three years."

"Only three?"

So little time.

"It's at least two and a half more than he would have had." Alan's eyes flicked back and forth as he scanned ahead. "He's the first person to win the Nobel Prize posthumously. He died, and then he won it."

Three years. But if that was in the '70s, surely by now they've got the treatment working even better. Of course they do.

Alan's voice was calm, but with a confidence that boosted my courage.

"This is what we need to pursue, Pam," he said. "I need what Ralph Steinman pursued. I need dendritic cell therapy."

I went to sleep that night smelling the jasmine beside my bed, but the sweeter smell was hope. I'd known from the moment I hugged Alan that afternoon that I would do whatever it took to save my husband. Now I had the beginnings of a strategy.

I just had to figure out what the hell a dendritic cell was, and how we could get hold of a gazillion or two as lethal weapons against Alan's tumors.

Chapter Fifteen | The News Isn't Good

The next morning, Alan underwent a liver biopsy and a port insertion at MD Anderson Cancer Center at Orlando Health (Orlando Health's cancer affiliation has since changed, and is now UF Health Cancer Center at Orlando Health).

The purpose of the biopsy was to retrieve tissue from tumors in his liver. We knew the growth's locations, but Alan needed the biopsy to confirm which kind of growths we were up against. We hoped—if anyone could hope to find they had a particular kind of pancreatic cancer—that Alan's tumors would turn out to be the less common, slower-growing neuroendocrine type, the kind Steve Jobs had. It was "better," in that it was easier to treat.

The surgically inserted port was necessary to give Alan's doctors an entry point for the chemotherapy he would soon begin. The doctor who did the procedure was a man whom Alan knew well. They had treated one another, and Alan trusted his skills. The anesthesiologist gave him a light sedative so Alan remained conscious during the biopsy, which used a needle longer than some adult hands.

Caroline and I waited in the recovery room with Alan as his head cleared from the sedation. One benefit of undergoing procedures like this one at the hands of Alan's peers meant we didn't have to wait as long as most patients for test results; we got them reviewed and hand-delivered almost immediately by doctors we already knew.

In fact, Alan was more than a peer who had both treated and worked with many of the doctors and support staff now treating him. Beyond their professional relationships, these healers were his friends. Not only that, but at different times, for two years he'd been chief of ENT at both Florida Hospital and at Orlando Regional Medical Center.

Alan's doctor came into the waiting area almost immediately after the procedure and delivered the preliminary results right away. When he walked into the room, I thought, "We're so lucky to get this attention. I'd go out of my mind if we had to wait any longer."

But his somber expression told me before his words did: The news wasn't good. Alan's diagnosis wasn't the hoped-for neuroendocrine type. He had adenocarcinoma, the least responsive, fastest-growing kind of pancreatic cancer.

*   *   *

I was now Alan's advocate, a role I would play with increasing frequency and ferocity during the months to come.

As soon as we learned that Alan had the most aggressive type of cancer, I called my neighbor Mary. Her husband, Mark Roh, was the president of MD Anderson Cancer Center in Orlando. The week before, Alan had treated their daughters. Mary assumed I was calling to see how her girls were doing.

"I'm glad they're feeling better, but that's not why I called."

"Oh. How is everything going, Pam?"

"Mary, it's not good. Where's your husband right now?"

"I don't know, but I can probably track him down. Is everything OK?"

I told her the story.

"Let me go find him."

Ten minutes later, Dr. Mark Roh walked into Alan's room.

Ten minutes after that, Mark called oncologist Dr. Omar Kayaleh. Another ten minutes later, Dr. Kayaleh entered the room.

"I want a sample of that tissue. We're going to do genetic testing on the tumor."

We all sat there, Alan recovering from the biopsy sedative, Caroline and I Googling everything they told us about as fast as we could.

At this point it was too soon for the doctors to have all the pathology reports back. We still needed to verify the tumor of origin. There was still some question whether this tumor had started in the colon.

"With cancer," they explained, "we have to find the tumor of origin. If it's all spread out, we have to find out where it began in order to treat that particular type, whether it's lung, pancreatic, or colon."

The genetic testing Dr. Kayaleh ordered on the biopsied tissue would have to be sent to the FoundationOne lab in Cambridge, Massachusetts, where they specialized in the genetic testing of tumors.

In other words, it would take time before we knew this cancer's genetics. And by the looks of Alan's CT scan, time wasn't something we could afford to squander.

Every doctor in the room—including the patient—agreed that having a PET scan ASAP would reveal a detailed view of what the tumors themselves looked like, and whether they had spread into Alan's bones. That insight, in turn, would shape the course of his treatment. Trouble was, getting approval from our insurance for the $8,000 test would require more time.

Chapter Sixteen | Praying for Colon Cancer

Word spreads quickly in the medical community. In addition to serving as chief of ENT at Orlando Regional Medical Center, Alan had also held the same position at Florida Hospital, the rival health system across town.

So, it was no surprise that the day after we were told Alan needed a PET scan, an administrator at Florida Hospital learned about the holdup getting approval for the test. Despite being Orlando Health's biggest competitor, the administration offered to perform the test that day—and free of charge! Now that was a surprise.

I squeezed Alan's hand.

"See, honey? Everything is going to be fine. We've got people at two hospitals willing to do whatever it takes to get you better."

We were elated—until we got the results. The PET scan confirmed two tumors in Alan's ribs.

But there was still a slight chance his prognosis wasn't as grim as he'd first thought. Alan's tests had shown spots on his colon. There was hope he might have colon cancer.

What a horrible thing to say!

If his tumors had originated in the colon rather than in the pancreas, his odds for survival increased.

Oh, how I prayed he had stage IV colon cancer, with its comparatively generous 11 percent survival rate.

After the PET scan, I took Alan home. He was worn out and needed to rest. But he was sick as a dog, so I worried he might be unable to sleep.

*   *   *

It had been only two days since Alan's diagnosis, and I was exhausted. The emotional roller coaster of hopes rising, falling, and rising again took such a toll on me. And I already felt the physical strain of taking on Alan's usual weekday duties.

I'd never been a morning person, but now instead of running one early carpool, I had to get our kids up and off to both schools. All I wanted to do was crawl into bed, but I had to get supplies from the pharmacy for Alan to prep for a colonoscopy scheduled early the next morning.

In the car, I grappled with guilt—for leaving Alan alone at home, for dividing my time from our kids, and for not being at my mother's bedside most of that day and the day before. I reminded myself Alan was in good hands with all the friends and family at our house.

While waiting for a green light, I gave myself a pep talk.

"You don't need to feel bad about time away from our kids. They're getting attention from their grandmother and uncles, and their aunts too. Besides, they have homework and after-school activities to keep them occupied."

Caroline's ongoing presence assuaged my guilt a little over being absent from Dorrie's bedside. I knew Caroline wouldn't let Mom's care fall short any more than I would, that her watchfulness was better focused than mine could be given my state of mind over Alan.

But after Dorrie's surgery on Saturday—God, *was it only four days ago?*—I'd been determined to stay beside her until she was out of the ICU and back to herself again.

Then Alan's diagnosis. *Only two days ago? Really?* It seemed like a whole lifetime. Undermining my attempts to forgive myself for letting down everyone around me was the ridiculous, unforgivable, awful sound of my own thoughts hoping and pleading, "Please God, let my husband have colon cancer."

I would bargain anything—anything at all—for Alan's survival odds to jump from only one in a hundred to a whopping 11 percent.

I pulled into the first pharmacy I saw, a Walgreens, instead of the CVS we usually used. I entered the store, list in hand, to pick up the nasty-sounding prep supplies for Alan's colonoscopy.

"My poor husband's already sick enough," I muttered as I glanced at it, walking down the aisle. "How's he going to drink all this stuff to empty him out?"

I got the dreaded, essential items, paid for my purchases, walked a few steps … and the whole day hit me. Just like that.

I slipped to the ground. I sat on the cold tile, crying. Thinking and not thinking, on the pharmacy floor.

Chapter Seventeen | An Unexpected Kindness

As horribly as this day was going, I had to remind myself of the compassion I had been shown only a few hours earlier.

I had to drop something off at Trinity Prep, where Miles and Nat went to school. I was in a hurry to get to the pharmacy for Alan's colonoscopy supplies, so I kept my head down on the way to the front desk, hoping I would not be noticed and could get in and out as fast as possible.

However, Sherryn Hay, the beautiful, elegant head of admissions poked her head out from her nearby office doorway and said, "Pam, hey, can you come in for a minute?"

Damn the luck.

I didn't feel like talking to anyone, but I liked this woman.

"I'm so sorry. I'm in a rush, Sherryn." I made the mistake of glancing at her, and I couldn't ignore the unmistakable disappointment shading her features. "I guess I can spare just one minute."

She beckoned me into her office.

"Since yesterday, I've been trying to call your husband's practice to set up an appointment with Alan. They wouldn't schedule me with him, and they wouldn't say why. What's going on?"

Damn them.

Why weren't Alan's partners doing as he'd asked and telling his patients he was on medical leave? I didn't want to have this conversation myself.

So much for being in a hurry.

I closed my eyes and inhaled deeply. Exhaled. Faced Sherryn.

"I need to close your door, and you need to sit down."

"OK, now you're scaring me, Pam. What's wrong?"

"Alan's been diagnosed with stage IV pancreatic cancer."

She gasped. "What can I do?"

"We're just ... We're in for the fight of our lives." I couldn't think of anything more to say.

A few heartbeats passed. The look on her face shifted from shock to sadness and then added something akin to determination.

"Well …" Sherryn blinked rapidly and wiped at her eyes. When she spoke again, she said the last thing I'd have expected from an old-school administrator.

"Let's consider your tuition overpaid for this year. We'll be sending you a refund."

*   *   *

The night before Alan's colonoscopy, Caroline and I continued Googling for ideas.

"You know, Pam," she said, "I keep going back to that article Alan showed you the other night. Something about it sounds familiar. There's something about that name … I might know of somebody who may be able to help us."

"Oh my god, Caroline. Really?"

She nodded. "Let me call my friend Lindsay. Her kids go to school at Sidwell Friends with mine. I think Lindsay knows Claire Dwoskin. She's got connections with NW Bio, a lab outside of D.C. that is doing research for brain cancers and other types of cancers using dendritic cells."

As my sister spoke, her voice grew faster and louder.

"Can you call her? Do you think she can help us?"

"It's worth a try."

In what seemed like no time, Caroline had tracked down Claire's number. I held my breath as it rang.

In as few words as possible, Caroline explained to Claire who she was and why she was calling. Even though Caroline had her phone on speaker, I wanted to hold it so I wouldn't miss a single word.

Claire said, "The lab is doing dendritic cell trials right now for solid tumors, so the researchers may be able to help. You'll have to talk to the CEO and head researcher on the project, Dr. Linda Powers. And of course, you'll have to get FDA approval for a trial targeting pancreatic cancer tumors with dendritic cell therapy."

"How would we go about that?"

She sighed.

"It's not going to be easy. You'll have to find a medical facility willing to host the procedures of such a trial, and then they'll have to make a formal request and application to have the trial approved."

"Then what?"

"Let's just start there. I'll give you Dr. Powers' number and you can coordinate the details with her, though you may have to wait until morning. I don't know what time she leaves the lab for the day."

My watch said 6:30.

Please stay late tonight.

I jotted down the number and thanked Claire before I hung up, but I was already looking ahead to my next step.

Claire said we'd need a medical facility willing to host a clinical trial in order to secure dendritic cell therapy for Alan.

I knew just where to ask.

Chapter Eighteen | Hoping Against Hope

While Alan was getting his colonoscopy, we hoped that his physician, Dr. Marlon Ilagan, would not find a clear colon, but instead would discover the origin of Alan's tumors. If so, his survival rate would be a little better.

For the third time in as many days, I waited as Alan underwent another procedure.

Dr. Ilagan stepped into the waiting room. His family had been Alan's patients, including children who were near our kids' ages.

Dr. Ilagan walked toward me, eyes filled with tears, shoulders hunched. He sat beside me. Hugged me. Cried.

"I'm so sorry, Pam. I'm so sorry. There were none."

Which meant it was pancreatic cancer. With only a one percent chance for survival.

It was all but a death sentence.

*   *   *

Alan and I were originally supposed to be married in the summer of 1994. The venues were rented, the invitations sent, the dress fitted.

But there was a problem: I was ill.

The past year had been a whirlwind as Alan and I dated, and the year of our engagement looked to be just as busy as we planned our wedding for the following year.

Not long after Alan proposed, I played in a tennis match at Interlachen Country Club. In the middle of a set, I suddenly felt lethargic. Am I dehydrated? I didn't think so; I always took care to drink plenty of fluids, especially in the mid-summer Florida heat.

I didn't feel at all myself, but I didn't call the match, either. That wasn't my style. After, I skipped lunch with my teammates and went straight to bed, really sick.

Sometimes, I felt almost like myself again, but without warning I'd be unable to lift my racket, let alone swing it at a flying ball. Fevers came and went, and my face became gaunt, as I lacked an appetite for even my favorite foods.

Meanwhile, Dorrie helped with the wedding plans when I was up to it, and she stayed with me all day, every day, to take care of me when I wasn't.

We went to doctor after doctor. Nobody could figure out what was wrong with me. They even did a CT scan of my brain to make sure I didn't have a brain tumor.

Alan told my mom, "I think she's got adult mono." He discussed the idea with one of his partners, who agreed.

That night, Alan relayed his colleague's confirmation.

"She needs to see an infectious disease specialist."

It was April before we got in to see the Mayo Clinic doctor Alan recommended. Of all the physicians I'd seen, he was the first who thought to test for the Epstein-Barr virus.

The test confirmed what Alan already suspected.

Finally, a diagnosis!

"How long will the treatment take?"

I imagined taking a ten- to fourteen-day course of medication and making my vows to Alan while feeling good again.

"Ms. Thompson," the doctor said, "mono can take longer for an adult to get over than a child."

"Mono? I thought you said I had Epstein-Barr..."

"Precisely. That's the virus that causes mono. And you've been ill for so long, it's going to take your body some time to get over it."

"How long?"

"I can't give you a time frame."

"But I've got a wedding in a couple of months. Will that be long enough?"

He shook his head and looked at me with compassion, but he spoke slowly and clearly, as if explaining a difficult concept to a small child.

"You're going to need longer than a couple of months resting—maybe much longer."

We'd have to postpone the wedding 'til I was well enough—but who knew when that would be?

There wasn't much I could do beyond resting and waiting. I spent what felt like years of my life lying on the sofa thinking thoughts that didn't help.

This is the worst thing that's ever happened to me. I'm never going to get better.

For nearly a year I'd pushed my body beyond its limits just to function, never realizing that was the worst thing I could have done to it. Now, forced into rest, I succumbed to the inertia.

Before the Epstein-Barr virus took me down, I'd never been forced to face the reality of life's unfairness.

When I was working toward my master's in counseling, one of my professors required we write a paper on the topic: "What is the worst event that's ever happened to you?"

I sat in front of a blank page in my upstairs study, tapping my pen and my foot at the same time.

For a moment, I considered writing about how homesick I was that first year—and every year from ages twelve to eighteen—when my parents shipped me off to Nick Bollettieri's fledgling academy, where he made us practice our tennis drills longer hours per day than we had in school. Into the middle of the night, too. But I dismissed the idea at once.

That training was what made me a champion.

I tried wresting some traumatic occurrence from memory.

I don't have anything to write about.

I went downstairs and told Dorrie about the assignment.

"Mom, I can't think of anything."

"What about…" Her brow furrowed and she tried again. "Or maybe…"

"I've always known I was blessed, but this is almost embarrassing."

"Embarrassing that you've lived a good life so far?"

"It's not that I don't appreciate it. I always have—you taught me to be grateful—but I can't write down that nothing bad has ever happened to me. The professor will claim I'm in denial."

So together, Mom and I brainstormed a paper's worth of made-up problems.

Chapter Nineteen | Gaining a Foothold

If only I could be so blissfully naïve again, I thought, as I speed-walked down the street to the home of our friends Mary and Dr. Mark Roh.

Just yesterday, Dr. Roh, president of MD Anderson Cancer Center, had come to Alan's hospital room to discuss treatment options after we got the results of Alan's liver biopsy. Tonight, I was taking my glimmer of hope for another approach straight to our neighbor's home.

I saw the Roh family through their window as I approached the house. They were eating dinner, a vegetable lasagna, but I couldn't wait until later. By the time I reached the door, Mary, who'd seen me passing, was already opening it.

"Pam, what's going on? Is it Alan?"

"No change—but Mary, I'm so sorry to interrupt your family time. I really need to talk to Mark right away."

"Of course. Come in."

"Mark, I am so sorry to interrupt your dinner, but I need your time."

He left the table and came toward me.

"That's OK. What can I do to help?"

"We may have a solution. We may be onto something we can use, because if Alan said it, it's got to be true."

I could tell by the confusion on Mark's face I needed to calm down and explain myself.

"Can you do a conference call with me right now? With this lab in Washington, D.C. It's called Northwest Biotherapeutics, and we need to talk to them about starting a dendritic cell therapy trial here as soon as possible."

Mark blinked once and his eyebrows rose. "Absolutely."

I pressed the number I'd already added to my contacts. As soon as I put it on speaker, my phone flashed a warning: *Low battery. Low battery.*

It was 6:30.

For the second time that night, I said to myself, "Please stay late tonight."

While we waited for someone—anyone—at the lab to pick up, I mouthed a plea to Mary, "Do you have a charger?"

She scrambled around and found one just as Dr. Linda Powers herself picked up.

Our timing, she said, was fortunate.

"We've already been doing dendritic cell trials on glioblastoma, and we've been looking to start a new trial at a major hospital for solid tumors. Pancreatic cancer would certainly meet our parameters."

I have to admit, I tuned out as Mark and Linda talked through details of the battle plan of lengthy procedural details that lay ahead. The hospital board would have to vote to allow the trial, the lab would have to coordinate with the hospital, and the Food and Drug Administration would have to sign off on the whole thing before Alan could even be considered as a candidate for the therapy.

When Mark ended the call, he nodded his head.

"This sounds promising. Let's go to work on it."

We didn't yet have this weapon in hand to fight Alan's tumors, but it felt like we'd just won the first skirmish.

*　*　*

By the end of that first week, I was exhausted beyond anything I'd ever experienced. Even as we followed all the suggestions and sought all the tests Alan and his doctors had recommended, and even though we'd been getting results back as fast as possible, part of my own weariness centered on my shock and disbelief.

How can one week make such a difference? How can everything change so fast?

Alan had a complete blood workup for his insurance company back in August, just eight months earlier.

"Honey, you have perfect bloodwork," I'd said when we got a copy of the results. "I'm going to hang onto this, since you haven't been to a doctor in ten years."

"You can keep it if you want it, but we don't need it. You might as well toss it, but do what you will."

"I'm keeping it. You never know when it might come in handy."

I guess that's silly since he never goes to the doctor.

In fact, he'd seen only three doctors in twenty-one years; and two of them were over the same tachycardia scare six years earlier.

It hadn't taken long to determine Alan's caffeine intake was the culprit. Coffee in the early morning before rounds, on rounds, after rounds before taking the boys to school, first thing when he opened up the office, between patients—Alan had been drinking a lot of coffee.

"You've got to cut back on the caffeine," his doctors told him, so he did.

Just. Like. That.

He was so disciplined about health, he never touched it again. Instead of arguing with his doctors, he did what they asked of him.

Now, six years after he quit caffeine, I wanted to argue against what Alan's current doctors told us. When I'd showed Alan the eight-month-old insurance blood workup, I'd insisted, "Alan, don't you understand? This proves your body's in good health. Everything is in the normal range."

"Was, Pam." He kept his voice calm, gently contradicting me. "It *was* all normal, but now...it's not normal anymore."

Chapter Twenty | A Scramble at Dinner

Caroline had to fly back home, but continued reaching out to the friends in D.C. she had called from my house. We needed to connect with anyone at the FDA who might be instrumental in fast-tracking a dendritic cell therapy trial.

Meanwhile, my house was like a train station.

At the beginning, I could not even get into my kitchen. There were people in and out bringing food—Ensure for Alan—all the meals you could imagine. It was a constant blessing, but required more coordination than I had the energy or concentration to manage.

Once my childhood friend Cia arrived, she set up a train of helping hands to organize meal volunteers online. Somehow, though, at one point there was a slight glitch.

One night, a kind family dropped off a delicious dinner of barbecued chicken and said their goodbyes. We started eating when the doorbell rang.

Oh, shit. Who's stopping by at dinner time?

I peeked out and saw it was another group of friends, and they were carrying a big pot. I ran back to the others.

"Quick, we have to hide this. There's another dinner at the front door." Everyone else jumped up from the table and scrambled to shove our current dinner into bags, which we then hid in Ella's bedroom.

I answered the door without letting on theirs was the second dinner we'd received that night.

"Thank you, this is so nice, and it smells wonderful."

That homemade chicken stew was every bit as good as the takeout meal we'd already started.

And for leftovers, we had plenty of chicken.

*   *   *

Alan knew he was in for the fight of his life.

"I'm not going back to work," he told me the day he was diagnosed. That night he also called his partners.

"I'm going on medical leave, so please let my patients know you'll be seeing them for the duration. I'll let you know when...if...I'm coming back."

As spring yielded to summer, at times Alan felt well enough—for brief periods—to check in by phone or email with friends, family, and business associates. A few colleagues still contacted him for referrals or opinions on perplexing cases. Occasionally, though, he switched his phone to silent mode so he could rest, or more often, to spend uninterrupted time with our kids.

By contrast, it seemed I was always on the phone—my battery ran down several times a day. I scheduled Alan's doctor, laboratory, and treatment appointments. I followed up with his doctors for ways to ease his chemotherapy side effects, meanwhile researching how to obtain dendritic cell therapy for him.

His family wanted to be apprised of the latest developments, and because Alan wasn't always up to talking after his treatments, that also fell to me. I checked in more often than daily with Dorrie's doctors and caretakers (unless they sought me out first), and I relayed her current needs and condition to my sisters while updating them about Alan too.

When I wasn't driving them myself, I coordinated getting our kids to and from school and extracurricular commitments. As the busy summer tourist season approached, I also managed my mother's primary source of income, the rental property on Sea Island.

And then there were the calls from patients complaining that Alan's practice wouldn't let them make an appointment with him, and they wouldn't tell them why not.

"I tried to call," they'd tell me, "and nobody would give me any answers. They just wouldn't tell me. Could you please persuade Alan to work me into his schedule?"

At first I was astounded.

But the more it happened, the more annoyed I became—not at his patients, but at his partners. In spite of Alan's request to his colleagues, none of his patients were told he was on medical leave. It seemed the staff was instructed that all inquiries about Dr. Saffran were to be answered with a standard response: "We can schedule you with one of the other doctors."

One employee at the practice told me of an office blowup early after Alan began his medical leave. When an elderly woman arrived for her appointment, she was told, "Dr. Saffran is not available, but you can see one of his partners."

"Oh, no. I made my appointment with Dr. Saffran, and that's who I'm here to see."

"I'm sorry, ma'am, but he's not available. You'll have to see one of the other doctors if you'd like to keep your appointment today."

"I don't want to see those idiots—today or ever. I want Dr. Saffran. I've been a patient of his for thirteen years, and I'm not changing now."

By this point, the woman was shouting loudly enough for everyone in the waiting room to hear.

"I am mortified that you have brought me here, that my husband had to drive me here, and Dr. Saffran isn't even available. You haven't been upfront with me. Well, I demand to know—what is going on with Dr. Saffran?"

As far as we knew, Alan's partners never told her, or any other patients, why Alan was on medical leave.

Chapter Twenty-One | Your Money is No Good Here

A week or two after Alan's diagnosis, I pulled into the drive-through at the CVS pharmacy near our house. For years, I'd bought all our family's medications at the same location. Even though the staff had always been friendly, I'd come to think of the place almost as an automated medicine machine, a pharmaceutical factory stop-off on my to-do lists.

Picking up our family prescriptions required little thought: waiting in line, approaching the window, waiting for the drawer to open, inserting payment and removing medicine when it opened again, and driving away so the next behind me in line could approach the window.

I'd been there so often they knew me by sight, so I didn't have to show ID before they placed my Synthroid in the drawer and extended it toward my car. I pulled out my credit card to pay and asked, "How much is it today?"

Instead of answering, the pharmacist pulled the drawer back into place and spoke into the speaker. "No. No, no, no. You're good, Mrs. Saffran."

I said thank you and pulled away, perplexed.

What the hell just happened?

The next time I drove to pick up a prescription, it was for one of the kids who'd developed a stomach issue. The gastroenterologist called in an expensive medicine that cost around $200. I wasn't looking forward to pulling out my wallet for that one.

It was the other pharmacist at the window that day who said, "You're good, Mrs. Saffran. Have a nice day."

"I don't understand."

"We know about your husband's illness, and we know his reputation. I can't tell you how many of our customers talk about 'that nice Dr. Saffran' when they pick up their prescriptions. It happens all the time. This is our small way of helping you and your family."

The drawer closed with a smile from the person behind the glass.

I sat there, credit card and medication still in my hands, unmoving.

Behind me, an engine revved and I glanced at the rearview mirror, only half aware of the long line of cars waiting for their turn. But I didn't trust myself to drive.

I inched my old Suburban to the side of the drive-through, just far enough out of the way to let the next car in line take my place at the window. I threw the gear into park and laid my arms across the wheel. No longer blinking away my tears, I let them pour down my cheeks, splashing onto my legs.

At first, I wasn't sure why I was crying. In part, I realized the bad news about Alan's illness had spread like its own epidemic throughout the medical community. I still, deep down, didn't want to believe this fight for his life could be real—but these pharmacists already accepted it as fact. More than that, though, the kindness of their gesture pierced the emotional armor I'd donned as soon as I'd gotten over the shock of Alan's diagnosis.

There was something in the tenderness of their generosity that allowed me to set aside my ferocity on Alan's behalf.

But it didn't end there.

Often, I returned to the pharmacy for Alan's nausea medicine to help him through chemotherapy. Time and again, the pharmacists wouldn't let me pay for it, or for any of the other prescriptions our family needed during the rest of his treatment.

In his career as a physician, Alan had touched countless people's lives. Patient by patient, he'd offered his best bedside manner and skill, treating every one with equal respect, whether they were high-end celebrities or impoverished children. It seemed his many kindnesses were now coming back to him.

* * *

In the very beginning, I didn't care how far we had to travel or what it would take to get there, as long as we found someone to help Alan beat the cancer inside him. Besides working through Caroline's D.C. contacts and reaching out to local specialists, I contacted MD Anderson Cancer Center in Houston and arranged a second opinion appointment with Dr. Robert Wolff.

I also called a clinic even farther away that worked with the pancreas. I left message after message for the head researchers. When they finally returned my call, Alan and I were walking down a long hallway at Florida Hospital. I recognized the number and dropped everything to take the call.

"Yes, this is Mrs. Saffran. Yes, I'll hold." I grabbed a chair from a nearby room for Alan. "Honey, sit right here. It's that place in Arizona."

I sloughed off my huge bag with all of Alan's paperwork and medical stuff, *thump* onto the floor alongside my purse. I watched my husband, who'd been chief of his field in this huge hospital, rest his head against the wall behind him and close his eyes as I paced, pleaded, argued.

They wouldn't open a time to work him in for another two months.

Chapter Twenty-Two | Alan's First Chemotherapy

I wasn't supposed to be here.

Our firstborn son, Miles, had worked hard all season to earn his position at the state varsity tennis finals. Either Alan or I had been at almost every match along the way, and I was supposed to be there today, at this most important match of the year, cheering him on. He wasn't alone. Cia took him for me, and the director of athletics and the headmaster at his school also went to show their support.

But that didn't assuage my guilt. Our boy's mom and dad and grandma were supposed to be yelling encouragement and pride where he could hear us.

Instead, we were all at one hospital or another.

A week ago, I'd rushed Dorrie to Florida Hospital, where she still lay in a coma. As much as I longed to be with Miles today, I yearned to wait at my mother's bedside. I worried constantly whether she would make it—we still hadn't cleared the critical first ten days the neurologist warned my sisters and me about. I didn't care what the doctors and nurses said, that it didn't matter to her whether I was there. On a visceral, emotional level, I felt my physical presence was necessary to ensure Mom would wake up.

I'd had to put those concerns physically and emotionally behind me. I had to convince myself the doctors were right; my mother, unresponsive as she was, probably wouldn't know or care who was in and out of her room. My husband, though, needed me here now, front and center alongside him, a good thirty minutes away from Dorrie, as he began chemotherapy at Orlando Health's MD Anderson Cancer Center.

Although my physician husband's specialty wasn't oncology, he knew far better what to expect than I did. Even after all the examinations and tests he'd undergone since his diagnosis on Monday—God, *has it only been since the beginning of last week?*—I hadn't yet recognized the inevitable rhythms of diagnostic and treatment practices: The hurry to schedule treatment and cut through cross-town traffic for on-time arrival. The flurry of paperwork to verify patient identity (even when the doctor-patient was personally known to the staff), to confirm which symptoms and diagnoses were being treated, to guarantee financial coverage. The worry over whether this procedure or that course could cure at best, or do no harm at least. And the waiting.

At every one of the steps before, during, and after treatment, there was always the waiting.

Until cancer attacked my husband, I'd never given more than passing thoughts to what it meant for someone to "have cancer." What a horrible, understated, passive phrase for such a dispassionate, aggressive, relentless invasion against one's body.

Now I sat alongside my husband, where I wanted to be, inside the oncology unit where nobody wanted to be, wishing we could both be at the match we'd much rather see.

Waiting for Alan's doctors to poison the tumors inside him. Other patients, they forewarned us, would come and go all day receiving their individual chemo protocols, but Alan's doctors had him on a four-medication regimen.

It would take six hours to infuse.

*   *   *

In late 1995, I was a visiting psychologist for twelve nursing homes. One day I got a call from my supervisor.

"It has come to my attention that you're in your first trimester of pregnancy. We cannot let you see TB or AIDS patients anymore. We're going to have to pull you out of the nursing homes."

I was crushed.

"I can't believe this," I told Alan that night. "I love my work, and I know I'm helping people. I don't want to be sidelined just because I'm pregnant."

"Of course you're good at what you do, and I can see why you don't want to stop, but you've got to think about the health of our baby."

"I know," I sniffed, not wanting to cry, but unable to suppress my sadness over no longer working with these patients.

He said, "Since they won't let you keep working there, why don't you just take it easy the rest of your pregnancy?"

That's when I quit working as a full-time counselor to focus on the unpaid job of being a full-time mom. I didn't look back.

Chapter Twenty-Three | The New Normal

Mornings took on a new pattern. For one thing, I didn't have Alan available to help with carpool anymore—he just wasn't capable of driving—so Miles had to get his license. Up until now, our sons had been too busy with school, tennis, and speech and debate every day to learn to drive. Besides, Alan had looked forward to his early mornings with them in the car.

Now, though, I needed Miles to transport himself and his brother to and from high school because I, already not a morning person, could only stretch myself so far. Between my children still in school, my eighty-one-year-old mom still comatose after multiple aneurysms, and my fifty-two-year-old husband undergoing chemotherapy to fight an aggressive form of cancer, I didn't know how much more I could manage.

After I took Ella to Park Maitland at 7:30 every school day, I started my "rounds" at the hospitals. I visited with Dorrie every day in the Ginsburg Tower ICU at Florida Hospital, checking with the nurses to see how she fared overnight and whether there was any change. I told her I loved her—in case she might hear it somewhere deep inside her as yet unresponsive mind—kissed her gently goodbye, and went back to advocate for Alan's care.

Of course, if it was a day for Alan's chemo, I delayed seeing Dorrie until later in the day; but I started even earlier, trading Ella's drop-off with someone else while I took Alan to MD Anderson early enough to sign in on time for his six-hour treatment.

Arriving by 7:30 in the morning was never a big deal for Alan, since he'd been out the door early every day of his career. For me, though, it was still a struggle, another unwelcome intrusion on our normal lives. I was used to leaving the house later in the day for Ella's ride to school, and in the summer, to get the kids to their tennis lessons and other activities.

Harder to adjust to than the demands of the clock, though, were the physical changes in my husband. Between the chemotherapy and the cancer, Alan's weight had dropped from a fit just-right to a pale gaunt, and his energy level and endurance had dropped with it. Now, instead of bounding out the door like every other day, we moved at a pace that would have infuriated him four months earlier.

Although his chemotherapy treatments were scheduled two to three weeks apart, by our second visit, I recognized the routine.

Two down, eight to go.

Each time we returned, I kept a mental countdown running in my head.

Three down, seven to go. Four down, six to go...

The first step in the process began as soon as we'd signed in: the phlebotomist drew Alan's blood and analyzed its makeup. Most weeks the news was good.

"Dr. Saffran, your white blood cell count is high enough, so you can proceed with your scheduled chemo today."

*   *   *

As good a husband, father, and doctor as Alan was, he was still a guy. He loved sports. He had been the sports announcer when he was a student at Columbia University, a young, medically-oriented version of Bob Costas. But he especially loved baseball, and when he was at Columbia, Alan started a fantasy league with his baseball buddies and called it the Roach Motel League.

And so, he was not there in 1998 when I was in the maternity ward ICU, anguishing in more pain than I'd ever felt in my life.

Dorrie held my hand as I cried.

"I wish Alan was here with you instead of away having fun with his fantasy baseball friends this weekend," she complained.

Secretly, I felt the same, but I wasn't about to admit that to my mother. Through gritted teeth and shallow breaths, I defended him.

"He planned this months ago. He couldn't have known."

"No, but with you seven months pregnant, it's silly for him to be playing pretend baseball drafts with his college friends."

"Other men do far worse things." I gasped, fresh tears of pain spilling down both cheeks.

"Of course. I'm sorry. I'm just worried about you and the baby."

I was relieved when my doctor interrupted us.

"The good news," said the doctor, looking not at me but at a printout in his hands as he bustled into the room, "is your baby appears to be doing fine. And your pain isn't anything serious for your long-term health. It's just a kidney stone."

Just.

"I...can't...take...this...pain."

I could scarcely hear myself, but the doctor must have caught my words.

"I wish there were something I could give you for the pain," he said, "but anything strong enough to be of any help to you would be too strong for your baby."

I had never imagined the human body could hurt so bad—and I'd already given birth once. But as excruciating as the pain was, being hospitalized for that kidney stone was a good thing. The routine maternity blood workup showed I had developed gestational diabetes.

They would need to induce our second son as soon as he reached full-term.

I remember thinking, looking out the window as we drove home from the hospital after Nat's birth: *He's already so much like Alan, the glue of our family.*

Everybody loved him the moment they met him. Just like Alan.

Chapter Twenty-Four | Dorrie's Miracle

While Dorrie recovered from her aneurysm and the surgery to repair the bleeding in her brain, she needed every kind of physical care. Tubes entered and left her body from one end to the other. She had a catheter, a G-tube for direct stomach-feeding, and a drain for blood and fluid from her brain. She wasn't conscious enough to swallow her own saliva, much less water or food.

Around the second week in May, Dorrie showed initial signs of reawakening. Her eyelids fluttered open—briefly, but more often. When they fully opened, she appeared to stare without seeing. We were elated that she was physically awakening from the coma, yet also disconcerted by her obvious mental disconnect.

However, with Dorrie's body settling into more stability, my sisters were finally able to spend more time back at home with their own families.

She gradually seemed partially aware of the people around her—at times at least. Rediscovering her voice, she made babbling sounds, as if mumbling in her sleep. Most of it, like "Naanaanaanaanaa..." was pure gibberish. We doubted she knew what she was saying—we certainly didn't—but we were elated she was trying to interact in her own incoherent way. Babble by babble, Mom gave us incremental thrills of hope for her recovery.

The hospital staff covering her unit agreed: That she woke up at all was a complete miracle.

Dr. Baker, after examining her, grinned broadly. "I'm very pleased at her progress. It's been gradual, but steady, and that's a good thing. I think she's out of the woods."

He turned toward Dorrie, not expecting a response but nevertheless addressing her directly.

"And you, Mrs. Thompson, you keep getting better. Every day you show even slight improvement, your recovery prognosis gets better, too."

Day by day she improved. They sent in speech therapists and physical therapists and gradually pulled out tubes as she became a bit stronger. Every day, I updated Alan about her recovery.

"The fewer tubes she has in there, the better," he said. "The more her body can regain strength and do its work, the better. That means she's on the road to recovery."

* * *

Despite our tremendous respect for Florida Hospital, where Dorrie was being treated, we chose the MD Anderson Cancer Center at Orlando Health for Alan's treatment for two entwined reasons. First, MD Anderson in Houston already had dendritic cell therapy trials underway, which made it more likely we could get one approved at its affiliated hospital here in Orlando.

Second, we already had the president of MD Anderson Orlando—our neighbor, Dr. Mark Roh (whose wife, Mary, was my good friend)—on our side, determined to help.

When Dr. Roh first introduced us to Dr. Omar Kayaleh, the broad-shouldered oncologist talked us through a general overview of what to expect through the course of Alan's treatment. Before each round of chemo began, he told us, Alan's doctors would check the levels of tumor indicators, called markers, in his blood. Those levels would reveal whether the chemotherapy was working. The higher the marker numbers, the stronger the cancer; the lower the markers, the healthier the patient.

Every time he underwent chemotherapy, Alan's doctors would verify whether Alan's treatment worked by regularly measuring the carcinoembryonic antigen (CEA) level in his blood. If Alan were a typically healthy, cancer-free nonsmoker—as we'd thought only days ago—his blood workups for CEA would have registered below three nanograms per milliliter. If lab work revealed a CEA density above one hundred, it usually meant the patient had metastasized pancreatic cancer.

The first time they measured Alan's markers, his CEA indicators were near 700.

We had to fight this disease with every weapon we could find, but what his doctors told us about the prescribed treatment frightened me almost as much as the diagnosis.

"You mean this chemotherapy is so toxic you can only give it to patients who, except for their cancer, are otherwise considered to be in great shape?"

"Technically, Mrs. Saffran, FOLFIRINOX is a combination of four medications administered intravenously in a precise sequence. But yes, it is dangerous, which is why it is fortunate Dr. Saffran is in excellent condition. He will be here under close supervision during each treatment, but it's the current first-line treatment against metastasized pancreatic cancer."

First-line treatment.

Except for that one semester in college, I'd always played line one tennis, the first line, against the toughest, most skilled opponents. They were harder to beat than their teammates, but I'd conquered them. If line one medicine was what Alan needed to conquer the tumors inside him, I was on board.

Even so, knowing how necessary it was, when I watched Alan sicken from the drugs, I had difficulty accepting that in order to save my always health-conscious husband, we were poisoning him.

Chapter Twenty-Five | Finding Time to Laugh

After Alan began medical leave, he wanted even more quality time with our kids. He'd always been as involved with them as his long work hours permitted, savoring evenings and weekends in family activities. Now, except during his chemotherapy treatments, he was home, waiting to see them as soon as they came in the door from after-school extracurricular activities.

They came into our room and sat beside him on the bed to talk, dropping their book bags on the floor. Some afternoons he spent one-on-one time with each of them, sometimes with Ella and the boys together.

As the school year wound down, Miles was a junior, Nat a freshman, and Ella a fourth-grader. In eleven years, Alan hadn't been able to attend any of their school-day activities. Now he wanted to take advantage of his time on medical leave to be there for them.

The boys were doing speech and debate, finishing up the season, and Ella had a big event too. I brought Alan to watch her complete a state fair project in the gymnasium at Park Maitland School. Alan's grin while watching her was as big as it had been in weeks, but he had so little energy, he had to rest. The only place he could sit was on the steps to the stage where Ella presented.

He was too sick to do much else, but he was able to go with me to events like this one, even if he could stay only for short periods.

Alan wasn't always ill from chemotherapy, but he lacked the energy to exert himself, and I hated the thought of him staying in the house, alone all day when I had to run errands. I'd say, "Honey, I'd like you to ride in the car with me so we can talk. I just want to talk with you."

Throughout our relationship, in spite of Alan's long hours at the medical center and hospital—or maybe because of those hours apart—we'd always made the effort to talk over the phone several times a day. He asked about everything from the kids and their schooling, to where I wanted to go for date night that week, to which home repair we needed to tackle next. He called me so often during lunch breaks or between morning surgeries and afternoon office hours that when I was with friends, they commented on it.

"Oh, Pam's phone's ringing. Alan must be between surgeries." "You're always on the phone with him, aren't you?" Once in a while they complained, "My husband never talks to me like Alan talks to you."

But now with Alan at home, our whole family piled onto the bed in our room at night. Countless evenings that summer I silently thanked my sister Caroline for her long-ago advice: "Buy a king size bed. It'll change your life."

I'd glance over at one or the other of the kids leaning up against one side of Alan while another snuggled against his other side, all of us cracking up at something on the TV. I also silently thanked Alan's best friend, Jeff, for setting up Netflix so Alan could access comedies day or night.

Before Alan got sick, he seldom sat down to watch TV—except for baseball, of course—unless it was something the kids wanted to enjoy with him. He'd rather spend any on-his-own free time reading a book than staring at a screen.

Alan made me laugh. He had an intelligent, wicked, Woody Allen-type sense of humor. An avid fan of *Monty Python and the Holy Grail*, Alan quoted lines from the movie whenever his quick wit spotted relevant, real-life situations.

Laughing through painful circumstances helped Alan channel anxiety that plagued him since childhood. That humor he'd learned to rely on served him as an effective coping mechanism while he endured chemotherapy that summer; he laughed his pain into the back of his mind watching hours of *Saturday Night Live* sketches on YouTube by day, and sitcoms with the kids and I by night.

We all needed the shared outlet of humor. It kept at arm's length the somber mood that threatened to settle over our house in Dorrie's absence and Alan's illness.

*   *   *

Alan's chemotherapy infusions took so long—six hours—that we often had nothing better to do than watch people come and go. While we waited, the oncology staff ran further tests on the blood they'd drawn that morning.

When I wasn't at Alan's bedside, I would pace between him and the staff station.

"Has the blood work come back?"

A while later, I'd return to the technicians, my feet overriding my resolve not to rush them.

"How about now? Can we tell yet whether his treatment is working?"

Even after he finished at the cancer center, Alan's treatment would continue at home overnight. The final step in each round of chemotherapy required a twenty-four-hour infusion. Once discharged for the day, Alan would be sent home wearing a pump secured around his waist, in a bag like runners carry—a pharmaceutical fanny pack. We called Alan's pump "the cat," because its motor purred the whole time it pushed the final chemotherapy into his body.

But maybe that cat had claws, because two weeks after Alan's first round of chemo, his CEA level dropped 200 points to 500. When they checked his levels again two weeks after the second treatment, Dr. Kayaleh practically skipped into the room, a huge grin on his face.

"Your CEA markers are down to 300 now, less than half of where they started. The chemotherapy regimen appears to be working."

I knew, I just knew—we could beat this. Set one, Alan.

Chapter Twenty-Six | Is Anyone Listening?

Alan was innately gifted at diagnosing patients' illnesses. It seemed as if every week his partners sought Alan's objective insight on difficult cases. Yet, a handful of times over the years, I witnessed him grapple over an elusive diagnosis.

We hadn't been together very long the first time it happened. Alan was getting ready for an evening out, and I heard him muttering incomprehensible words in the bathroom.

"What's that, honey? What'd you say?"

"Nothing, Pam. I'm just whispering in the dark."

Not understanding, I teased him.

"And yet, you've got the light on, which is probably a good thing while shaving."

The corners of Alan's mouth turned up as his reflection looked at mine through the doorway.

"I'm talking myself through a persistent case of laryngitis. I haven't found what's causing it, so I don't know what medicine might work. I feel like I'm grabbing at straws. It just about kills me not to be able to figure it out."

Then he went on about it, talking through his patient's symptoms as if I were one of his colleagues, though I understood little of the anatomy he referred to. When he finally paused, I tried to reassure him.

"I'm sure you'll figure it out."

So often, I too felt like I was whispering in the dark, listening for the universe to echo back an answer.

I spent every possible hour researching treatment methods and facilities, but it seemed at every turn I met with another obstacle.

"Sorry, ma'am, that person's on vacation," or "No, you'll have to wait until tomorrow. She's in a meeting all day."

Half the numbers I found went straight to voicemail. Between calls, I'd sometimes lower my head, just for a second, and gripe at the universe.

God, this is just so exhausting.

I had no idea who was listening on the other end of my emails and phone messages or whether any of my attempts would stick to a source that could help us fight Alan's cancer. So, I pushed myself harder, faster. I had to seek as many specialists as I could; the more people and places I contacted, the better the likelihood something helpful would happen.

Something, somewhere, had to stick.

*   *   *

The more I learned about dendritic cell therapy, the more excited I became.

"It's incredible," I told my dear friend Cia, "because there are no toxic side effects. You don't lose hair. You don't lose feeling in your fingers. You're not tired. It's like the wave of the future. It's called immunotherapy—using your own cells to fight cancer."

The dendritic cells, each patient's own white blood cells, were harvested, re-engineered, and revamped to target specific cancer cells. That meant patients could undergo chemotherapy and dendritic cell therapy at the same time; they could start traditional treatment right away, while awaiting approval from the Food and Drug Administration for the experimental therapy, which turned out to be a better theoretical than practical benefit.

We started the process to get FDA approval for the Orlando dendritic cell therapy trial at MD Anderson in early April, a few days after Alan's diagnosis; MD Anderson finally got the go-ahead in July.

In the beginning, I didn't know one thing about the FDA—not one thing—except that everybody said, "It's going to be really hard."

I had no idea how many hurdles I'd have to jump over or how many people we'd have to convince to get dendritic cell treatment within Alan's reach.

I quickly learned that lining things up was far more complicated than organizing a championship tennis tournament. There were hordes of players and reams of rulebooks involved, and we had to get everybody on board with the plan; onto the same side of the court, so to speak. Immunotherapy with dendritic cells was such a new concept that a lot of people (even in the medical community) had never heard about it. I had to educate myself, so I could educate them. More often, though, I acted as the coach who coordinated which new-to-the-circuit players should be teamed up with which veteran experts for individual games within matches.

Having MD Anderson Orlando's president as our friend and neighbor helped, but it wasn't up to Dr. Roh alone to bring an FDA dendritic cell therapy trial to our city. The hospital board had to approve the idea, and that meant he had to persuade the hospital's board members.

We also needed a qualified doctor willing to take on the enormous responsibilities (and hassles) of being the lead principal for the trial (if it were approved). In our case, again, we were lucky we'd already met Dr. Kayaleh, who stepped up to the project. But it took time to connect him with the lead principal at NW Bio, and with their laboratory researchers, and their oncologists.

And we needed a team of researchers with the skills to take on the myriad testing and analysis tasks required by the FDA. It seemed I was constantly entering offices, on the phone and in person, to connect people so they could talk to one another. I needed their minds working together, because that was the only way anything was going to happen. As much as I'd learned, I didn't have the scientific terminology or background they had.

During one conversation after another, I called Claire Dwoskin, the woman who had connections with NW Bio.

"Claire, I need you to talk with..." and then I'd hand over my cell phone to whoever needed convincing, telling them, "Here you go. Talk to Claire, and she'll explain what this is."

In turn, Claire then tracked down the lead principal and got her connected at their end.

For many of those involved in the critical decision making, this "new" approach to treating cancer was such an unknown. It wasn't as if great strides were being made in leaps and bounds from year to year.

"It's almost like we've been stuck," I told Alan one day, after making who knows how many phone calls. "They've been doing the same things since the first chemotherapies were tried. 'Let's try this chemo and that chemo' is what they want to do, but for crying out loud, Alan, why haven't they been working harder with dendritic cells since they found them back in the seventies?"

To some of those I approached, I must have looked (and at times sounded) like the lunatic I resembled, talking to everyone I could, persuading them to give me "just one more minute" of their time, even if they'd already told me no.

I had to battle my own frustration as fiercely as the red tape and ignorance we encountered. It seemed trying anything new frightened those who didn't understand it—especially doctors. Few were willing to put themselves (meaning their patients and their reputations) on the line for something no one could guarantee.

I didn't—couldn't—understand that attitude. Over and over, I lobbed the question, "How are we ever going to move forward if we don't try new things?"

If MD Anderson in Houston hadn't already been participating in a dendritic cell therapy trial, it would have been much harder to win the support and approval we needed there.

Chapter Twenty-Seven | My Amazing Oldest Sister

I would have understood if my sister Maryann said she was too busy to spend so much time helping me with Alan and Dorrie. She is one of the premier female architects in the country, and employs more than a dozen top architects at the firm bearing her name. Even while working on high-profile client projects, she traveled in a fluid north-south loop, one day flying to Florida to lend her steady hand with our latest crisis, the next jetting back to Cambridge.

In the hectic months after Dorrie's aneurysm and Alan's cancer diagnosis, Princeton University commissioned Maryann's company to design a child care facility for their professors' children. One Monday morning, a member of Maryann's staff said, "You have to make a site visit to Princeton this week."

"No, I can't do that," Maryann countered. "My brother-in-law is having another chemotherapy treatment. I'll be with my sister and their kids."

Another time, a different employee implored her to do an on-site review of her company's progress on a multibillionaire's house.

"No. Can't do that," Maryann said again, but with a different explanation. "My mom is getting an emergency pacemaker today. I'll be in Florida by then."

To her staff, it seemed as if her every absence was for reasons of increasing doom and gloom. To our family, her priorities offered blessings of light—and lightheartedness.

Maryann was funny. During her multiple visits, she draped herself, often fully clothed, across whatever mostly horizontal furniture she found unoccupied overnight; she refused to put any of us out of our beds, and making Dorrie's room fit for guests was a long-term project. As many chuckles as Maryann's literal sleep profile provided, the effort she put into physically supporting us (through the craziness of juggling Dorrie's care and Alan's treatments) made a serious contribution to our family's morale.

She didn't let her work get in the way of our family, but in spite of her many absences, she took care not to neglect her clients, either. Once, after getting Alan settled back at home after chemo, I returned to Dorrie's hospital room to relieve Maryann, who'd been there all day.

I shook my head as I entered the transformed, paper-covered space before me. There were pages of architectural plans everywhere; across the furniture, covering Dorrie's unconscious legs, torso, and arms, and balanced across the tops of her life support equipment. All day, Maryann had worked quickly while monitoring and talking to our snoring, unresponsive mother, refining the plans for a $20 million building project.

"This will become a Catholic headquarters complex," she explained. "And here they're going to have the wing for conducting silent prayers."

*   *   *

With three older sisters, it was only natural for me to want to do what they did. And I've always been mischievous, too.

One day when I was ten or eleven years old, my mother, just waking up from a much-needed nap, looked out an upstairs window and saw her car driving back and forth on the main thoroughfare in front of our house.

Even though she was still half-asleep, she quickly left the house to see who was behind the wheel.

There I was, taller than I should have been (sitting on a stack of phone directories) with eight other girls in the car, screaming their own terrified delight.

My poor mother was exhausted by the time I came along—four daughters in five years—so it's no surprise I got away with things my oldest sisters probably didn't. We still laugh over that one.

Chapter Twenty-Eight | Behind the Scenes

From the moment Dorrie's aneurysm was discovered and Alan received his diagnosis, I was in constant motion. I was either on the phone or running back and forth between doctors, hospitals, and other facilities. At any given moment, I had to think about my husband or my mother, putting each in the forefront of my thoughts. I learned to briefly summarize their medical histories for each new provider to bring them up to date right away, because things changed very quickly with both of them.

Juggling their case histories in my head was complicated. Sometimes I mixed them up, especially when I was tired beyond exhaustion and frazzled beyond frustration—as I was after our flight to MD Anderson in Houston to get the second opinion from Dr. Wolff.

We'd waited forever for the appointment, so I'd already thought out how to begin our introduction.

When he walked into the room I said, "Dr. Wolff, it's such an honor to meet you. I'm Pam Saffran, and this is my husband, Dr. Alan Saffran. Now, my husband has very high blood pressure, so I want…"

"Pam," Alan interrupted me. His voice was unusually sharp. "I don't have high blood pressure!"

"Oh my goodness, Dr. Wolff. I'm so sorry. That's my mother I'm talking about."

The rest of the visit went more smoothly. During the examination, Alan pulled several pictures from his wallet. They were photos of Miles, Nat, and Ella.

"Dr. Wolff, I want you to see these. Do you see why I need to live? I live for these children. They're everything to me."

Dr. Wolff nodded solemnly, then confirmed his agreement with the course we were already on. When he learned we were also pursuing approval for a dendritic cell therapy trial in Orlando, he said, "Excuse me one moment," and called the lead researcher there at MD Anderson. To our surprise, he arranged for the man to come meet us.

When the lead principal investigator on the Houston dendritic cell therapy trial arrived, he spoke briefly with us about the clinical process. Then he asked, "Would you like to meet some of the researchers working on this trial?"

I was eager to see what I could, but Alan declined, looking back and forth between the researcher, Dr. Wolff, and me.

"I'm tired, Pam. If you don't mind, I'll stay here and speak with Dr. Wolff a little longer."

On the way down the hallway toward the room where all the researchers were, the man in charge of the trial said, "It's people like you, Pam, that can make a difference in the world of cancer."

I must have looked as shocked as I felt, because he explained as we continued walking.

"I say that because personal involvement is why childhood cancer mortality is reaching an all-time low. Their mothers have insisted and pushed and nudged and begged and pleaded for their children. And it's made a difference in childhood leukemia and other cancers."

He introduced me to the many behind-the-scenes researchers working on the dendritic cell immunotherapy trial—all in this room by their computers and microscopes. For the first time, I saw the clinical trial as more than a pile of paperwork acting as a gateway to a select matching of a few patients, doctors, and laboratory technicians in a faraway "somewhere." These were women and men who'd dedicated themselves to studying, researching, and fighting a pernicious killer—the same killer stalking my husband from the inside.

Again, just down the hall from Alan's room, the lead researcher spoke with urgency.

"You keep it up, Pam. It's going to be people like you who won't take no for an answer that will make a difference in the world of curing cancer."

*　　*　　*

Sometimes I suspected Alan and his doctors didn't tell me everything, like they were keeping me in the dark. Maybe they rightly assumed I wouldn't understand their technical, medical jargon, and therefore wrongly assumed I wouldn't want to hear it.

Maybe they kept quiet because Alan meant to protect me; he had wanted to shield me from the beginning, that first day when he said it was hopeless and he wanted to begin only palliative care right away.

I realized it would have been easy for Alan to communicate with his peers without me knowing.

Maybe that's what happened during our first visit to see Dr. Wolff in Houston. Perhaps when I left the room to talk to the researchers about their dendritic trials, Alan said to Dr. Wolff, "Look, I don't want her to know how bad it's going to get for me."

I'll always wonder. When I returned to the room, Alan's expression was unreadable. But when I told him about my visit to the hospital's research department, he smiled warmly.

"What did you and Dr. Wolff talk about while I was gone?" I asked. Then someone else came into the room, interrupting our conversation.

He never did answer me.

Chapter Twenty-Nine | Girls are Different

Even with his medical training, Alan wasn't quite prepared when we brought our daughter into the world. Neither was I, for that matter.

One night, though, I confessed my insecurity to Alan.

"I don't know anything about raising girls." He looked at me like I'd just spoken a foreign language.

"You are a girl, and you have three sisters."

"But we were all young together, and I never, ever did any babysitting when I was a teenager. I was always at tennis camp or practice."

"But at least you've been a little girl. When the boys were born, you didn't know anything about raising boys, either. Neither of us did."

He grinned as he put his hand on my swelling belly. "And we're pretty good at this parenting thing–both of us."

I sighed in relief. Our sons were a constant joy to us, and we'd learned as we went with them. Still, it had been five years since Nathaniel was a newborn, and I wondered how well I'd remember all I'd learned about caring for newborns.

When Ella was born a few months later, in February 2003, one of the first things Alan said to me in my hospital room was, "Look at her, Pam, she's as beautiful as her mother."

I agreed about her beauty, and I appreciated the compliment, although at that moment I knew I looked like crap. But how I looked didn't matter, as neither of us took our eyes from our new daughter's tiny face and body.

She nursed well and slept soundly, but after a few hours Alan's new-father-glow began fading. His brows moved closer together, and he checked her diaper every few minutes, pacing between rechecks.

"Alan, what's the matter? Is something wrong?"

"No, of course not." But he answered too quickly, averting his face. "You should try to get some rest."

I sat up higher in the bed.

"What aren't you telling me?"

For a moment, his lips pursed as if straining to keep him from speaking. Then his shoulders slumped and he stepped closer to my bed.

"Pam, Ella's diaper is still dry."

"But you've changed it several times."

"No, sweetheart. I've checked it. That's all. It's just as dry as when it went on."

For one long second I looked up at him in confusion. Then it hit me.

"When the boys were born, they peed all the time."

As a brand-new mother, I'd been startled the first time the front of Miles's diaper warmed my shoulder as I gently patted his back, and I'd been amazed at how many times his tiny body needed changing each day. It hadn't taken long to learn how the outside of a wet diaper felt, and Alan and I quickly became as expert as every new parent.

"If she hasn't peed yet...give her to me, Alan. Give her to me now!"

He handed me our precious new daughter, but the look on his face said letting her out of his arms cut him to the core. As soon as she was in my arms, I felt the too soft, too dry material. Not willing to believe what my fingertips told me, I laid her in my lap. My hands shook as I undid the tiny fasteners covering her body and undid the diaper. I pulled it open and looked at the un-yellowed surface, then tucked it back around her.

Alan had already opened and closed it so many times, the tabs wouldn't stick.

"Get me another one," I said as I hit the call button for the nurse, pressing it over and over.

Alan put a fresh diaper on our daughter while I throttled the call button with both hands. I was crying too hard to see more than a blur as Alan scooped our baby girl back into his arms, guarding her against his chest.

"Baby Girl," he crooned, "sweet Ella. You've got to be OK. You've got to be."

I'd never heard Alan so scared as he turned toward the door.

"I'm not waiting for them. I'm taking her to find..."

"Hello, Dr. and Mrs. Saffran," the nurse said as she rounded the doorway. "What can I do for you?"

"There's something wrong with our baby!" I screamed.

At the same time, Alan's frightened voice slipped back into doctor-speak. "The baby hasn't voided!"

All business all at once, the maternity nurse ordered the ENT surgeon out of her way as she pulled our precious baby from him. It took only two seconds for her to check Ella's just-applied diaper.

"Is this still her first diaper?"

"Ye—no. The other one wouldn't stay on anymore."

She bent over the trash can and pulled up the diaper Alan discarded, a puzzled smile tugging at her lips.

"Dr. Saffran, Mrs. Saffran. Your baby's fine. This diaper is soaked."

"But I just checked it."

"I did, too. It was dry!"

"Try again."

She didn't try to stifle her laughter as she continued.

"This time, feel the *back* of the diaper."

"The back?" We couldn't have spoken in better unison if we'd practiced beforehand. We reached for the curled diaper at the same time. Sure enough, the backside of the diaper had hardened into a sodden mass.

"But..."

"How..."

"You two have two little boys, right?"

The nurse was trying so hard not to laugh, I could hardly understand her.

"Think about the anatomy, Dr. Saffran. Little boys pee into the front of their diapers, but with little girls, it runs into the back."

"Ohh..." we both said, then laughed along with her, having just learned lesson number one about raising our daughter.

Chapter Thirty | It Never Hurts to Try

Now that Dorrie was considered to be on the road to recovery and showing more awareness of her surroundings, her doctors informed us a hospital setting was no longer appropriate.

She still could not communicate any of her needs—and we weren't sure whether she was even aware of them—so she required round-the-clock skilled nursing care and physician monitoring.

I visited one facility after another, each more depressing than the last. They all seemed to smell of body fluids, disinfectant, and despair. I couldn't imagine allowing my mother to languish in one of those places.

Eventually, I found one place that seemed promising. The Mayflower Healthcare Center in Winter Park was pricey, but it was also clean and well-maintained.

"I have to admit," I told the person giving me a tour, "the patients here seem happy in spite of their health issues. Let's go back to the office, and I'll sign my mom up."

"Wonderful," she said. "We can get the paperwork started right away."

As I began filling out the small ream of forms, I made an offhand comment between pages.

"I'm so relieved I found this place when I did. If all goes well, my mother's being discharged in a few days."

"Oh!"

I looked up, startled by the alarm in the woman's voice.

"I'm sorry. There's been a misunderstanding. I didn't realize you needed placement so soon. We don't have any vacancies at the moment."

I put the pen down.

"How soon do you expect to have an open room?"

"Well, it's hard to say, but even then, we have a waiting list."

Maybe we could find somewhere temporary until a spot opened up.

"What are we talking, a few days, a couple of weeks? Maybe a month or two?"

She shook her head. "I'm afraid it's a four-year waiting list."

Four frickin' years?

By then she wouldn't need full-time care, I hoped, but in the meantime, I'd have to get back to my search.

"I'm sorry to have taken up so much of your time. I'll be on my way now."

"Please don't apologize. If you'd like, you can still fill out an application to put her on the list for somewhere down the road."

I hesitated. *Now* is what I needed, but if the last six weeks had taught me anything, it was how unpredictable—and unfair—life could be.

Pen to paper again, I filled out the remaining paperwork.

"Thanks again for your time."

I left the center, feeling the unfamiliar frustration of defeat adding to the familiar guilt over spending so many hours away from Alan, Dorrie, and my kids. I knew it had to be done—there was no other way to prepare for Dorrie's discharge—but once again I felt the pressure of juggling too many balls, keeping them aloft and bouncing between too few rackets.

I closed the car door and looked at the brochures in my hand. This place would be perfect for Dorrie, who'd taught me to never give up and never take no for an answer.

What the hell. It can't hurt to try.

I dialed the number for one of the head administrators. I told the secretary who answered, "My name is Pamela Saffran, the wife of Dr. Alan Saffran. I just toured your beautiful facility and I understand there is a waiting list, but I wonder if there is any way you can make an exception and move someone in sooner. My mother is being discharged in a few days, and I'd be so grateful if we could secure her a bed in a place like yours."

After leaving my number, I tossed the phone into my purse and headed back toward Alan.

I'd no sooner parked the car than my phone rang.

"Mrs. Saffran, I think we can help you."

It was the administrator returning my call.

"I recognized your name as soon as I heard your message. Your husband diagnosed a rare cancer and saved the life of someone dear to the top of this center's administration. I'm so sorry to learn of your mother's condition, but we will make room for her here."

I couldn't believe it.

"Thank you! This is wonderful. I'll make sure the hospital staff knows to coordinate her release with you."

"And how is Dr. Saffran? Will you please give him our best?"

Elation flatlined. Was this a casual inquiry, like those I'd had from others who knew Alan over the last twenty years, or was this a more knowing question from someone in the healthcare field who'd learned of his condition and hoped for a positive update?

I never knew how best to respond, which question to answer. This time, I felt, considering the huge favor this woman had just conceded, the full truth was best.

She was silent for a moment after I told her.

"My best wishes for your husband, Mrs. Saffran. And please know we will always have a bed available for your mom."

But it wasn't to be.

Chapter Thirty-One | A Plan for Us All

Dorrie had piano lessons as a child, but that was all. As my sisters and I grew up, she lessoned us to death. When any of the four of us complained, we all got the same lecture. There were charts all over our kitchen, outlining classes for all four of us. Overseeing our family calendar looked like planning a military invasion.

Despite our repeated protests, Dorrie refused to lighten up.

"I don't want you girls to let anything—especially a man—get in the way of fulfilling what you want to do and what your dreams are. And I don't want you to ever have to depend on a man for your livelihood. That's why I'm making sure you'll specialize in different things."

We had scant free time, hardly any at all, but what precious little we *did* have, Dorrie used to study our strengths and interests.

As frustrated and overbooked as we all felt, being lessoned to death was also wonderful—the reason we became so good at what we did. For me, that was tennis.

My mother had me on the tennis court when I was five. I could barely hold the racket. Lessons for such a young child were unheard of back in the sixties, and they certainly wouldn't have been available to girls, but my mother—and her plans for her daughters—were ahead of her time.

While I was learning to swing a too-big racket at a moving ball, my sisters were being pushed toward perfection as well. Mom saw from an early age that Maryann was a gifted artist. Dorrie would call her to come in for dinner, and Maryann would be outside, sitting in the middle of a field of wildflowers, sketching.

With a flash of insight, Mom said, "She's going to be an architect. I'm going to guide her toward that so she can use her artistic talents to take care of herself."

And Cynthia, her second daughter, was always up for—and able to—debate with everyone. Cinny constantly argued topics. With uncanny second sight, our mother declared, "She's going to be a lawyer. Or a judge."

So, Dorrie encouraged (and insisted) Cinny pursue the skills that would lead her in that direction.

My sister Caroline could have gone in as many different ways, as she was brilliant. As with my other sisters, Dorrie enrolled her in all-academic extracurricular and camp activities, each of which helped shape her path toward becoming a lawyer.

Besides my aptitude for tennis, Dorrie noticed I was an empathetic listener who eagerly helped people and animals. So, when I floundered after a year of realizing law school wasn't something I felt passionate about, Mom guided me toward becoming a psychologist; a career I loved.

All my life, my sisters and I have benefited from our mother's wisdom, and I really wanted that back.

*   *   *

The chemotherapy, hard as it was on Alan's body, seemed to be working. His important CEA markers dropped to around twenty, and I allowed myself to hope that a normal, single-digit, cancer-free score was within reach.

"Remind me never to complain about the cost of our health insurance premiums again," I told Alan one day, as I opened yet another hospital invoice. "How do people get through something like this without a decent policy?"

I added this latest $15,000 chemotherapy bill to the growing stack of medical statements awaiting processing by our insurance company.

Alan, resting in bed, shook his head and said, "Too many don't. The best they can hope for is that someone will waive their fees and help them anyway."

I looked at my husband's drawn face, and at once better understood things people had told me about his way of practicing medicine over the years. Often, I'd call his office and say to the staff, "I know the doctors' schedules are busy, but could you possibly work in a friend of mine?"

I referred so many patients to them they developed a code for my calls. I'd hear one say to another, "Got another F-O-P. Where can we put them?" before telling me a date and time to relay.

One day I had to ask, "What does F-O-P mean?"

The woman on the other end of the line chuckled.

"Oh, that. An F-O-P is a Friend of Pam. We always make room somewhere to fit in all the people you refer to us, just like we schedule Dr. Saffran for the patients no one else wants to see."

"I don't understand."

"I probably shouldn't have said that." Her words tumbled out in a flustered rush. "It's just that, well, we get calls about some of the migrant farmworkers from Apopka."

She lowered her voice to a near whisper.

"The ones without insurance can't pay much, if anything. Dr. Saffran told us to schedule them with him so they wouldn't be turned away."

"I didn't know about that."

"Oh! I don't think I was supposed to say anything. Please don't tell him I brought it up."

I hung up the phone that day wondering how many lives Alan had improved quietly, behind the scenes. How many lives had he saved because he was willing to treat those who couldn't afford his services?

Chapter Thirty-Two | Not Again

Even though Dorrie was improving, she had not been released from the hospital.

Her gibberish still wasn't making any sense, but she began to seem more aware of her surroundings. As the staff worked with her, they'd say, "Mrs. Thompson, Mrs. Thompson, can you hear me?" and she'd make sounds like, "Nlaa, nlaa, nlaa, nlaa." The closest she came to forming any intelligible words was in response to the same question. Slowly, deliberately, she learned to reply, "ah-ess."

She even sat propped up a few times, which we knew would greatly help reduce the risk of pneumonia. She was doing so well that one morning in the middle of May, the hospital staff said, "Now, we're going to see if she can handle swallowing something with a slight thickness, like applesauce or pudding." Prior to that, we were just giving her liquids. They were worried about her choking. But now they were confident enough to schedule another swallow test.

I went along for the exam, following the transportation employee who pushed her wheelchair down into the bowels of Florida Hospital. We took so many turns, I'd have never found my way out again on my own. I watched and waited as they had Dorrie sit up, and the therapist gave her a little bit of applesauce. The radiologist took pictures in segments as she swallowed and the food began going down.

"Yeah," they said, "it looks like she can start swallowing again."

It was great news—another milestone.

As we wheeled her back upstairs, I said, "OK Mom. I've got to pick up Ella from Park Maitland now." I patted her on the shoulder. "But I'll be back later."

The sun blazed as I hurried from my car to the school entry a few minutes early, hoping to circumvent the carpool line. It wasn't just that I hoped to avoid the heavy traffic and waiting in the long, long line. It was all the other moms. They were wonderful, but the news about Alan had spread like a brush fire, and curious concern flared whenever they saw me.

Between Alan and my mom, I just really wanted to be incognito (but it almost never happened). I wanted to dash inside, sign Ella out, and get out of there before one more person could ask me how either of them was doing. Even when I had good news, like today's triumphant swallow test for Dorrie, sometimes I just needed to center on myself and whichever child I was with in that moment, pretending everything—or at least one thing—was still normal in our lives.

When my phone rang on my way inside the school, my first reflex was worry. The caller ID listed an unknown number. My mind raced into a loop that was becoming increasingly common.

What's happened? Is it a lab or a doctor or a researcher for Alan? Has something happened to one of the boys? Is it the new speech therapist with a question about Dorrie?

I answered immediately. "This is Pamela Saffran."

"Hello, Pam? This is Dr. Gilles Chemtob."

I breathed again, relieved. Like so many physicians in the area, Dr. Chemtob, a pain management anesthesiologist, was one of Alan's friends and also his patient. They'd operated together many times, and our children were close in ages.

"Hello, Dr. Chemtob. How are you and your family today?"

"Oh, Pam, I'm so sorry. This isn't a social call."

Oh no, oh no, oh no, oh no. Is it Alan? Is it Mom?

"I happened to be walking by your mother's room while I was doing my rounds, and all of a sudden she started coding. Since she didn't have a living will in place, I did chest compressions, and I may have broken some of her ribs."

No, no, no, this can't be happening. Why can't my family catch a break?

"I had to intubate her to keep her breathing. She's on life support, but it doesn't look good. They pulled in a portable CT scanner, and it confirmed she has rebled. Her blood pressure skyrocketed to two hundred."

"But I was just there! She was fine."

There was no time for what-ifs or how-coulds or the concerned looks of the people I passed. I had to wipe my tears, get my daughter, and rush back.

Just like before, the neurosurgeon ran another catheter up Dorrie's leg to see if he could stop the bleed through her artery, but again there was too much blood.

Her doctor was so upset after the procedure, he slammed a door.

To re-clip the burst blood vessel, he would have to enter Dorrie's brain again.

*　　*　　*

The miniature petting zoo in the Saffran household was as much my doing as my husband's or our children's. I grew up with a lot of animals. In my childhood, I thought I had access to every animal known to man. I brought home and rescued any strays I found; Dorrie said I developed my psychologist's empathy by tending to their many and varied needs. Rabbits, doves, horses, dogs, cats, gerbils, hamsters...I think we had everything but chickens.

Alan, on the other hand, grew up in cramped quarters inside a modest apartment in the Jackson Heights neighborhood of New York City. His parents had one bedroom; Alan and his brother Bruce shared the other. All four Saffrans shared the small kitchen, bathroom, and living area, so there wasn't a lot of room for pets.

However, Alan had pet mice at one point—he loved those mice!—and he talked about them all the time. Once, though, they somehow got out of their cage. His poor mother had a fit, and as much as he wanted them, Alan never had pets again.

Until we married.

Almost as soon as we became Dr. And Mrs. Saffran, we bought a golden retriever puppy. Sammy, a great family dog, moved with us from my little house in Thornton Park to our new home; where one by one, our children were born and learned to crawl alongside him. Sammy lived a long time, but eventually his health failed and our vet had to put him down.

We thought no goodbye could ever be as painful.

In spite of that, we welcomed other animals into our family. Who could have known that we would have to give them away?

Alan's doctors cautioned us that chemotherapy meant he could not live with the bacteria associated with house pets. I'd gone home that same day in April and first farmed away our sweet little parakeet, Budgie, then found new homes for our three cats and as many of the gerbils as we could.

We even sent our beloved black lab, Hershey, to live with dear friends, the Bibliowicz family. It broke all our hearts, but if their presence endangered Alan, they had to go.

Chapter Thirty-Three | We're Not Pulling the Plug

After Dorrie's second, unexpected surgery to stop bleeding in her brain, we found ourselves waiting through ten terrifying days, hoping she would pull through. She'd come so far only to be once again laid out on the bed, inert, with her head newly shaved and bandaged.

My sisters came as often and stayed as long as they could. A few days later, Dr. Baker insisted we have a difficult talk about Dorrie's condition. "I'm sorry, but it's time," he said.

"Time for what, exactly?" I asked.

"For you to let go."

I was stunned.

"But you said the surgery went well, and the first ten days would be touch and go. It's only been four days."

"Yes, but she's eighty." His frown voiced his disapproval even louder. "At her age, the odds of her even making it through the surgery were fifty-fifty. Much less recovering after. It's over. You need to think about her. If this was my mother, I'd let her go."

"She's our mother, and we're not pulling the plug."

"Your mother has basically been in a coma since the beginning of April. She's never entirely resumed full consciousness in between, and now after this second bleed, she's only being kept alive via life support."

He took a deep breath and let it out before continuing.

"There was just too much blood in her brain with the second stroke. I think it's time you ladies let your mom go. It's time to pull the plug."

I was too stunned to speak, but Maryann didn't hesitate.

"No, we're not pulling the plug," she said. "When I got here this morning, I saw her toe wiggling. You told us before that was purposeful movement, so no, we're not pulling the plug. We're going to give her time to recover."

With Dorrie's neurosurgeon unable to persuade us to end life support, it seemed the hospital staff felt there was nothing more they could do for her in the eleventh-floor brain injury ICU, where the level of one-nurse-per-two-patients typically reflected the overwhelming cost of $40,000 per day. (I thanked God every day for Medicare, but I had no idea yet how much we'd have to cover out of pocket).

After my sisters and I refused to terminate Mom's life support, the hospital stepped her down to the seventh-floor ICU to finish out her observation period.

A week later, the discharge nurse was kind but firm.

"We're transferring your mother to an interim care facility; it will have to be up to her there. Doctors will still see her daily, the same as here in the ICU."

The implication was clear: the new facility would keep Dorrie alive on life support while the hospital freed up her room for a new patient whose progress was more likely.

They transferred Dorrie—trach tube and all—into Select Specialty Hospital, which stood across the street from Florida Hospital.

At least my commute to see her is no different from before.

The building was lousy with people like her, still in comas and helpless.

She lay mostly unresponsive for the better part of two months. In the meantime, she also had three rounds of pneumonia, and a host of infections, including MRSA.

However, after an excruciating reprise of our previous watching and waiting, it was in Select where Dorrie finally, truly woke up and began working toward her own recovery.

At the end of July, Dorrie's therapists again tested her swallowing ability and allowed her to begin eating applesauce. It felt like a huge victory, though they kept her on the feeding tube much longer for supplemental nutrition. Eating was too difficult and slow for her to rely on her own chewing and swallowing. To open and close her jaw, then swallow a few mouthfuls, exhausted her.

The pressure to see to everyone's needs was constant. Sometimes the medical staff needed gentle reminders—sometimes outright reprimands. It was a never-ending balancing act to make sure I was getting Alan what he needed, and Dorrie what she needed, and my kids what they needed; standing as their fulcrum, I too often neglected what I needed.

I couldn't have gotten through it without our families' support. My sisters Caroline and Maryann, of course, were there to help whenever they could. In many ways, we'd lost our mother and needed each other. For months (while my husband grew gravely ill), Dorrie lay nearly as unresponsive as if she were dead.

"If she ever awakens," her doctors cautioned us, "we'll see what kind of damage was done. She may never be like herself."

I couldn't face the possibility that she might never again be there for me and my kids.

If I can't make her well, I can at least give her the best shot possible.

I threw myself into searching for quality care facilities, because I was back to square one. The promised Mayflower opening closed to us during the long weeks and months of her second post-op recovery.

For a while, from the Select facility, I moved Mom into a nursing home I'd once worked in, East Orlando Rehab Center. As I signed the admission paperwork, I thought, "It's crazy how life is. Crazy that I'm back here where I used to treat people, with Mom as a patient."

She had extensive physical therapy there, but it was a longer drive for me to make. Worse, she caught additional infections, so we transferred her to the nearer Gardens at Mary Lee DePugh Nursing Center.

My poor mother was constantly sick: urinary tract infections, MRSA, multiple bouts of pneumonia. Each time my phone rang, adrenaline pumped sweat into my palms as I braced against the threat of more bad news. She'd faced too many near-misses.

* * *

In what seems like a lifetime ago, Alan was coming home from work one evening and stopped his car in front of the house instead of pulling into the garage.

"Why is the front door wide open?" he called out, clearly annoyed. "Do you expect me to air-condition the entire neighborhood?"

Dorrie answered him from the kitchen.

"Wasn't me. The cat must have opened it."

"Uh-huh. Dorrie, why'd you leave it open again?"

"I already told you, Alan, it must have been Daisy or one of the others."

He shook his head, not wanting to argue about it, but they repeated the conversation almost daily over the course of a week or so. More than once in that same period, I'd return from taking Ella to school and drive up to find the animals playing by themselves in the front yard—with our entry door wide open.

One weekend, I heard Alan yell, "Aha!" from the other end of the house.

"What on earth are you shouting about?"

"I just saw her do it. I can't believe she's that smart."

"Saw who do what? Ella? Of course she's smart."

"No, I mean, yes, she is, but that's not what I mean. It's Daisy."

"What about her?"

By now I'd joined him. He held the calico in his arms, stroking her behind the ears.

"She just jumped up and held onto the levered handle until it went down—*click-click*—and opened the door. What an amazing, smart kitty."

"Really? I thought Mom was making that up."

"I did too." Right away, he went and apologized for not believing her.

"Told you so," she smirked.

Chapter Thirty-Four | Thank You, Dorrie

A few days after Alan's third chemotherapy treatment at MD Anderson, he insisted on coming with me to Florida Hospital to see Dorrie. This was not long after his diagnosis, and Dorrie was still in a coma from her first surgery to stop the bleeding in her brain.

My husband, who'd once been *the* Dr. Saffran, chief of otolaryngology for the entire hospital, refused the help of a wheelchair, too proud to be seen needing it. At the same time, he was too humble to presume his need for help might be greater than that of any other patient. Fortunately, Alan was relatively young, indisputably strong, and otherwise physically fit before he started chemo. He walked the maze of corridors under his own power—slowly—except for leaning on my arm.

Alan hadn't seen Dorrie since the weekend of her surgery, right before his own diagnosis. Even now, I'd protested against him coming. It wasn't that I didn't want him to see her; I just thought he shouldn't come yet and expose himself to all the germs in the hospital, even if he did wear a surgical mask.

"Don't worry, Pam. If it's good enough to protect patients from catching my germs while I'm operating on them, it's good enough to keep me from catching anything while we visit your mom."

Since Dorrie was comatose, "visit" implied far more interaction than took place. I didn't put two and two together about Alan's intentions on our way there. In my mind, I viewed only the literal, practical level of his request.

Oh, he needs to see Dorrie. He hasn't seen her in ages. Of course he wants to go.

I was too entrenched in warrior mode to think clearly of what motivated him. My own mind was continually engaged in strategizing. Between Alan and Mom, I had two fronts of healthcare battles going on. It seemed my every conscious thought was, "How am I going to save them?"

As we entered Dorrie's room that day, I went about my usual routine, announcing myself to her unresponsive ears, kissing her forehead (feeling her temperature as I did so), and straightening the covers around her feet. I'd thought Alan might want to speak to her nurse for a clinical update, but he only shook his head.

At first, he didn't say anything. He looked at my mother, taking in the changes from the vibrant woman who'd lived with us since Miles's birth. Then he held her hand. After a few minutes of silence, he thanked her for everything she had done and how she had helped us with the kids.

It wasn't until we reached the car and started for home that I realized why Alan had come. His words made me wish I wasn't behind the wheel.

"She's going to outlive me."

"Alan, how can you say that? She's still in a coma. We don't even know if she's gonna wake up. And you're going to get better. Your markers are already better."

He didn't argue with me, but he didn't agree, either.

In his mind, he'd accompanied me to say his goodbye to Dorrie.

*   *   *

Early in Alan's diagnosis, his doctors strongly urged him to have genetic testing done on his biopsied tumors. The testing would help determine which treatments would be most effective. Later, we had to have a second round of genetic testing.

One mixed benefit of Alan's genetic testing was confirmation that Alan carried the K-RAS mutation present in more than ninety-five percent of pancreatic cancer patients. While it was true that every bit of information we learned about the disease riddling his body gave us another way to treat it, the knowledge came with a sobering cost.

Alan's own DNA made him likely to develop this horrible disease. The same set of genes that produced Alan's brilliance, determination, and resiliency were also the source of his body's self-betrayal.

The Saffrans were just riddled with cancer. Alan's first cousins and an uncle tested positive for the BRCA-1 and -2 genes and developed glioblastoma and kidney cancers at younger ages than Alan. His grandfather died of lung cancer in his fifties.

As Alan relayed his family's medical history to the oncologist, the doctor commented, "That's your Ashkenazic lineage," referring to Jewish people whose heritage is primarily from France, Germany, and Eastern Europe.

At that moment, I felt like a light bulb exploded above me. I wished we'd realized back then the prevalence of cancer in the Saffran family.

How did we not see this coming? Why didn't we test Alan's genes before he got cancer? Why didn't he leave work early and get a CT scan the first time he felt sick to his stomach?

In school, I'd studied Freud's famous axiom, "Anatomy is destiny."

If only I had known. If only we had looked behind at the Saffran family's history and thought ahead to its ramifications, we could have checked Alan sooner, just in case. We could have bought a CT scanning machine and used it enough to catch the first possibility of a tumor. "Get into the CT scanner," I'd have begged him every week.

It would have been the only way to catch his tumors early, before they'd spread. By the time Alan felt the first symptom of illness, a CT scan found he was riddled with tumors.

Chapter Thirty-Five | Patients Come First

Come hell or high water, Alan was not going to let his patients down—even if he was sick himself.

Late in 1996, when our firstborn Miles was still an infant, we took a weekend trip to Antigua in the Caribbean. We went with our friends William and Beth Lu, who had their two children along as well.

A terrible storm delayed the first leg of our return flight Sunday afternoon. As the hour grew later and later, Alan became more and more agitated. By the time our plane left the island, we knew we wouldn't make it into Puerto Rico in time for our connecting flight to the mainland.

Meanwhile, Alan broke out in a sweat. Before long, I realized what he already knew: He had a high fever. His pallor and sickness only grew worse throughout the flight.

When the plane touched down in San Juan near eleven o'clock that night, Alan turned to me and said, "I've got to get back to the mainland. I've got nine surgeries scheduled tomorrow morning."

From his nearby seat, William, a neurosurgeon, said, "Listen, Alan, just cancel your morning appointments. That's what I'm doing."

"I will not do that. I'm not inconveniencing any of my patients."

We'd been married for a couple of years, but I hadn't yet fully realized I couldn't interfere when Alan had patients waiting for him; or in this case, if he had patients who would begin waiting early the next day. They needed him, and he wouldn't let anything as inconvenient as a high fever get in his way.

I didn't like it, but what could I do?

"Well, Alan, OK then," I finally said, hoping that one pointed jab at his personal conscience might lift a chink in the armor of his professional code. "If you're sure you'd rather leave your wife and baby on an island with nowhere to go in the middle of the night, even though you're clearly too sick to travel, then you just go right on."

"I knew you'd understand. I'm going to find a flight right now."

Alan was determined to be at work by the time the rest of us might catch a morning flight. He kissed the back of Miles's head and gave me a chaste, contagion-limiting peck on the cheek. His fever-warmed lips burned my skin.

"I'll meet you back in the United States, but I can't wait for morning. I've got to get back tonight."

He ran ahead as we exited the plane, ditching me and eight-month-old Miles.

In spite of the late hour, taxi drivers outside the San Juan airport swarmed around us in their frenzy to attract passengers. Shouts of "over here, over here, over here" and waving arms bombarded us as the Lu's and I juggled our children and luggage. At last, one ambitious driver squished all six of us into his car and in a great rush, piled our luggage atop the vehicle as fast as he could.

I worried about Alan, but this was back in the days before cell phones became more common than car keys. I had no way to learn whether he found a flight, and I had no way to let him know where we headed either. With a sudden lurch, my concern shifted from my absent husband to my baby and myself.

Our driver took off into the night and within seconds, we flew eighty miles an hour down one of San Juan's major highways.

Unfortunately, in his haste, our driver failed to secure our luggage. *Ka-thunk. Ka-thunk.* Beth and I jumped, startled as one by one, our suitcases toppled from roof to trunk to pavement. Our flying luggage forced speeding drivers to swerve all over the roadway. We didn't try to recover the bags. It would have been too dangerous.

From the back of the car we cried out, "Holy crap!" as our driver went even faster. Horns blared from every direction.

Oh my god. This is the end of us. We are going to die. Thank god, my purse is in here with Miles so they'll be able to identify our bodies.

Against all odds, we reached the hotel intact and napped a few fitful hours—still wearing yesterday's clothes—before we crammed our disheveled group into another taxi. Our rescheduled flight was so early, seven o'clock in the morning, I hoped I might find Alan still in the airport, maybe even boarding the same plane. Alan was nowhere to be found.

After we landed in Orlando, I hurried through the airport, glad for the first time that our luggage stayed on a San Juan highway. Not having to wait at baggage claim meant I'd be home that much sooner. When I unlocked our front door, I didn't care whether I woke my husband from a fevered sleep; I called out to him while pushing open the door.

"Alan! We're back. Are you OK, sweetheart?"

No answer.

I searched all over the house, still toting Miles in my arms. No husband, no luggage, no note, nothing. Frantic, I called the surgery center.

"Oh, yes, Mrs. Saffran, he's here, but he's in surgery. Do you want me to put the call through on speaker?"

Relief flooded me. He'd made it safely, and he must have been feeling better to be operating on patients.

"No, that's OK. Just tell him I called and I'll see him when he gets home."

Around dinner time, I heard Alan drive up. I was so eager to tell him about our adventures I ran to greet him, but pulled up short when I saw him.

"Alan, you look terrible. What were you doing at work?"

I hardly recognized his raspy voice.

"I had to take care of my patients, Pam."

"It looks like you should have been taking care of yourself." I felt his burning forehead, got him a glass of water, and listened to his story.

"I made it onto the final flight out of San Juan last night. I barely made it onto the plane before they were ready to take off. We got into Miami at midnight. The rental car companies all closed down about the time we were touching down."

Alan wiped his brow with the back of his hand and took another sip of water.

"I finally found one woman at a rental counter packing up to leave for the night and talked her into renting me a car even though they'd officially closed at midnight. Then I drove straight to the surgery center."

"You drove all night from Miami to Orlando with a fever of—how high is it?"

He shrugged his head to the side.

"It doesn't matter."

"It does to me."

He sighed.

"One-oh-three."

"Oh, Alan. Why didn't you come home?"

"I figured I could get a better nap if I was already there."

He tried to hide a yawn behind his hand.

"I got to the surgical center about four, pulled a gurney into my office, and grabbed a solid couple of hours before my first procedure at seven."

Chapter Thirty-Six | Pulled in Two Directions

The last Monday of July was another day of needing to be in two places at once. On Friday, three days earlier, I'd cringed when the caller ID showed the physician line at Select. Every time they called, I feared the worst for Dorrie.

"Mrs. Saffran, I'm calling about your mother. Her heart rate is dropping dangerously low, sometimes under fifty beats per minute. She needs a pacemaker."

"Oh my god. I'll be right there."

"No, you don't need to rush. We've scheduled her procedure for early Monday morning."

Sunday night they'd transported Dorrie from Select to one of the surgical floors at Orlando Regional Medical Center, across the street from where I now brought Alan for his fifth chemo treatment at the MD Anderson Cancer Center. For Alan, it would be another day of the now familiar routine: arrival and sign-in, blood draw and white cell count, hours of chemotherapy medications dripping into his veins, analysis of the blood drawn earlier in the day. He at least knew what to expect.

My part in the day, however, was to be anything but routine.

Alan signed in and joked with the nurse taking his blood as part of the pre-chemo process. When she left the room, I realized I'd been holding my breath.

"How can you be so calm about this? What if your white count is too low?"

The oncologist would not allow Alan to undergo today's round of chemo if his white cell count was not high enough for his immune system to handle the chemotherapy. On the other hand, if it was too high, that could mean he was already battling any infection on top of the cancer.

"It'll be fine, Pam, not like last time."

He waited for me to return his smile, though mine didn't match the confidence his held.

"Don't worry so much. I've had my shots." Alan laughed, but I didn't think it was funny.

Last time he'd been scheduled for treatment, they'd postponed it on account of too few white cells. Instead of chemo, he'd gotten an injection of Neupogen to stimulate the growth of his immune-boosting cells.

I'd hated the idea of waiting—of giving his tumors even a few days of rest from our attack. The delay gnawed at my insides, but after listening to the oncologist's explanation, I understood we had no choice.

A quick knock against the doorjamb sent my heart into overdrive.

The door opened and the same nurse peeked around it. By the look on her face, I anticipated her words with a relieved sigh.

"You're good to go, Dr. Saffran," she said, as the rest of her body rounded the doorway and entered the room. "Let's get you started so you can get out of here before midnight."

I checked my watch and tried to smile at the hyperbole. Once he was hooked up and began his fifth of ten scheduled rounds, he wouldn't leave the room for another six hours. For a while I sat with Alan to keep him company throughout the long day, just as I'd done four times before.

As the chemicals worked their way into Alan's body, he grew increasingly tired.

I made sure he was as comfortable as possible, but I was getting antsy about Dorrie and her surgery. I needed to be here with my husband—but also there with my mother. After fidgeting myself into a frenzy, I pecked Alan quickly on the lips.

"Honey, I've got to go. I'm gonna go check on Dorrie now. I'll check back in with you as soon as I know anything."

He knew well her surgeon's reputation and glanced at the time.

"Of course, Pam. She should be in recovery by now."

"Love you. Call me if you need anything."

I was already out the door, half-running toward the elevator, when I heard Alan call out, "Take the fifth-floor bridge between the buildings—it's a shortcut! You'll get you there faster."

I couldn't help chuckling. Alan knew these hallways as well as I knew the grid on a tennis racket, and even from the middle of chemo, he still wanted to help me navigate them.

*　　*　　*

"I don't see why we have to do this now, Alan," I complained. I hadn't let up on him even while driving us to the attorney's office. As we got out of the car, I kept at it.

"Your CEA markers are going down, and you told me if you keep feeling better, next month you might see a few patients. So, I don't understand why we can't put this off."

Alan's jaw muscle tightened in the same rigid line it showed yesterday.

"I know you're still angry I made the appointment without telling you, but I suspected you might put up a fuss about it—and I was right. In spite of how you feel, though, we have to get this done now, Pam."

I could have refused to drive him, but even in his weakened state, when Alan put his foot down about something, there was no swaying him. He didn't do it often; he preferred letting everyone around him come to their own decisions in their own time, which made his rare insistence all the more implacable.

Inside the office, I grudgingly listened as carefully as I could, only because of how important this meeting was to Alan. I leaned back in the comfortable chair, arms and legs crossed, the outward picture of calm compliance. But my mind whirred in a storm of arguing emotions.

I can't believe we are doing this. Having a will is a good thing—everybody says you need one. But why now? We're fighting the cancer. We're going to make him better than better, because losing Alan isn't an option. We're not gonna need this for a long, long time.

Our meeting with the lawyer dragged on and on. My body tensed. The man across the desk from us was no longer an attorney, but a ball machine aiming projectiles at my head. Instead of tennis balls I could have redirected in my sleep, he lobbed legal terms I either understood only in part, or too well. I flinched at the relentless blur: Partnership. Ownership. Practice. Distribution. Rental. Shareholder. Proxy. Survivor. Estate. Beneficiary.

While Alan signed and initialed the pages of his newly drafted will, I numbly inked my own signature onto lines naming me as the future executor of Alan's estate. With every silent stroke of the ballpoint in my hand, "I hate this, I hate this, I hate this ..." repeated in my head.

On our way home, Alan's mood was as light and warm as the June afternoon. I tried not to let the storm I felt rain on his relief, but I still resented feeling coerced into my husband's estate planning.

Later, I'd thank God Alan insisted; there was soon going to be a third front in the war I was fighting for Alan and Dorrie.

Chapter Thirty-Seven | Battling the Partners

Looking back, I realize my antenna should have been up, warning me that something was amiss. But I was so fixated on getting Alan and Dorrie better that it went right over my head.

Not long after Alan's diagnosis, we got a notice from one of Alan's partners that our cell phone plan was being cut off. For years, the partners and their families had shared the costs and the benefits of a group plan. Because Alan was on leave, they said, our participation was over.

"We can pay our own bill," Alan told them, "but don't cut us off. We need to keep our numbers the same for the kids and our family."

"And your doctors," I ranted. "Don't forget we're still waiting to hear back from some of the specialists I've got calls out to."

That incident ended in a truce, but it was just a precursor to what was to come with Alan's partners, men he considered friends.

One night after a particularly exhausting round of chemo, Alan was recovering at home in bed. After the kids settled into doing their homework, I went to check on him again.

"Can I get you anything to eat or drink, sweetie?"

"No, thank you, but I need to talk to you, Pam." I sat on the end of the bed.

"I just got off the phone with James."

"That's nice," I said, glad Alan's partners were staying in touch with him. "Was he calling to wish you good luck with this round of chemo?"

"Pam, I think we're going to have to sell the house, because the guys are not going to buy you out."

"What?" His words were such a non-sequitur it took me a moment to process what he'd said.

"James said they're not planning to buy out your share of the practice and the properties when I die."

For once, I ignored the worst of his assertions, responding only to the financial implications of what he said.

"Well, that wouldn't be so bad, would it, because I'd still get your share's worth of the income to pay the kids' school bills, right?"

He thought a moment, then slowly nodded.

"The twice-a-year distribution checks from the rental income on our buildings should be enough to cover their tuitions. But you'll still have the mortgage and property taxes, plus all the other bills. The rental income will take care of the kids' school expenses, as long as they don't go up."

His brow furrowed and his eyes clouded in a pain.

"James said they don't have the money without me doing surgeries. He said if they did offer to buy you out, they would only go as high as fifty percent of what it's really worth. So, you shouldn't count on that money."

Alan kept the discussion factual, no matter how much I speculated or asked, "What if...?" I asked him to call James back and clarify this and that, but Alan refused.

"No, Pam. I'm not going to fight them. We'll find another way."

Sometimes I admired Alan's ability to turn away from a fight. He'd rather acquiesce, giving people the benefit of the doubt rather than going head-to-head with them. At other times—like this one—the undefeated champion I'd trained to be was just plain frustrated by him acting that way.

As I thought it through this time, though, I understood why Alan was willing to step back from this fight. He was already fighting the battle for his own life— at my insistence. He didn't have the strength to take on another, even for the good of his wife and kids.

"Alan, don't worry about me. I will be able to take care of my side of the finances. Let's just get you better."

*   *   *

As I walked the hallways waiting to see Dorrie after she had the pacemaker implanted, I was fully aware of the irony: My mother's slowing, weakened heart required a pacemaker, yet mine raced. My footsteps could have outrun a singles player competing against an accomplished doubles team.

What seemed like hours later, Mom's cardiologist emerged from the operating suite. "Her surgery went well, but we're going to have to keep a close eye on her. With the dormant aneurysms in her brain, there's always danger from potential re-bleeds."

"Right. That's what her neurosurgeon said. He told me we can't ever let her blood pressure go above 150/90."

"Absolutely. They'll move her into the ICU recovery soon, and you'll be able to see her."

It seemed like forever before they let me see her. I worked my way around the nurses milling in the middle of the floor area. Whether they were having a staff meeting or it was their social hour, it seemed as if every nurse on the floor was clumped together like links in a human barricade.

At last, I found my mother—and gasped at what I saw.

The machine displaying her vitals flashed 190/120.

"Someone get in here now! My mother's blood pressure is too high!"

One of the nursing techs glanced my way, and pulled by my eye contact as much as my waving gestures, sauntered over to the door of the room.

"Oh, that's OK. It's normal for it to go up a bit after surgery."

"It's not OK. Get me the nurses now. Her doctor said her BP can't ever get that high."

"Relax, ma'am. We know what we're doing."

I elbowed my way around her and charged at the clustered group.

"My mother needs help *now*."

"We'll be with you in a minute, ma'am." She turned back toward the group.

"No, you'll come with me this second." I was so upset, I may have pulled her by the arm. "My mother's blood pressure isn't supposed to get that high. Haven't any of you read her chart?"

"Ma'am," she said, her voice loud and cold now, "we'll be with you in a *minute*."

Fear and frustration spiked my own blood pressure. Later there would be time for losing it, but my mother needed these people's help for who knew how long before I even got here. I channeled my fury into clenched fists and clear words, forcing my voice to speak as rapidly yet calmly as I could. I was stern and to the point.

"I'm so sorry to interrupt you. I can see that you guys are having an important meeting here. But my mother has had multiple brain aneurysms. Her neurosurgeon, Dr. Chris Baker, is a friend of my husband, Dr. Alan Saffran, who used to be chief of ENT at this hospital. Dr. Baker warned that the six aneurysms around the sentinel bleed he repaired are ready to blow if my mother's blood pressure ever goes above 150 over 90. Well, it is currently 190 over 120. So, if you want her to die on your watch during this little meeting, then so be it, but if none of you wants to explain to your boss why you let this woman bleed out in her brain, I suggest one of you get her blood pressure lowered. Right. NOW."

It was as if I'd hit a tennis ball into an ant hill. Two of them dropped their clipboards and ran immediately into her room.

Chapter Thirty-Eight | Cruel Irony

A week after Alan's fifth round of chemotherapy treatment, we returned to his oncologist's office at MD Anderson, just as we'd done four times before and as we'd do yet again after every one of Alan's ten scheduled treatment rounds. Last time, his antigen markers had been down to twenty. I couldn't wait to see how much they'd dropped in two weeks.

My heart tightened when Dr. Kayaleh walked into the room. A big, broad-shouldered, good-looking man, he usually stood straight, radiating confidence and optimism. This time, he slumped.

"I just went over your blood work." He sat face-to-face with my husband. "My friend, I don't have good news on this one. Your markers are back up to forty. The FOLFIRINOX regimen is not working anymore."

Forty—doubled. Not working. That can't be.

I couldn't breathe. Alan, his doctors, everyone, had called FOLFIRINOX the big kahuna of chemos, the court of last resort, where they threw everything they had at pancreatic cancer tumors.

The first line of defense.

And where there was a first, there had to be a second. "So, we switch chemos now, right? How soon can we start him on the second line?" I asked.

Both men turned to me. Alan's gaze drifted to the floor. I thought he shook his head slightly. Behind Dr. Kayaleh, the second hand on a big white wall clock ticked from one stark black number to the next. I concentrated on the tone of Dr. Kayaleh's measured words. "The gemcitabine-Abraxane combination. Yes. It's achieving positive results with many pancreatic cancer patients, and the FDA is allowing us to proceed with it even before they announce it as a preferred regimen, but we will need to wait several weeks before Alan's body will be able to have that added to the chemo that's already in him."

Weeks?

I looked from Dr. Kayaleh's compassionate expression to Alan's mask of resignation. That he might give up punched air back into my lungs. I lobbed it back out in a question, aiming it as a request rather than a demand.

"Doctor Kayaleh, Omar, don't you think in the meantime maybe Alan should start the dendritic trial?"

Before, the oncologist had been subdued; now his face paled, then reddened. He looked stricken, as if I'd slapped him. If I lived another hundred years, I knew I would never forget the look on his face as he said, "Oh, I am so sorry. I can't get you into the trial treatment yet. You're third in line—there are people in line—two other patients already waiting ahead of you, Alan. The timing's not going to be good. It's not going to work for you. We have to wait a full two weeks to observe the other patient who just got his dendritic cells. You'd have to wait... too long."

Alan sucked in his breath and lowered his face into his hands.

My eyes blurred and refocused on the clock beyond Dr. Kayaleh.

"Omar, you're the principle investigator," Alan said. "Why can't you start me on the dendritic trial now that the chemo protocol is no longer working?"

We're out of time.

"My hands are tied by the FDA regulations. As soon as they gave us approval for the trial, we started two other patients on it. You were doing so well on the FOLFIRINOX."

"If it's already underway, why not add me?"

"The FDA built a mandatory two-week waiting period between procedures. In this phase one trial, after every insertion, the patient has to be closely monitored for side effects and symptoms before..."

"That's bullshit, Omar. We both know the dendritic cells are from the patients' own bodies. It's not the same as injecting foreign substances."

"Of course I know that, Alan. But you know how the FDA is. If we don't wait the full two weeks for each patient before we begin on another or even resume with the first, they'll cut the whole trial"—he snapped his fingers—"faster than that. We have no choice but to wait."

No. Alan doesn't have time to wait. I've got to get him this trial. I've got to get myself into gear.

I blinked, drew in a breath, and found my voice again.

"What do you mean, we've got to wait? There wouldn't even be a trial if I hadn't gotten it here for Alan—he's the reason MD Anderson applied for the fricking dendritic therapy trial in the first place. It was because I went to Mark Roh and convinced him to get the hospital board to agree to do this trial for Alan! And now you're telling me he can't have it?"

"Pam, I'm very sorry, but the others have already started the protocol. We can't interrupt their treatment to start it for Alan."

My arms shook with the effort of keeping my balled fists at my side. It was early August, four months into Alan's projected six-month lifespan. I was furious.

"They wouldn't even know about the dendritic therapy, let alone be a part of the trial here, if it weren't for Alan, so... How. Are. We. Going. To. Fix. This."

In all our years together, I'd never seen Alan lose his temper in front of a colleague. He was all about decorum and professionalism. But after we left Dr. Kayaleh's office and got in the car, his anger erupted.

"I cannot believe that guy. You worked so hard to win this trial, and now I can't be a participant in it?"

"Alan, we're not gonna let that stop us. We're gonna figure this out. I'm gonna figure this out."

We'd already won MD Anderson the right to its dendritic cell therapy trial. Now I just had to figure out how to win back Alan's right to what we'd fought for.

*   *   *

The day after our disheartening and infuriating meeting with Dr. Kayaleh, I happened to glance at Alan's iPad. He'd left it open in the middle of composing an email to Miles, Nat, and Ella.

From: Alan Saffran

Date: Monday, August 5, 2013, 1:56 p.m.

Subject: This is for my children

You have been the focus of my life for as long as you have been here. You may have noticed that I do not have many active hobbies—my baseball league aside. I have never felt the need to pick up golf, improve my chess game, take up oil painting or pursue other relaxing or challenging activities. This is because of my dedication to you. I have always wanted to make sure that you had the proper basis for being fine, honest people throughout your lives. I hope that I have emphasized enough that it should be substance over appearance, honesty and dignity over opportunism, long-term planning over immediate gratification. I tried to make sure that you had discipline in your lives, not

It ended there, mid-thought. *What he was going to say next? Why didn't he say it?*

I didn't know what kept him from sending–or even finishing–his message to them. It was so unlike him.

Alan told our kids as they grew up, "The three most powerful words in the English language are *never give up.*"

And he'd always lived them.

Chapter Thirty-Nine | Dorrie's Awake!

I may have caused a scene with the nurses, but at least they were paying attention to Dorrie and had stabilized her blood pressure. Gradually, as the blood pressure readouts on the monitor approached safer ranges, the numbers of people in the room also diminished. One by one they left, none of them looking me in the eye.

But something good, something amazing, had happened in the meantime.

Dorrie woke up.

With her heartbeat newly regulated, and in spite of the chaos that nearly cost her another aneurysm, she finally, truly began to wake up.

For months, I'd waited and waited to tell my mother about the traumatic turns our lives had taken since early April. I had yet to tell her about Alan being sick. She'd only recently demonstrated conscious awareness, and then they'd rushed her from the Select care center into surgery at ORMC.

I'd seen her face every day, but I'd missed *her*. Dorrie had always given me such sage advice all my life. If I'd ever needed my mother's wisdom, it was now, and she was waking up—at last! Dorrie was talking, responding to me and to the doctor and nurses. Most of her words made sense, though a few didn't; but she clearly knew who I was.

After the doctors and nurses cleared the room, I pulled a chair as close as I could to her bedside.

"It's so good to finally have you back, Mom."

She smiled and asked me to tell her what she'd missed.

I told her everything that had happened to her. Everything I'd done to keep on top of her doctors. Everything that was happening with the kids.

She watched me intently as I spoke, nodding her head and *mm-hmming* as she listened. She really was starting to finally come out of it.

"Mom," I concluded, finally saying the words I'd wanted and needed to say to her since April 8, "Mom, I have something really important to tell you."

"What, Pam? What is it?"

"Alan's been diagnosed with stage IV pancreatic cancer." I told her everything we'd done, everything I was doing to fight for his life. "What am I going to do,

Mom? What should I do, Mom?"

She turned toward me. I'd waited four long months for her to wake up, to regain consciousness so I could ask her advice. And now she was finally, truly awake.

Her face showed pensive concentration, but she answered almost immediately. I strained, leaning closer to distinguish the words she worked so hard to form.

"Well, Pam, you need to get Alan into the best animal hospital. His coat needs to be shiny like a cat. And he needs to get into that cat hospital as quickly as possible."

I couldn't respond.

Oh my god, oh, my god. What am...I can't do this...

Until that moment, I'd held out hope that in Dorrie's ongoing recovery, I'd draw on her strength and wisdom to help me through my husband's life-and-death struggle.

I forced myself to breathe again.

OK. I'm in this by myself. I'm in it alone.

I couldn't count on my mother to mother me anymore.

*   *   *

I left Dorrie's room, my legs wooden, and went back to join Alan. He was nearly at the end of his chemo session, and though drained, the first thing he said was, "How's Dorrie?"

"Well, she's awake now."

"That's great! Wait, do you mean she's awake-awake?"

"More or less ... The cardiologist said the procedure went fine. Her heart is working well with the pacemaker."

My own heart couldn't bear to tell him any more than that.

I got him home and into bed. Exhausted from his treatment, he fell asleep right away. After the kids also went down for the night, I lay awake.

Only then did I reflect on the day. Once again, I'd been pulled in opposite directions. I had to manage the demands of mothering, but I also had to be a constant health advocate, fighting to keep my mother and my husband alive.

I didn't know how much more I could take.

Chapter Forty | Tumor Fever

Alan's family, including his mother Dolores and brother Bruce, had been staying with us the week that we were told he couldn't get into the dendritic trial. They were leaving soon to make the three-hour drive south to Boca Raton.

Meanwhile, I sat with Alan at the table. I'd made him a bowl of soup for lunch, but the meal wasn't progressing as it should.

"Honey," I said gently, "you don't look well." His hands shook, and his face was an ashen, almost colorless yellow.

He continued lifting the spoon to his mouth, but his hands trembled too much for the broth to reach his lips.

"Here, honey. Let me help."

I fed him a few spoonfuls before he stopped me.

"I don't feel well. I think I'm going to go lie down."

On his way to the bedroom, Alan walked slowly to the front door and said goodbye to his mother, brother, and the rest of his family. By the time he went to lie down, he looked so drained I worried he might not make it all the way to bed.

Knowing how much he needed the rest, I left him undisturbed for a couple of hours. Around two or three o'clock, I went to check on him. Even from the doorway, his face looked flushed. I touched his forehead with the back of my hand and recoiled. Alan was burning up. I grabbed a thermometer from the accumulated medical supplies on the nightstand and took his temperature. It was 104 degrees.

As angry as I still was with Dr. Kayaleh over the fact that Alan couldn't yet actively participate in the dendritic trial, he was still Alan's oncologist, and I needed to let him know what was happening. By now Dr. Kayaleh and I were on a first-name basis, as with many of Alan's other first-name colleague-friends.

"Omar, Alan's fever's so high. What should I do?"

"Make him as comfortable as you can. Meanwhile, let's wait and watch, and if it doesn't get any better, you can bring him in."

I did all the usual things we'd done before; applying compresses, offering sips of water, and letting him rest.

About five o'clock, though, he became worse. Instead of continuing his small movements of feverish restlessness, he writhed in pain, holding his back. His whole body thrashed, and he spoke only with great difficulty.

Cia was visiting at the time, and I asked for her opinion of Alan's condition.

She took one glance and said, "Pam, look at him. You've got to take him to the emergency room. It's time. I'll stay here with the kids."

She was right, of course. I'd known already, but somehow, I needed to hear it myself.

I eased Alan through the garage and into the car, cringing at every sound he made. Every movement, every touch tortured him. I tried reassuring him, the way I'd done with our kids when they were little—"It's OK, sweetheart. You're going to be OK"—but I think I was trying to reassure myself as much as him.

I grudgingly pressed the brake at the egress from our cul-de-sac, right beside the Roh's house, waiting for rush-hour traffic to let me onto the connecting road. With the Roh's panoramic windows, they couldn't avoid seeing who came and went on the street, and before I had an opening, Mary Roh flew down the walkway from her house.

"Pam," she yelled, "is everything all right?"

"No, it's not. Is Mark around?"

Within moments, Dr. Roh rushed out to our car too.

He leaned in the window and spoke with Alan briefly.

"I think it's just tumor fever. You both know how crowded the ER is. You should go back home and manage the pain as best you can from there. You'll be a lot more comfortable. I'll talk to Dr. Kayaleh about evaluating him in the morning."

Reluctantly, but with Alan's agreement, I turned the car around and went back home. As we stepped into the house from the garage, Cia said, "What the hell are you doing back here?"

I guided Alan inside, letting him lean heavily against my arm. He could hardly walk. "Dr. Roh told us it's just tumor fever. He said the ER won't be able to do him any good overnight."

"Tumor fever? What does that even mean?"

"I have no idea."

Later, I'd learn it was a generic term. When cancer patients like Alan spiked a high fever that couldn't be attributed to a specific infection, tumor fever was the catchall term most often applied. But that night, I had no inkling beyond what Dr. Roh said.

Meanwhile, by six o'clock, Alan was getting worse.

He was aware, but in so much pain that making any further decisions was my call. In many ways, I felt like everything had already been my call, from the moment he got sick. It wasn't that he didn't want to take responsibility for his own healthcare decisions—far from it. But it was important to him that I feel empowered, and that he not try to put his views above my own. He made suggestions, of course—like the mention of dendritic cell therapy—but he never pushed anything onto anybody. That's just how it was with Alan.

Over our years together, many times I'd wanted to talk through questions or issues I had about friends or acquaintances. I'd ask Alan, "What should I do about this?"

Every time, he threw the question right back at me. "What do you want to do about it?"

That was his way of helping me, of helping everyone.

That night I wished he were able to give me not only a suggestion, but a decision. I was desperate for any type of feedback, but he was in too much pain. I even called Alan's mom.

"I need help, Dolores. I don't know what to do. Is there any way you can come back?"

"This isn't right," Cia said, as Alan groaned. "I'm calling my brother."

I'd known him since Cia and I were kids in Cincinnati, and I respected his view. An eye physician in North Carolina, Cia's brother, Dr. Bryan Allf, had a bedside manner much like Alan's—calm and gentle. But his words this time were stern, like nothing I'd ever heard from him.

"Cia, I don't like what you're describing. I think you need to tell Pam to take Alan to the emergency room."

This wasn't the first (or last) time Alan and I got conflicting advice about his illness. However, with the intensity of his distress, and the rapid swing from one medical opinion to the other, this was the most telling. In a span of under two hours, we'd consulted with two doctors, though neither of them physically examined Alan. One, the president of a local hospital, counseled us through the car window; and the other, an eye specialist in another state, counseled us through the phone. And from them we'd gotten opposite advice.

Hearing Alan's agonized sounds and seeing his writhing body, I knew we had to act. We'd already given the former wait-it-out advice a try. Now, we'd heed the latter.

This time, I remembered to call Alan's oncologist to let him know we were heading to the hospital. By the time I got Alan back into the car that night, it was late. When we arrived, Dr. Kayaleh had already arranged to have a bed ready for him.

After a few minutes in the room observing Alan, Dr. Kayaleh paced back and forth. His patient's pain was palpable. Alan writhed and writhed, involuntary moans escaping from his usually controlled voice. At a slightly lower volume I heard Omar's voice, as he verbally wrestled with himself, changing the direction of his pacing and glancing over at Alan with each repeated sentence.

"What can we do to alleviate these symptoms?" he asked himself. "What else can I try? How can I help him? If only we didn't have those other patients' built-in waiting periods..."

I'd kept myself together all afternoon and evening, watching my husband's increasing suffering. Now, seeing his oncologist visibly shaken by the severity of Alan's symptoms, I felt my brave front crumble. But I couldn't let Alan see me fall apart.

"Sweetheart, I'll be back in a couple of minutes. I've got to...use the restroom."

I stepped from his bedside into the floor's family lounge and collapsed onto the sofa.

What the hell is going on? What am I going to do? What is he going to do?

Awful, horrible thoughts intruded and raced through my head. Worst was the unthinkable.

Maybe we're coming to the end.

But I couldn't, wouldn't accept that.

I may have been in denial, but it was my defense mechanism—one of the few things keeping me together.

I got a drink of water and then splashed some on my eyelids. I wiped my nose, dried my eyes, and straightened my shoulders before I stepped back inside the room.

*   *   *

I'd been racking my brain and wringing information from everyone I could think of to figure out a way to get Alan into the dendritic trial at MD Anderson in Orlando. Like the tennis tournaments I'd always visualized winning before stepping onto the court, in my head I could see that there must be a way to get Alan the dendritic cell therapy he needed. I just couldn't see what that way was—yet.

For days and days, I searched nonstop for answers. I made phone calls to every agency and administrator I could think of. I ran around from offices to laboratories to medical facilities, like a mad woman, talking to hordes of different people in the field about what we could do.

It seemed like I made phone calls 24/7. There was no time limit on when I called anyone, because we were running out of time. Day and night, as soon as I thought of someone who might be able to help us, I dialed them. But so far, phone calls, web research, office encounters had turned up only more questions, more roadblocks, and more frustration.

Then an idea struck.

"Alan, I figured out a way we can circumvent the FDA's own rules—this will work!"

"Go on ..." he said, tilting his head to one side as he listened.

"They call it 'expanded access,' for people who can't get into an established trial but who are in critical need of whatever benefit the not-yet-approved treatment might offer."

"But I *am* in an established trial, Pam. Granted, I haven't started yet, but I'm in it."

"You're in line, but that's all. Alan, you can't wait around for all their blah-blah-blah timetables and rules about watching to see if anybody in line before you gets any side effects from their injections. We need to get those dendritic cells in you ASAP."

"I can't argue with that."

"So, we'll withdraw you from the clinical trial and get you your own..." I looked again at the FDA website to see what they called it. "'Individual patient emergency compassionate use.' Alan, you alone will be a trial unto yourself. You'll have your own deadlines, not other patients.'"

All I had to do now was fight the FDA to let him out of the trial we'd fought for—and to let him have his own.

The next day, Alan's ultrasound revealed an unexpected development in his gallbladder.

"It appears contracted, perhaps surrounded by fluids that shouldn't be concentrated there." Dr. Kayaleh looked up from reviewing the test results. "We don't have a definitive answer, Alan, but your continued fever indicates there is an infection. For now, I'm sending you home on oral antibiotics and steroids. Meanwhile, we'll take a watchful, waiting course to see how you do."

For a couple of days, Alan's pain improved, lifting everyone's spirits, but the fever never subsided. Night sweats left him drenched head to toe; each morning he needed fresh bedclothes and linens.

But a few days later, the pain resurged.

Back to the hospital.

More tests, more evaluation, more treatment, few answers.

The next week felt like an unending loop. Cultures came back negative as we sought the source of Alan's fever, but a CT scan of his tumors showed a slight worsening compared to one he'd had a month earlier. The images suggested sludge—or possibly small stones—in his gallbladder.

Once again, I was pulled by the daily stretch between Dorrie and Alan at separate facilities while I struggled with the bureaucracy of the FDA, trying to find a way Alan could have the benefit of the dendritic cell therapy trial we'd won for the hospital. Thank god Cia was there to help with the kids as their new school year began.

Chapter Forty-One | All About Saving Alan

It's such a very big, but very small world. Of the hundreds of millions of people in the United States, only a fraction work in the medical research industry; even fewer wield the authority to make FDA-level decisions equal to FDA-level red tape. The chances were astronomical that I could reach and persuade such a person to order emergency, single patient, compassionate use access for Alan alone.

I didn't care. I was getting that dendritic cell therapy for Alan, no matter what.

They say it takes a village to raise a child. That may or may not be, but I can attest it takes an army to raise the FDA's approval. An army of experts individually recruited and rallied to engage in a forward movement of phone calls and emails.

One of the first calls I made was to Maryann and Caroline, enlisting their help in contacting their widespread networks.

"It's an emergency compassionate use access we need granted," I explained. In the background, I heard odd noises. "Where on earth are you two?"

"Don't worry, Pam," explained Maryann. "We're at the Martha's Vineyard Ag Fair today, but we'll get right on it from here."

I was in Alan's room, still on speaker phone with Caroline and Maryann, when Dr. Brian Haas walked in. I waved briefly at the eye doctor, a friend of Alan's from Columbia, but quickly returned my attention to my sisters. I angled myself into the corner of the room, concentrating; they spoke as precisely as ever, but I strained to hear them over the merry-go-round music surrounding them at the fair.

"It's just so frustrating," I told them. "It seems like everyone we talk to gives us a different answer with a different way of going about it. How are we going to make this happen? How are we going to get approval on this so we can get him the dendritic therapy?"

Caroline's voice chimed in over the calliope music.

"I'll find a way to reach Margaret Hamburg for you. Her daughter's at school with one of my kids, and I believe she's now the FDA commissioner."

I breathed a sigh of relief, knowing that even though we had a mountain of work ahead of us, my sisters would do everything in their power to help me move heaven and earth—and more importantly—the FDA.

Above the background music, one of my sisters said, "Pam, before we can get to the next step, you're also going to need to get a doctor—any doctor—to sign off on this."

I turned around and looked toward Brian. He and Alan already had eyes on me. Without my having to ask, Brian said, "I'll sign off. Not a problem."

I felt the weight on my chest ease up a notch.

"Thank you, Brian."

Thank you, God. One thing down.

For a handful of minutes, my sisters and I discussed our next steps. They still had people they were trying to reach on their end, while I had my hands full of contacts to make and red tape to cut through here.

When I hung up with them, I picked up my tote bag and faced the men in the room. I stepped over to the bed and gave Alan a quick kiss.

"OK, sweetheart. I'm off to go talk to the researchers. Brian," I added, extending my hand, "it was great to see you again. Thank you for stepping up to sign off on this."

He shook his head.

"Not at all. My pleasure."

Then he called out as I reached for the doorknob. "Pam, can I ask you a favor?"

I paused, eager to be on my way, but grateful for Brian's support.

"Sure, Brian. What is it?"

"After hearing what you and your sisters are doing, and after what Alan's told me..."

"Yes?"

"My god, Pam, if I ever get sick, could you be my healthcare advocate?"

"Absolutely, Brian. I'd be honored."

While my sisters heated up the phone lines in their part of the country, at MD Anderson Orlando I lugged my big, floppy cotton beach bag with Alan's medical documentation everywhere, as I rushed up and down the hospital's multiple floors and hallways. It seemed I needed to cover every one of them.

Back in April I'd toted around a notebook and file folder to help me keep track of Dorrie's and Alan's medical information; now my bag bulged with so many medical records it pressed grooves into my shoulders and the crooks of my elbows. It weighed at least fifteen pounds; including pens for writing, phone chargers, a water bottle, and granola bar. That day, I might as well have thrown out the latter items to save myself a bit of hauling–I had no time to use them.

I had so many different battles to fight on so many different fronts, but right now I had to set aside all my worries over Dorrie and the kids. It was all-or-nothing time for Alan.

I went downstairs to the hospital president's office, but his staff said, "Oh, no, Dr. Roh is in a meeting."

"OK, where's the meeting?"

I rushed up to that floor and waited for him to come out. When I told Mark what I needed for Alan, a few minutes later he placed his first call, throwing us his all-in support as he had from the beginning.

While I hurried from one office to the next, I made calls. Florida Hospital's Dr. Lee Zehngebot soon agreed to contact the FDA on Alan's behalf and promised to enlist colleagues to add their voices.

I was off to find the lead researchers to see if they'd gotten any news yet, but they were in a totally different building.

I felt like I was racing against a monstrous, invisible clock like the one in Dr. Kayaleh's office. With every tick, the tumors were eating away at Alan's body, and his organs were starting to shut down. We had to rush–had to get the FDA to remove him from the trial we'd fought so hard for. It usually took years to get clinical trials established, but we'd accelerated the process and gotten it within months. Now we needed even greater speed to allow Alan his own individual use of the dendritic therapy. With the state of his tumors, the sooner the better.

Even once we got the approval–which we just *had* to get–I knew Alan's own blood would have to be harvested. Then the dendritic cells would have to be shipped out for re-engineering. And I knew that was all going to take too much time for me to take mine now.

I called anybody I could think of with important connections, whether I knew them or not. I called a pancreatic specialist at MD Anderson in Houston, eventually eliciting his promise to make phone calls for us. I even called the past president of MD Anderson Orlando–a man I'd never met or spoken with before.

"Dendritic cell treatment will benefit cancer patients in this area," I told him. "And my husband was chief of ENT here at the hospital you once headed. He's the reason we got the trial brought here in the first place. But unless they allow him to have his own, non-trial access to the treatment, he'll have to wait too long. So, I need you to please, please call them on our behalf and let them know you support him having his own trial."

It was such work, and there was so much red tape, and at first it seemed like everybody said no. Everybody. Nobody wanted to be on the line for something like pulling an approved participant from an FDA trial to try and start their own.

Nobody wanted to go out on a limb against the government and the FDA.

But I'd learned early in life not to take no for an answer.

"Here is this physician," I pleaded over and over, "who was chief in his field in this hospital. He's been such a well-known and well-loved figure in the community. If he doesn't get this therapy in time, he's going to die. You don't want that happening, do you?"

I rushed in and out of elevators and offices. I made calls. Checked back in with Alan, at least every hour. Touched base with my sisters. Doctors' offices. Called again. Staff offices. Alan's room again. Not taking time to eat, to drink, to go to the bathroom.

There was no time.

I ran from person to person to plead Alan's case, until they relented and I heard a yes. I didn't pause between one person's agreement and the next one I sought. I could feel how close we were to getting the FDA to approve Alan's emergency dendritic cell therapy. I dared not lose momentum. For Alan's sake, I dared not stop for anything.

On my way from one floor to another, I half stood, half leaned against the back wall of a packed elevator, grateful for the few seconds of upright rest. Stacks of paperwork—even more than my bag already held—filled my arms. All at once, a warm trickle slid, then streamed down my leg.

Oh my god. What's...? Oh my god, I haven't been to the bathroom—I've got to...

But it was too late. My bladder let loose as urine streamed down both legs inside my pants.

Thank god, I'm not wearing shorts.

I'd just peed my pants in public.

I could have been mortified; but instead, that's when I realized what a warrior I was, how strong my focus was.

Since April, I'd worn the same "uniform" most days: Jeans and one of several plain T-shirts I rotated through a bedside pile. I was in warrior—not wardrobe—mode. I was in battle. Right now, it seemed the enemy was winning, but it was far from over.

I wouldn't let it be.

When the elevator opened for the next person to get out, I elbowed my way out and found a bathroom on that floor. Cleaning up as best I could (and as fast as I could) with paper towels and dispenser soap, I looked myself in the mirror and said, "You're fighting the clock, Pam, but you also have to take care of yourself."

I said it, knowing I should believe it, but I didn't really give a shit about myself.

I didn't care about myself at all. It was all about saving Alan. It was almost like my body, and needing to take care of it, got in the way.

Tossing another wad of paper towels into the trash, I gave myself the kind of stare I'd practiced against opponents on the court.

OK, body. Keep up with me. I have more important things to do than deal with you right now.

I hurried out to make more calls. I enlisted anyone and everybody's help.

"Can you please make a phone call for me? Can you please put something in an email to the FDA? Can you please call the board at...?"

I called Dr. Wolff at MD Anderson in Houston. I even went to the American Cancer Society in Orlando. And I had to run everything through the researchers at MD Anderson.

There were so many roadblocks.

At one point, it didn't look like we were going to get it. Mary Roh called me one morning and said, "Pam, when we were going to bed last night, Mark told me he thought it wasn't looking good to get the approval for Alan, but I told him, 'Mark, you get that for Pam and Alan. You push that through.' And Pam, he promised me he'll do everything he can."

Finally, one morning, at least a decades-long week after we started, lead researcher Casey Anderson's number lit up my phone screen.

"The FDA approved him, Pam. We've got Alan scheduled for six dendritic cell therapy treatments." He sounded as elated as I felt.

"How soon can we get him started?"

"As soon as we can get everything ready for him—shouldn't be long, but there's a lot of red tape."

No matter. We did it!

Within forty-eight hours, we thought, Alan would begin a procedure—leukapheresis—to separate his white blood cells. It would be the first step in the process.

*   *   *

Since the problem had been discovered with Alan's gallbladder, he had been on IV antibiotics to control his tumor fever. For a while his pain improved, but just when his symptoms seemed under control, his fever began to spike. Then, on the sixth day of testing, an MRI revealed an increase of tumor tissue in Alan's liver.

Once again, doctors attributed his high temperatures to tumor fever—tumor fever, tumor fever. They just kept saying "tumor fever." I never wanted to hear that phrase again.

We brought him home that afternoon, hoping for an uneventful weekend of recovery, subdued by the knowledge his tumor mass had increased, but nevertheless riding high on the knowledge that dendritic cell therapy was now within sight.

Chapter Forty-Two | Help from an Unlikely Source

With Alan resting at home, his close friend Jeff busied about in the kitchen behind me, cleaning out our long-neglected refrigerator. I sat hunched over my laptop—again, still, always—researching ways to save Alan's life.

I looked away from the screen long enough to see that I received a text from Alan's aunt, Roberta Saffran. At first I thought she wanted another update, as we'd been keeping the whole family aware of all his fever relapses, hospitalizations, and tests.

Then, I read her message: "Hey, Pam, I just saw a segment Dr. Oz did on pancreatic cancer. He interviewed a female surgeon who says it doesn't have to be a doom and gloom diagnosis anymore, that there are new ways to treat it."

Aunt Roberta included a YouTube link and added, "I think this could maybe help Alan."

I pulled up the excerpt from *The Dr. Oz Show*. They'd filmed a special week of programs on pancreatic cancer. I leaned forward, nodding, as Dr. Oz said, "Pancreatic cancer is the one doctors fear most."

I laughed in mirthless agreement.

How many times have I heard that in the last four and a half months?

I listened as he added, "Dr. Sarah Thayer, director of pancreatic cancer research at Massachusetts General Hospital, is joining me to discuss your biggest pancreatic cancer risks and the best solutions that are out there."

I glanced over my shoulder as Jeff approached, peering toward the monitor.

"I know that name. How do I know that name?"

Seconds later he said, "I've got to talk to Alan." And he was gone. He'd left the kitchen. Food covered the counter tops, and the emptied refrigerator doors gaped wide open.

Odd, I thought, but returned my attention to the show. The guest expert talked about prevention, diagnosis, and treatment of the deadly disease.

This woman is beautiful and brilliant.

Then Alan called me from the bedroom.

"Pam! Pam, come in here."

I slapped the space bar to pause the video and ran to our room.

"Alan, what's wrong, are you all right?" I stopped short inside the doorway. Jeff stood next to where Alan lay on the bed.

"Pam," Alan asked, "you know that clip you were just watching on YouTube?"

Calm down. Everything's OK.

"Sure, I just stopped it to see what you wanted."

"That's Sarah Thayer. The woman I dated for about a year, bridging my UVA residency with my first six months in Florida."

My heart pounded even harder.

Of course. I should have recognized her.

I'd first seen a picture of Dr. Sarah Thayer the year before we married. Not long after Alan moved into my little house in Thornton Park, I'd come across the worn photograph when I was putting away some of his things.

Her image was striking, as I should have expected from the way he'd spoken of her. I took one look at the photo and remembered my discomfort at the loving respect in his voice when he spoke of her. Insecurity had chafed like new, ill-fitting tennis shoes. Not for the first time, I thought, *I can't compete with this. She's going to be a surgeon, for God's sake. I can't compete.*

But I hadn't heard much about Sarah after Alan and I became serious. I'd all but forgotten those early insecurities. For twenty years, I'd had no need of them, as Alan devoted himself to me and our kids.

My thoughts fast-forwarded from those memories to now, with Alan sick.

Jeff said, "I recognized her from when they were dating back in Charlottesville." His head inclined toward Alan, but he faced me. "I had to tell him."

"I thought she was going to become a thoracic surgeon," Alan said. "I can't believe she's a pancreatic cancer surgeon."

I couldn't believe it either. From what I'd just seen and Googled about her expertise, it was clear she was one of the foremost physicians in her field. And Alan knew her—knew her well. She could help me save him.

"For God's sake, Alan, we are calling her right now!"

But Alan, sick or not, was still Alan. He shook his head. "It's Sunday, Pam. We are *not* bothering her on a Sunday."

"Are you kidding me? This is no time to worry about whether we're imposing on anyone. We are calling her now. Give me your phone."

I tracked down the number to her office at Mass General and reached her answering service, leaving a message to page her.

"Please tell Dr. Thayer that Dr. Alan Saffran is calling. She'll know that this is a personal call."

It wasn't a gamble. I knew she would remember Alan. Nobody ever forgets Alan.

She called back within fifteen minutes. I answered.

"Hi, Dr. Thayer, my name is Pam Saffran. I'm married to Alan."

"Alan, Alan Saffran?"

"Yes, Alan from UVA."

"Oh my god. It's so nice to meet you over the phone."

"Sarah, I'm so sorry, this is not—I can't thank you enough—this is not a very positive phone call. What I'm about to tell you is not good. I'm calling because Alan is sick, and I think you can help him."

"Alan has pancreatic cancer?" She was already crying.

"It's stage IV. I just saw you on Dr. Oz. Is there any way..."

"Please, let me help you."

I put Alan on and for the next forty-five minutes, she took a full medical history over the phone while he lay against his pillows. They discussed short- and long-term treatment and goals, and I felt the burden of uncertainty and sole responsibility lighten on my shoulders.

It's amazing how life comes full circle.

From that day on, Dr. Thayer became my long-haul advocate for Alan, as determined as I to save his life. Until then, so many times along the way, I felt like everyone else had just given up on him. In hindsight, I realized it was because many of the others already saw Alan as a dead man.

But Sarah didn't see him that way. Once I got her on board, it no longer felt like I was the only one fighting for Alan's life.

Now, I had a new ally.

The next morning, as soon as the hospital records office opened—and nearly every day thereafter—I faxed or FedExed Alan's lab and test results directly to Sarah's office in Boston; PET and CT scans, MRIs, blood workups, everything. She wanted not just the reports, but the actual scans, so she could read and interpret them for herself.

I loved her aggressive, thorough, personal approach, and I took pleasure in the hours I spent in the records room at ORMC. I developed friendships with the people working down there. More importantly, I felt I was making a real, tangible contribution to Alan's care.

Sarah called us that night, after she'd had a chance to review everything I'd sent her.

"I recommend," she said, "not starting chemo again until the infection issue has been ruled out."

"But wouldn't it be dangerous for him to wait longer?" I asked, ever leery of any delay that might let the tumors start growing again.

"It's a hard call either way. Ultimately, of course, it will have to be Alan's decision—as long as his cell counts allow, that is."

Alan spoke up.

"I'm already slated to start back tomorrow. If my blood counts permit, I'm going through with it. I'm not going to mess up their schedule."

Typical Alan. If his mind was made up in order to avoid inconveniencing colleagues, I knew not even Sarah could change it.

*　　*　　*

Arranged in front of me where I sat on the bed, number-filled pages spread out in an arc. With Alan unable to work since the beginning of April, our income for the year halted at less than a third of what he'd been making—and what we'd budgeted for. Upcoming payments for property taxes and three kids' tuitions totaled nearly $50,000. That wasn't counting Alan's out-of-pocket medical expenses and money for us to live on.

Rifling through the substantial stack of daunting educational bills alone, I was making a list of all the things I needed to do, things I needed to make work, and I was beginning to realize how much I had yet to figure out.

For most of our marriage, I handled all the finances. Alan just handed me his checks. The bank probably wouldn't have recognized his signature, because I endorsed them for him. If he'd actually signed his own stereotypical doctor's signature, they'd probably have thought it was a fraud.

In almost any case, Alan let me do what I wanted with our budget. Only rarely would I come up with an idea that would make him say, "Uh-uh. No, that's crazy. We're not doing that."

Now, although Alan was too ill to weigh in on money matters, he'd insisted on going over all our finances with me. Lying on the bed beside me, he worried—not for the first time—about his partnership in the medical practice.

I reached over and felt his burning forehead—104 degrees, the last time we checked it with a thermometer—and offered him a sip of water. No matter how "normal" it was for him to spike a fever these days, I didn't think I could ever get used to it. My husband's body had been pumped full of toxins and poisons to attack the cancer, but it seemed at times the treatment was worse than the disease. Witnessing the toll on his body, I felt hopeless, helpless. I sat beside him, grasping at straws. For anything. For any help. From anywhere.

I felt so alone.

Even sitting beside him.

I'm going to be alone.

The intrusive thought wouldn't stay away.

In the early days after Alan's diagnosis, once I'd gotten over my initial shock, I'd consciously donned a brave mask of capability and optimism whenever I was near him. As long as I kept my spirits up, I thought, I'd keep his right up there, too. I'd never let him see me feeling sad or vulnerable.

Until that evening.

I saw our house and the kids' education and my out-of-it mother and my poor husband with this terrible disease. I felt it all on my shoulders and saw everything tumbling down around me.

I couldn't stop myself. Rocking back and forth with my arms wrapped tightly around myself, I cried.

"What am I going to do, honey? What the hell am I going to do?"

Alan groaned, as hurt by my distress as by the warring chemicals and tumors inside him. His fevered hand touched me, and I looked over at him through my tears.

He looked at me with such sad eyes. I could tell he felt worse about the idea of leaving me and the kids than his horrible physical pain.

The realization of how much precious energy he'd expended on my behalf made me cry even harder.

"You'll be OK, Pam. You know you will. You're a fighter. A champion."

"I don't know how to do this on my own."

"But you will. We'll figure it out, and you'll manage."

I wiped my eyes in the silence that followed, and when I turned to look at him, I half expected to see him asleep. But his eyes met mine with a shimmer of hope.

"I just remembered something. No matter what, you'll always have help with the kids' tuition."

"What do you mean?"

"The buildings, Pam."

"Oh. You mean the rent on the medical center properties?"

My mind flashed back to the picture of Alan, standing alongside his partners, holding a golden groundbreaking shovel when we were first dating.

"Exactly. January first and July first you'll get the distribution checks for our share of the rent from both medical centers. If you're careful, those payments should cover the kids' tuition through high school. It may not cover everything, but it should help some with their college expenses when they're ready, too."

"It won't be long for Miles."

"Has he decided where he's applying early?"

"Not yet, but he has to make his decision before the end of September."

Alan was quiet again, long enough for me to feel ashamed of my outburst.

How could I have let him see me that way? I have to stay strong for him and the kids.

"Alan," I said aloud, as much for myself as for him, "I'm not going to have to figure this out alone. We've already won against the FDA. You're getting your own trial for dendritic cell therapy, and it is going to make you better."

Whether he believed it or not, I had to.

Chapter Forty-Three | So Much Pain

We'd gotten the kids off to school, and had already been to MD Anderson and back for Alan's first infusion of the new chemotherapy called gemcitabine-Abraxane. Fortunately for him, this treatment was shorter—only an hour and a half compared to the six-hour ordeals of the FOLFIRINOX regimen that he had been taking to this point. It seemed odd to be back home while it was still morning.

At first, Alan felt OK—relatively, that is, compared to how awful the last couple of weeks had been. But about four hours later, before the kids were due home from school, his body shook with chills. I checked his temperature; it was 104 degrees, just like last time.

Unlike last time, though, we wondered if it was due to the new chemo. Then again, it could have been another bout of the tumor fever, or it could have been some other mysterious infection yet to be unmasked. We just didn't know.

Worse than the fever, though, was the pain. When evening came, its onset was sudden and excruciating.

"Honey, that's it," I said. "I'm packing the bag again, and we're going to the hospital."

I called Omar to let him know I was returning Alan to the MD Anderson emergency room that night, and I called Sarah to update her.

"Pam, you've got to tell them to order a goddamn HIDA scan this time."

"I've never heard of that. What is it?"

"It's a detailed imaging test. It will create images of Alan's gallbladder from multiple angles so we can see whether it's functioning—or not. I'm worried that may be a factor."

I promised I'd FedEx Sarah a copy of the scan as soon as it was done, and Omar agreed to her suggestion as soon as I relayed it. Unfortunately, no matter what Dr. Kayaleh said to persuade them, the earliest the hospital staff could schedule Alan for the hour-long test was the next afternoon.

With Alan hurting so horribly, tomorrow afternoon might as well have been a lifetime away. It was obscenely tragic seeing this proud man—who exuded dignity and honor—so vulnerable.

Even Omar seemed shaken and frustrated by Alan's agony. He strode back and forth in the small room; between Alan's bed and each piece of electronic equipment, and then back to Alan again.

"Omar," I pleaded, "can't you help him? He's in so much pain, and his fever's so high."

He seemed to speak more to himself than to me, as he paced.

"I don't know what I'm going to do for him. I don't know what the hell to do."

My own body screamed exhaustion. My stomach hurt. I wanted to throw up. Alan's agony was unbearable. Each time I watched his body writhe, it felt like pieces of my own heart were being plucked away. I knew that this—whatever was happening to him—was not good. Nor was the fact that his doctors didn't really know what they were dealing with at this point.

Alan hadn't eaten since noon the previous day. He was sick and in too much pain. But in preparation for the afternoon HIDA scan, he had to fast completely, meaning he could not eat or drink—or take any pain medicine at all. He'd been managing his meds on his own before this, trying to space out his pain pills to keep his head clear.

But now, on an empty stomach and without any pain medication in his system for hours, Alan's pain level soared from intense but manageable to intolerable torture. He remained conscious, still able to talk through clenched teeth, but every breath cost him dearly.

I'd have done anything to ease his anguish. Anything, that is, except leave him alone in the room. Anything but that.

It was late in the afternoon when someone from the imaging department finally entered the room and injected Alan with the radioactive tracer chemical that would allow them to make the diagnostic pictures.

"Can't you give him something for the pain in an IV?" I asked one of the staff.

"I'm sorry, but it's not on the orders, and we need to see Dr. Saffran's organs functioning without impairment."

As they wheeled him down the corridor for the time-consuming test, I couldn't help worrying. *What if he can't hold still for the scan?*

* * *

Alan and I were newlyweds when we met Frank and Joan Pohl, and their then-twelve-year-old daughter Allie, on the tennis courts at Interlachen. We became fast friends.

Not long after Alan's struggles with his gallbladder, Frank, who was also Miles' godfather, took me on the worst shopping errand of my life. That day, he said, "Let's go look at graves."

We drove to a beautiful old cemetery in Winter Park. For nearly four hours,

Frank and I wandered the entire seventeen acres with an employee, flagging where we looked at available plots.

As we stepped through the thick blades of green lawn between monuments, I couldn't help noticing the old, barely legible headstones dating back to the 1800s. They were links to a distant history; I far preferred them over the shinier, smoother stones with markings clearly denoting more recent deaths. I averted my eyes altogether from the far worse mounds where transplanted, yellow-tinged grass had yet to take root.

This is a horrible thing we are doing.

In spite of our purpose, Frank kept the conversation as light as possible.

"We want Alan overlooking the golf course. He's always worked too many hours to take up the sport, so he should be able to enjoy the view here."

I was upset just being there. But Frank's humor made it manageable—as manageable as buying a cemetery plot for my husband *could* be. Part of me found it easier to joke and kid around about why we were there; I still didn't fully accept as reality that Alan could need a burial plot before forty more years had passed.

Sometimes, I zoned out, only half-hearing his words as I grappled with why I'd come.

"...And we want you guys to be next to us." Frank turned to the cemetery employee and said, "Show us again, please, where are the four Pohl plots? We want the Saffrans as neighbors."

I bought Alan's cemetery plot that day, the worst land purchase I could think of, and for a purpose I still couldn't quite let myself imagine.

Chapter Forty-Four | Surgery–Stat

"What did they say?" I asked the minute the HIDA scan was completed and Alan was returned to his hospital room. He looked so drained, I wondered if he'd be able to answer.

"The technician said they couldn't see the gallbladder at all."

"Couldn't see…"

"…But not to worry, because the radiologist will give a clearer interpretation in the morning."

I helped Alan settle in for a rest, making sure he swallowed a few bites of food and swallowed enough water to wash down his pain pills. The minute he began to relax, I slipped out. I had to get copies of the scan and send them to Sarah.

I checked back in with Alan, then went home to the kids, thinking there was nothing more we could do until Alan's radiologist met with us in the morning.

I was so wrong.

Cia and I were clearing up after dinner and the kids were upstairs doing homework when I got the phone call.

"Pam, are you with Alan right now?"

I already recognized Sarah's voice.

"No, I'm at home. Why?"

"Pam, for God's sake, get back over there as fast as you can. Alan's got to have emergency gallbladder surgery."

"What, now? Tonight? What's wrong?" I peppered her with questions, not letting her answer any of them, while I grabbed my keys and the huge bag of Alan's records I lugged everywhere. "Have you been in touch with him at the hospital? Has something happened?" I rushed to my car and cranked the ignition, pausing only long enough to fasten my seat belt and put the phone on speaker before I pulled out of the driveway.

I hadn't even told Cia and the kids where I was going. I figured there would be time enough to fill them in later.

"It's what I saw on the HIDA scan, Pam. We've got to get him into surgery—and it has to be right away, before he becomes nadir."

"What the hell is nadir?" I didn't know what that meant, but her tone left no doubt as to how dire it would be. The word itself sounded like something nasty; just repeating it put a bad taste in my mouth, and when Sarah explained, I understood why.

"It means his white blood cell count will drop to its lowest point."

It was the reason chemotherapy had such a high risk of secondary infections from killing off the body's immune cells along with the cancer.

"Because he had the gem-Abraxane yesterday morning," she went on, "we only have a twenty-four to forty-eight-hour window to get him into surgery before he'll be ineligible. The chemo will make his white blood count plummet too low to operate."

"But why does he need surgery?"

"The infection, the tumor in his gallbladder. Pam, it's bad. If we don't get the damaged tissues out of him soon enough, it will kill him."

I sprinted from the MD Anderson parking lot into the hospital and ran straight to the elevator, punching the button hard—as if sending it through the wall would make its doors open faster. When the number above the door lit up at Alan's floor, I pushed my shoulder and knee into the widening gap before the rest of me could squeeze through. I ran down the hallway and burst into Alan's room.

Without saying as much as hello, I relayed her message, throwing the words out all at once.

"Sarah said you need emergency gallbladder surgery before you become nadir. We have to find you a surgeon now."

"What!? Why?"

I could have taken the time to explain, but from what Sarah told me, time was something Alan didn't have. I dialed her number and handed Alan the phone, figuring she could explain it faster from one doctor to another.

I leaned closer, overhearing parts of her explanation. "...Now, Alan. Tonight! If this infection continues and you get to the point where your white blood cells hit their nadir, you won't be able to have the surgery at all—and you need it, because antibiotics won't hold this off."

"I'll try, Sarah, but..." Alan hesitated. "I don't know whether I can get anyone from here to schedule surgery on such short notice based on the recommendation of someone in Boston."

"You've got to. You find them, and if they are at all resistant, let me talk to them. I will make it happen. You may need to maintain working relationships with the people down there, but I don't. I will do any hard pushing that's necessary."

"I guess I could call my friend who's a liver surgeon—he's the president of this hospital."

"That will do for starters, Alan. I'm going to hang up, and I want you to call him right now, OK? Please."

We called Dr. Roh at his house.

"Mark, the HIDA scan is showing something that worries Dr. Thayer. She's telling us to schedule emergency gallbladder surgery tonight, if possible, or tomorrow morning at the latest. Can you pull up the hospital portal from home and see what you think?"

In the background, I heard the clickety sounds of our neighbor's keyboard. Then he said, "Oh my god, the cancer—his gallbladder has already burst open."

No wonder Alan's pain has been so awful.

The tumor's exponential growth had already burst through Alan's organ.

"I wish I could help you myself, Alan," Dr. Roh said, "but I don't do laparoscopic surgery." He was silent only a beat or two before he said, "Marc Demers. That's who you want."

"Of course," said Alan, who knew oncology surgeon Dr. Marc Demers well. As soon as he hung up with Dr. Roh, he called Dr. Demers.

"Mark, I'd like to ask a favor of you. Would you be willing to take a look at my HIDA scan tonight and consult with Dr. Sarah Thayer over the phone?"

Alan gave Dr. Demers's number to Sarah, then we waited while she called him. He, too, studied Alan's scan from his home via the hospital's portal.

Within minutes, we heard back from Dr. Demers.

"Alan, you're first on my surgery schedule at 7:30 tomorrow morning."

*   *   *

I left the room to grab a coffee while the nurses prepped Alan for the emergency surgery. I'd only been gone a few minutes, but when I came back down the hallway, I did a double take.

Why are all these people here?

"Hello?" I said. "Excuse me? Can I get to my husband, please?"

As I gaped around at everyone and picked out snippets of words, all at once, it dawned on me who these people were and why they were here.

Alan had operated at least 300 times—probably more—in this same hospital over the years. Everyone there—from support staff to anesthesiologists to fellow surgeons—knew of Alan, Dr. Saffran, and they knew he was about to undergo an emergency operation.

They'd gathered around him to pay their respects.

I swallowed the lump of emotion in my throat without even knowing what it was. I was angry. I was sad. I loved that they came to support him, and I resented them for intruding on these moments I'd planned to spend with him. I felt so conflicted. I felt everything.

When the room finally cleared enough so that I could take Alan's hand and we could hear each other, he said, "Before I go into surgery, I want to alert you that afterward I'm going to probably have third spacing."

"I don't know what that means, Alan."

"There won't be anywhere for my fluids to go. There will be no space, because they won't be draining properly, so my body will fill up from the inside. And it will hurt."

As long as I'd known him, Alan constantly educated me, then our kids, and pretty much everyone around him. He was so brilliant that he often did it without knowing, just by the way he spoke about the world he'd so carefully studied.

But ever since his diagnosis, he'd made deliberate, intentional efforts, like this unwelcome conversation, to prepare me for each phase in his war against the malignancy claiming increasing ground within him. He'd say, "OK, this is what's happening to my body now, so we're at this point. Here is what's going to happen next."

It was uncanny how accurately he forecast his body's response to the pancreatic tumors—he claimed it was science, but it sometimes seemed more like soothsaying. I couldn't help thinking this third spacing phase he now foretold embodied the elements of an occult curse. It seemed unnatural that his own body might fill him first with fluids, and then with undrained pain.

When Alan came back from surgery, I tried to read Dr. Demers's face for clues as to how it went. In the months since early April, I'd become expert at reading doctors' expressions after procedures. Even before he spoke, I didn't like the look on Dr. Demers's face.

"I'm sorry. I'm so sorry."

In his hands, glossy photos shook.

"When I opened him up, the tumors were everywhere."

One by one, Dr. Demers shuffled the stack of photographs, pointing out the lesions attacking Alan's stomach and the linings of his lungs.

"I peeled one of the tumors from what was left of Alan's gallbladder, and I did another needle biopsy of the tumor in his liver to send it for genetic or other testing."

I'd never seen what a tumor looked like, but they were unmistakable.

"I wanted to help him more, Pam. I got in there, and..." His head hung low as he shook his head. "When I saw all those tumors, I couldn't help thinking how unfair it was. Your husband operated on my son and daughter. He fixed them. But all I could do for him was excise that burst gallbladder."

Chapter Forty-Five | Dorrie's Intuition

It was June 2012, less than a year before Alan's cancer was discovered. Mother's stubbornness was just as sharp as her mind.

Most days, I thanked God she was clearheaded and healthy enough to maintain her staunch independence at eighty. Frequent travels between my sisters' homes and her vacation place at Sea Island allowed her the freedom to come and go as she pleased, while keeping our house as her home base. She was with us often enough to help me with the kids, and she was away often enough so we didn't drive each other crazy.

I'd just hugged Alan goodbye then shuffled toward the coffeemaker as he exited the kitchen at exactly seven o'clock. My hands fumbled for the mug, since my eyes were only half open.

"Ahem." Dorrie snapped her newspaper shut, folded it in half, and *thwapped* it onto the table, staring at me as I moved about the room.

Still trying to wake up, I reluctantly looked her way.

"Mom. What?"

"I don't know what I'm doing today, but I know what you're doing."

"Oh, really? What's that?"

"You're getting life insurance for Alan. Today."

That was the last thing on my mind.

"What in the world would make you say that?"

She ignored the question. "You're doing it today."

"My schedule's already packed today. I have tennis practice in a couple of hours, and I'm going to lunch with the girls after."

"You can call and set it up the second you get home."

"When I get back, I already promised I'll help Miles look over some of the colleges he's thinking about, and Nat needs me to..."

"Then you're calling the company before you leave."

"Dorrie, I have a dozen other things I have to do."

"They can all wait. You have to do this today."

"There's no rush. He'll only be fifty-two next month, and you can see what great shape he's in."

"While he's in good shape is the time to buy a policy. You're doing this."

"It will cost too much, Mom. I've heard that policies for anyone over fifty are really high."

"Goddamn it, Pam." My mother slammed her palms against the breakfast table and growled at me. "Get. It. Now."

"OK, OK."

My face burned from what felt like a verbal slap. Shocked by her adamance, I backed out of the room to dress for the day, eager to put a bit of distance between us.

I hoped she would have cooled her fire before I re-entered the kitchen, but she already had the phone book open to "insurance companies." As soon as business hours began, she pointed wordlessly at the phone.

I'd have given up after the first inquiry, if Dorrie hadn't stayed within earshot. I no sooner hung up than she demanded, "Pick it up and call another one. You're getting that policy for Alan today, Pam."

I'd had no idea just how expensive it would be to purchase a term policy for someone over fifty.

It took half the day making endless calls, each prompted by my seemingly obsessed mother, but I finally settled on one life insurance company.

"Are you happy now, Mom?"

She thought a moment before answering.

"Mostly. But I'll rest better once you've got that policy in hand."

Neither of us realized, at the time, how difficult it would be to coordinate Alan's impossibly busy office hours and surgical calendar with the insurance company's required enrollment exam. It wasn't until August that the company nurse came to the house to draw his blood for the company's required workup.

Alan's policy was finally in effect on Sunday, September 1, 2012; it was another ninety days before the mandatory waiting period expired.

It had taken months to accomplish what Dorrie insisted I do in hours that day, and I wasn't happy about the expense. However, it was worth the cost of keeping my mother off my back.

From the day the policy was in place, she never said another word about it.

None of us, not even my intuitive, prescient mother, could have predicted what the next year would bring.

*　　*　　*

Because of his ruptured gallbladder, it took much longer than we'd hoped before doctors could begin harvesting—in a procedure called leukapheresis—Alan's white blood cells in preparation for the dendritic therapy.

In order for Alan to receive the dendritic cells, the lab first had to collect and then re-engineer his white blood cells. The procedure, they warned us, would take about six hours, and he would have to remain still the entire time.

I blinked and leaned backward when they wheeled in the leukapheresis machine, a piece of equipment so large the staff nicknamed it Hank. Alan lay flat in the bed with his arms stretched away from him like a T.

"You can't bend your arms at all until we are through," the technician reminded him as she inserted a needle into one arm and then another into the other.

Each needle connected to one of two tubes extending from the device. The first drained Alan's blood from his body into the machine, which spun the precious liquid, separating the white and red blood cells. The white cells went into a tiny collection bag, while the remaining components of Alan's blood exited the machine through the other tube and re-entered his other arm through the second needle.

The ghoulish setup was nearly as torturous as it looked. Because he couldn't move his arms at all until the end of the process, he was pinned in place by the needles, like a human specimen in an entomology display. Being laid out in that way was demeaning. During the second treatment, while Jeff visited with Alan, he needed his best friend's help peeing into a cup.

In spite of his embarrassment, Alan projected a brave front for everyone who came into the room—smiling and talking and laughing on the outside—but it was a battle he fought all day. Word spread fast among hospital personnel that Alan, their own Dr. Saffran, would be the first human with single-patient, compassionate access to dendritic cells to fight solid tumors.

Doctors from more departments than I could name came to his room to visit and wish him well. More than a few came to observe, making rounds with their residents to see a leukapheresis procedure firsthand. Alan, always instructing those around him, spoke openly, giving the inexperienced new doctors a physician's perspective on what it was like as a patient.

The moment Alan's procedure ended, a waiting air courier took custody of his collected white cells. The man closed the small bag inside an insulated cooler, and ran—literally ran—to board the private plane that would rush Alan's cells to the specialized manufacturing laboratory in Memphis.

For the first time since I'd fought to win Alan the right to this treatment, we had nothing to do but wait.

And wait.

It would take ten days for the return of Alan's revamped blood cells; ten nail-biting days, with Alan missing the majority of his immune-boosting white blood cells while the relentless malignancy within him continued to grow.

Other dendritic cell therapies returned the engineered super cells directly into the patients' bloodstreams, but Alan's was going to be shot right into his solid tumors. Because the procedure required such precision, it had to be done by an interventional radiologist.

Everything and everyone had to be ready and in position ahead of time, waiting for the courier's return with Alan's custom-altered cells. His interventional radiologist, Dr. Alexander Azbel (a family friend), explained why everyone had to be ready to spring into action.

"Time is of the essence for your treatment. As soon as we expose these cells to oxygen, we'll have only twenty minutes to get them inserted in the precise tumor site, or they'll die."

I watched the whole process, fascinated, holding my breath as Dr. Azbel's guided imagery showed on a monitor screen large enough for everyone present to see. He guided the needle tip into the center of the largest solid tumor mass in Alan's liver. As Dr. Azbel injected the dendritic cells directly into the cancerous tissue, this white glistening substance looked as cool as the science and hope behind it. White cells on the screen spread everywhere.

Chapter Forty-Six | A Terrible Kindness

As crazy as I sometimes felt with the stresses of managing one crisis after another, I thanked God Alan had such amazing doctors. They were great physicians to their other patients, too, but they also treated him like the esteemed colleague and friend he was. By extension, they afforded me the same generous courtesy.

During the second week of Alan's recovery from his gallbladder surgery, his nephrologist at MD Anderson Orlando, Dr. Jeffrey Cohen, and his wife, Dr. Lucille Belnick, gently coaxed me aside.

"Pam, we need to have a frank discussion."

At the time, Alan's Uncle Sy and his mother, Dolores, were visiting with us; they joined me, but these physicians' words were directed only to me.

"Pam, I want to tell you a story," Dr. Belnick said. "Once I called your house. You had no idea who I was, but your husband had operated on one of our children—he had removed our daughter's tonsils and adenoids—and she was bleeding. I called, hoping to talk to Alan, because I was concerned, and you were so kind. You said, 'Let me find my husband. I'll page him and have him call you.' And you didn't even know who I was. I'd just said I was a doctor in town, and you dropped everything to get me in touch with him immediately. I'll never forget that."

"I'm glad I was able to help." I didn't remember the incident, but I was touched that she did. "Was that what the two of you wanted to talk with me about?"

"It's about Alan's prognosis," Dr. Belnick said, nodding toward her husband.

"You need to know, Pam," Dr. Cohen said, "Time for Alan is winding down."

He looked at his wife, who fixed her gaze on him and then returned it to me.

"Alan's kidneys are starting to fail. His numbers are coming back less functional every day."

Kidney failure. No!

He spoke gently, but with authority.

"Little by little, tumors will make his organs unable to filter anything. They will shut down. He's probably only going to last a couple more weeks. Maybe as long as a couple of months."

This can't be right!

A faraway part of my consciousness heard Sy comforting Dolores, but I couldn't concentrate past Dr. Cohen's words.

This can't be right!

No other doctors had directly talked to me about what to expect.

He's going to live. This can't be right!

I didn't want to hear it, but even as I denied it, a horrified part of me warned I should listen to them.

*   *   *

Dr. Thayer and I debated the merits of having Alan transported by medical air ambulance to her facility at Mass General. After all, she'd been the one to diagnose his gallbladder emergency from Boston, so it made sense that maybe she could do more for him there. By the time we made that decision, though, by mutual consent, we agreed he was in no shape to endure the trip.

Alan stayed a full two weeks at MD Anderson after the gallbladder surgery. Before they sent him home the first week of September, they drained him in an attempt to alleviate the pain of his swollen, fluid-saturated tissues. Then they said there wasn't anything more they could do.

On the drive home, I tried not to stare. His bloated body was somewhat disguised when he had been lying nearly flat in the hospital bed. But it was obvious as he grimaced to put on his seatbelt.

Alan insisted on walking into the house unaided, weak and wobbly as he was. I tensed, watching his uneven footsteps. When he reached the step from the garage up into our kitchen, a step he had cleared thousands of times, he tripped—and would have fallen, if I hadn't been right behind him.

Despite his weakness, Alan had one more goal to accomplish before going to bed.

"Pam, I need a shower. Please. Help me."

I hesitated. He was so weak—he needed to lie down. Yet, I understood. He'd been in the hospital for weeks.

Torn between helping my husband straight into bed or straight into the shower, I listened to *him*; this articulate, intelligent man of such extraordinary manners and pride, reduced to pleading, unable to tend to his own hygiene unaided.

What he needs most of all is the dignity to choose for himself.

Undressing him wasn't easy. For several minutes, I couldn't get his pants down because of the bloating. Until a few months ago, Alan and I had often, eagerly undressed each other. He always made me feel beautiful, the focus of his desires. And he was so good-looking, so handsome, so striking.

I used to browse shops on Park Avenue in downtown Winter Park and say, "My husband looks like a TV anchorman. Can you please help me find a suit for him like Matt Lauer would wear on air?"

Now, immersed in the battle for my sweetheart's survival, I didn't think along the lines of the physical relationship we'd long enjoyed. All I wanted now was to save my husband, in spite of Dr. Cohen's precursive words.

One achievable thing I knew as I guided Alan, taking off all his clothes while easing him into the shower: He needed rest, so I had to get him into bed as soon as possible. I wouldn't waste his time by removing my own clothes.

I kicked off my shoes and stepped into the shower with him, supporting him in every way, but it was difficult to hold him upright. He was so big around the middle—swollen from undrained fluids—that I had a hard time reaching my arms all the way around him.

I crooned for him to keep his eyes closed tight as I shampooed his hair. I soaped and rinsed his sallow, jaundiced skin, wincing at how frail it felt, stretched taut beneath my fingers. I dried and dressed his distended middle as gently as I could, not wanting to add painful pressure to his tender, bloated torso.

Finally, I put my husband into bed, peeled out of my soaked clothing, pulled on dry shorts and a T-shirt, and curled up beside him. Exhausted though I was, sleep was long in coming. Every time I shut my eyes, my mind replayed the proof of Alan's physical deterioration.

I hadn't had time earlier to think about how our lives had spiraled. The physical chemistry between us had sparked and flamed from our first meeting, burning bright through all the years of work and raising kids and merging our lives.

Through it all, Alan had remained passionate and gentle, always sensitive to my needs. He stroked my hair when we talked, but he lacked the strength to do even that now.

I miss that.

Our mutual attraction had never waned, but that part of our marriage was currently all but extinguished by illness and fatigue and worry.

Even under the side effects of chemotherapy, before his gallbladder surgery, Alan had remained relatively up and about, helping me with the kids as much as he was able. He was young—only fifty-three—and except for his cancer, he had been healthy all his life, so his body kept springing back from hit after hit after hit.

But now, Alan couldn't get out of bed on his own. We brought in a bedside toilet because he couldn't make it all the way across the room to the bathroom, even with help. He had to be wheeled everywhere. He had no energy for walking or much of anything else.

Chapter Forty-Seven | An Honor, Nonetheless

One morning when I came in after dropping Ella off at school, I had something exciting to tell Alan.

"Honey, I just got a call from the headmaster at Ella's school. Park Maitland is renaming the science fair."

"Really?"

In spite of his weakness, I could tell Alan's interest was piqued. For several years, he had been one of the judges at the February event where hundreds of students created and displayed their projects at the Orlando Science Center.

I felt pride beaming from my skin as I told him the news.

"They're naming it after you, Alan. Starting this year, they're going to call it The Dr. Alan Saffran Science Expo."

With typical humor, he chuckled, and said, "Pam, when they start naming things after you, that's not a good sign."

*　　*　　*

One night while Alan was at home after his gallbladder surgery, he groaned constantly. I couldn't even doze as I listened to his awful, involuntary moans.

It sounds like a death cry.

Then, I berated myself for using such horrible words, even inside my head.

I couldn't function the next day. We hired a home health aide to stay with Alan overnight, so I could get the rest my body and mind desperately needed. I hated walking out of our bedroom as I told him good night, but I had to. I collapsed into the guest bed, unconsciousness until morning.

The next afternoon when the nurse arrived, she checked Alan's vital signs and frowned.

"This isn't good, Mrs. Saffran. His pulse and BP are all over the place." Her eyes held mine as she continued, "If he were mine, I think I'd be taking him in now."

I nodded slowly. "I'll call Doctor Z and tell him we're on the way."

At first, Dr. Lee Zehngebot hadn't wanted to take Alan on as a patient. They'd known each other for years, and "Dr. Z," as most called him, knew Alan's case had already advanced nearly as far as possible.

"I can't pick up the pieces and miraculously cure Alan at that point," he'd told me at the time, then turned to Alan. "If I treat you," he said, "you realize it will be strictly palliative."

Alan nodded. It was what he'd first suggested nearly six months earlier.

But I was so desperate for help. I'd fought the FDA, and I'd keep fighting. I'd try anything to save my husband.

So, we were back inside the Florida Hospital oncologist's office. Alan's hands were too weak to hold a pen, so I completed the forms for him.

Dr. Z examined the latest lab results and then looked over Alan, whose skin and eyes were the color of a Mountain Dew.

At last, Dr. Z said, "Well, there's one last thing we can do to buy some more time for now. The tumors are blocking almost everything, forcing your organs into this excruciating shutdown. We can have an interventional radiologist open up your bile ducts."

We did the surgery. We had to.

I paced outside the operating room, enveloped in an unpleasant déjà vu. The stark holding area was for families whose loved ones were undergoing surgery with a neurologist or an interventional radiologist. A few months earlier, Alan sat with me in this ground-floor lounge space, waiting and hoping the doctors could repair the bleeding in Dorrie's brain.

Now, I sat in the same claustrophobic waiting room without Alan. The same table, covered in the same brochures. The same pair of sofas. Same TV. Waiting and hoping.

Chapter Forty-Eight | Alan's List

Although Alan had been home for a short time, he had to be hospitalized again in the second half of September. Once more, I ran in nonstop mode every morning, rushing the kids out the door to their schools, checking in on my mother briefly, and then hurrying to Alan's bedside. The day after his admission, he had something on his mind when I arrived. He seemed preoccupied when I kissed him good morning, and I told him about the kids' night. I rambled on, sensing I'd prefer my own chatter to whatever he was thinking about. When he finally spoke, I saw I was right.

"We have to get the rest of our affairs in order before I die, Pam."

"We did that this summer, Alan. Don't you remember?"

"I don't mean my will. These are things you're going to have to take care of on your own."

"We don't have to do this now." I turned to reposition my ever-expanding beach bag on the ground, not wanting him to see my face. "Let's save your strength. There's plenty of time to talk about this later."

"No, there's not. I don't have that much strength left to save, Pam. I know you're not ready to hear it, but I won't be leaving here alive. We need to do this now, while I know I still can. I've got a list of things I need you to write down."

I didn't want to comply, but even more, I didn't want to wear him out with arguing.

"All right, Alan." I tried not to sigh as I pulled one of our son's speech and debate notebooks from my ever-present bag of medical records and to-do lists. "What do you want me to write down?"

"Before I die, I need you to take care of these things, and some you'll have to deal with afterward."

"I hate talking about this, Alan."

"I know, but it's necessary. You're going to inherit my ownership share of the practice and our properties, so you'll need to familiarize yourself with the bylaws of the operating agreement."

"I don't understand. Why do I need that?"

"It's in the bylaws that all the partners have to vote on any amendments to the operating agreements—any changes to the way we're going to run things—so you'll need to be familiar with it before anyone proposes changes."

"Oh my gosh, Alan. That sounds tedious."

He smiled, almost mustering the energy to laugh at me. "It is, but it's necessary. If you have any questions, Frank Pohl can walk you through the legalese."

"So, where are they?"

"I have copies of the originals in my closet. You'll see where the files are in the back."

"How long have you kept your business files there?"

"Since we moved in, when Miles was a baby."

I couldn't believe something so basic to our livelihood had been right there, just feet from where we slept, and I hadn't known.

But that wasn't all.

"I don't know if I told you about the gold coins in our safe deposit box."

"The what?"

Sick as he was, he had the good grace to look chagrined.

"They were my father's. I can't believe I didn't tell you about them. Maybe because we weren't married yet when he died."

For a moment, I forgot all about the need-to-know list Alan had me scribing and the valuables he'd been describing. All I saw was my sick husband, missing his twenty-years-gone father. A flash of angst washed over me as I thought of our children, twenty years from now, remembering their father. I buried the thought and prompted Alan.

"You were saying Murray had some coins?"

"Yes. My dad bought these Mexican gold coins as an investment—seven of them—a long time ago. They're worth quite a bit of money now, so they should help you pay off a couple of bills."

I scribbled the location of his copy of our safe deposit box key, also noting why I needed to know it.

"I can't believe you're telling me to do all this, Alan. You've really given this a lot of thought."

"I haven't had a lot else on my mind. You've had the fun of running back and forth between the kids and Dorrie and me while I've just been lying here, thinking up new ways to keep you busy."

Even with his eyes yellow from liver failure, he still knew how to twinkle them at me when he was teasing.

I wrote as he dictated, but my stomach churned as my husband continued to matter-of-factly lay out the pre- and post-death tasks he'd already thought through. A few I'd also privately stewed over, but others I hadn't yet considered, including family business matters and titles I'd need to put in my name, as well as passwords to things like his email account.

"You have to buy a new car, too."

"Alan, are you crazy? Here you are talking about me saving money so we can stay in the house and I can make sure the kids' tuition gets paid, and you want me to buy a car? I don't think so."

"Goddamn it, Pam, get rid of your car. It already has 170,000 miles on it. You've got to get another one, because you'll be driving our kids around by yourself, and I won't be here to help you..." His voice broke, and when he resumed speaking, only tenderness remained. "You need to stay safe for our kids. I need to know you'll be safe. Please, promise me."

I nodded, but I didn't trust my own voice. I was not going to let him see how much I hated imagining life without him, let alone listing the ways my life would be complicated when he died.

His list seemed to go on and on, Alan patiently speaking at a measured pace to allow me time to write everything he said, as if I were the ill one who needed accommodation. The nature of its contents—tasks I needed to manage before and after his death—dragged every syllable from his mouth onto the page with eternal finality. The pen in my hands felt dirty, as if forcing me to write what went against my conscience.

"There's something else I want you to make sure you take care of, but you won't be able to check it off for a long time, if ever."

I held my pen over the page, wondering at the serene gravity of his tone.

"I want you to make sure the kids stay moving forward on the path they were on before I got sick. Make sure they lead happy, healthy lives, all of them, but especially watch Ella."

My pen stopped as I looked at him. "It's just...she's going to need more guidance than the boys. I want her to know more of the essence of who her father is, and what I want for her.

Her brothers...I got to spend more years with them than I have with her."

Despite the quiet intensity of his words, I strained to understand as he repeated, "Make sure you watch Ella."

I didn't want to do this anymore. Writing Alan's last wishes for our children was a hundred times harder, a thousand times more real than sitting through the drafting of his last will and testament with our lawyer just months ago. In all our years together, Alan had never asked such hard things of me.

I blinked as hard and as fast as I could, turning aside in hopes he wouldn't see. I made my voice almost too bright.

"I think I'd like to take a quick break and stretch my legs down the hall, Alan. Is it OK if we finish in a few minutes, honey?"

"Wait, this won't take long. I'm worn out, but I'd rather get everything said before I rest."

I drew in what I hoped was an inaudible breath.

"All right. What next?"

"Pam..."

He didn't speak again until I looked him in the eye.

"I want you to have a healthy and happy life. I want you to try to be happy again."

Happiness was all he'd ever wanted for me. It was all he wanted now, when he wouldn't get to see me enjoy it. And it was the one thing I absolutely could not bring myself to promise him.

I still couldn't embrace the inevitability Alan had taken for granted from the day of his diagnosis.

"You might have to fight the life insurance company to pay you."

"Why? We bought your policy fair and square."

"Yes, but it was so soon after we bought the policy when I was diagnosed. It was barely past the waiting period." He shuddered. "Pam, if you hadn't made me get that physical for it when you did. Thank God for your mother. Thank God Dorrie insisted. It's almost like she knew.

There's one last thing I need you to take care of, Pam. I promise, no more. In fact, if you'll go ahead and do it now, you won't have to write it down. I'm worried about our health insurance."

Finally. Something I could reassure him about. I smiled and laid the pen down.

"You don't have to worry, sweetheart. Your hospital stays and treatments have all been covered. We've been paying through the nose for insurance premiums all these years. That's what we got it for, and we have enough saved to cover the co-pays."

His brows nearly touched as he moved his head in a weak imitation of shaking it.

"I mean for you and the kids. You have to call James about it. He will be able to give you the OK. Will you call him, right now? I need to put my mind at ease. Since you'll own my share of the business, I want them to let you stay on my plan after I die."

"Honey, we don't have to do that this minute. There's plenty of time."

"No, I need you to do it. Today, Pam. Please. Call him now."

Alan's chest heaved. Sweat ran from his forehead, and his heart and blood pressure monitors sounded off, lighting up like fireworks. "OK, honey. Just calm down. I'll step out to the hallway and give him a call right now, but please, please, Alan, relax. You get some rest while I get in touch with him."

* * *

I sat on the stone-cold floor of Florida Hospital's oncology unit with my back against the outside wall of Alan's room, waiting. I looked at the notebook in my lap, reading over the inked list of items. I'd waited for what seemed like minutes for James, Alan's partner of over twenty years, to answer my call.

"Alan asked me to check with you about the health insurance coverage he wants the kids and me to stay on after..." I swallowed, not sure I could bring myself to say the horrible, unacceptable words. But I'd promised Alan, so I continued as best I could. "He wants me to find out about coverage for us after I take over Alan's share of the ownership, after he isn't able to be a part of the practice anymore."

In the silence that followed, I wondered whether the call had dropped. Before I checked my screen, James cleared his throat.

"That's a complicated question, Pam. I don't have the authority to make that kind of decision on my own. I'll have to talk to all of the partners and get back to you."

Now, sitting on the floor like a child in timeout, except for the gravity of Alan's condition, I felt almost silly for making the call, like someone walking into a hospital and asking whether any doctors worked there.

What was I thinking? That was easy.

Of course Alan's partners would keep me on the practice's healthcare plan with our children. How could they not? Alan and I spent two decades of our lives building up that practice. We'd not only invested Alan's time and skills, we also made significant financial commitments for purchasing and developing medical properties the partners used and rented out to other healthcare providers.

My legs and rear end felt numb against the floor beneath me. I looked at my watch.

It's a wonder I reached him so quickly. I wonder how long it will take him to talk to everyone else.

Even with Alan's standing order to his staff to put my calls through to him, sometimes it took several minutes to figure out which patient room he was in during office hours.

If James had to consult with each of the other doctors in the practice before he got back to me, it would probably be a while. I hoped Alan would take a good, long nap while I waited.

My phone buzzed only ten minutes after we'd spoken.

I'd barely said hello before James interrupted.

"I checked with the guys. You're going to have to go to COBRA the day he dies."

He was referring to the Consolidated Omnibus Budget Reconciliation Act, which gives employees and their families the opportunity for a temporary extension of health coverage.

No hello. No regret. No kindness. Just a big, fat no. My stomach felt like a fist had punched and then twisted it.

"James, isn't there some way I can stay on the plan? I don't want a handout. I'm willing to work for the practice to keep our insurance. I'll go on the payroll and pay my own premiums, and I'll do anything you need or want done. I'll come in and file paperwork, I'll clean the bathrooms."

"No. We discussed all the options. You have to go to COBRA."

"James, I know you'll do the right thing. I know you will. Alan would do this for you."

"Goodbye, Pam."

The line went dead.

My husband's partners were cutting me off at the knees while he was dying in the room at my back. There was no yielding, no bending to meet me halfway. For a long moment, I looked at my phone, shocked and frightened.

But before I could wallow in self-pity, a more useful emotion stepped into play: anger.

I knew James hadn't spoken to all of Alan's partners that quickly, let alone discussed options with them. How could he possibly? At that time of day, all five doctors were in and out of performing surgeries and seeing dozens of other patients—including many I'd referred to them over the years. No way. He must have called Donald, the CFO and business manager of the practice.

Anger opened my eyes enough to see we were playing under different rulebooks. I'd counted on remaining a part of the team Alan and I had worked and played alongside for twenty years, since before we were married. We'd celebrated holidays and family milestones together in each other's homes, even vacationed together.

Now, the other members of what Alan and I thought of as our team were closing ranks. They'd crossed to the other side of the net. They saw Team

Saffran as opponents.

With that understanding came an isolating realization: I couldn't tell Alan. As certain as I was that James hadn't cleared his pronouncement with the other partners, I was just as certain that if I told Alan the kids and I were being cut off, the betrayal would kill him as surely and as painfully as the cancer.

I had to go back in and face him without letting him know. I drew on decades of muscle memory, channeling the self-control my tennis coach and mentor drilled into me. I knew how to mask insecurity, weakness, and fear from any adversary stepping onto the court against me.

It was much harder hiding my feelings from the man who knew me better than anyone.

Alan lay unmoving in the hospital bed, asleep I hoped, conserving his few remaining reserves of strength and delaying what I had to do. But almost immediately when I walked in, he opened his eyes and asked, "What did James say? Did you get hold of him?"

"You know what, Alan?" I made a big show of adjusting the covers around my husband. "I couldn't reach him. But I'm sure it'll be fine. We're just gonna focus on fighting this cancer. Let's just get you better. We're gonna get through this."

I'm sorry I lied to you, Alan. I can't ever let you find out.

When he finally drifted into sleep, I again sat with the notebook in my lap, looking at the list I'd written of all we discussed.

How am I going to support these kids or keep our house? We've got huge medical bills and school tuition payments coming up at the first of the year. Dorrie's still not here to help me, and she needs as much care as ever. I haven't worked in ages, and we've lost Alan's income.

In a whisper louder than Alan's breathing but softer than the noises of the machinery around him, I admitted to myself something I'd voiced aloud only once before.

"I'm up shit's creek. I don't know how I'm going to do this."

I kissed Alan goodnight before heading home, my heart still as heavy as the conversations we'd had throughout the day.

Overnight, Alan's already incapacitating pain intensified, and his strength ebbed further. His organs were shutting down, too filled with tumors to fulfill their functions. By morning, his doctors increased his sedation to a nearly comatose condition.

There wasn't anything left to lie about. It did neither of us any good for me to pretend he was getting better. By then, his energy and ability to function were nearly all eroded.

Once again, Alan had understood better than anyone—certainly better than I did—about the course of his disease; not just because it was happening to him, but because he was such a knowledgeable physician. He'd known the course of the disease within him long before he'd entered every phase. He'd tried to forewarn me at each step, but I hadn't wanted to believe his body could turn on him so violently. He wasn't exaggerating when he'd said he had no more time to delay that hard talk.

Chapter Forty-Nine | Counting Every Minute

Every morning I arrived at the hospital around eight o'clock, straight after taking our kids to school. I stayed by Alan's bedside, taking quick bathroom breaks only when someone else was in the room. Midway through the day, when Alan's pain medication nudged him into a fitful sleep, I'd rush to grab something from the cafeteria. I didn't care what or when or whether I ate or slept or changed my clothes, but Alan, sick as he was, noticed when I didn't.

"Pam," he said, "don't make me feel more guilty about all the time you're spending here with me. You've got to eat, and you've got to sleep, and you've got to start taking better care of yourself. The kids need you to be well for them since I can't be, and it'll make me rest easier if you do."

"Of course I will, honey. Anything you want."

"I don't want you to placate me, Pam. I want a solemn promise. I love you, and it hurts me to see you wearing yourself down."

His body may have been weak, but his eyes shone with strength in spite of the pain lines in his brow. He reached for my hand. "Promise me you'll take better care of yourself."

I closed my fingers around his and nodded. "OK, Alan. I promise."

But I didn't do it willingly, because I knew I'd be leaving him on his own too many hours as it was. For the most part, I usually stayed with him in his room until early evening. The kids, meanwhile, came straight to the hospital after school. There was a lounge directly across the hallway from Alan's room. Afternoons in the hospital visitor's lounge became our temporary normal.

Around five or six o'clock, I'd take the kids home and feed them, leaving him for what felt like a long part of the evening. After dinner, one or the other of our children sometimes came back with me to the hospital. I wouldn't leave Alan until it was time for the kids' bedtime.

So, midway through every day, placating Alan no matter what he called it, I grudgingly made my cafeteria run into a blurry competition with myself.

How can I get back to him faster?

Often, I returned with my disposable food cache within twenty minutes because the elevators and the food cashiers worked well. On other, infuriating occasions, we stopped at every floor while people shuffled in and out of the crowded, oversize dumbwaiters.

I had the route itself down to a blur of muscle memory: Rush from Alan's doorway to the elevator, pound the button all the way down, burst onto the cafeteria floor and grab whatever portable food was in reach, throw payment in the direction of the cashier, yell for someone to hold the elevator, smash the button back up to Alan's floor.

I always paused—briefly—outside Alan's doorway. No matter how frantically I'd completed the rest of the daily midday loop, I consciously reset my body language and facial expression before breezing into the room. In case Alan woke while I was gone, I wanted him seeing my "calm wife" look when I walked through the open doorway.

*   *   *

Alan was a perfectionist in everything he did—schooling, doctoring, and parenting—but that perfectionism carried a quirky cost: Procrastination. Whenever a big decision needed to be made or a project undertaken, he put it off because he knew how much effort it would cost him to get it done *right*.

The first time we planned a trip together, I had no idea it was a trait I'd learn to live with over the next twenty years. Whenever it was time to make vacation plans or arrange paperwork for important trips, my husband would have missed every deadline if not for me.

It shouldn't have come as a surprise that at least one of our kids—our firstborn—would take after Alan in that regard.

It wasn't procrastination that put off our summer plans that year, though. We'd intended on touring colleges and making a medical mission trip during the summer between Miles's junior and senior years. But the upheavals in April changed those plans, as we threw everything into balancing care for his grandma and father. We didn't visit a single school.

By the start of Miles's senior year, his classmates already knew what colleges they wanted to attend, and every week the school staff hounded him over the looming Nov. 1 early admission application deadline. With thirty thousand applicants vying for the relative handful of Ivy League openings in the spring, it was crucial that Miles commit to his one and only shot at fall early admission, where the field of applicants narrowed. That way, he'd be up against only five thousand or so of the best of the best; the valedictorians who'd played at Carnegie Hall or won the Nobel Prize during their summers.

As August's oppressive heat carried over into September, the pressure of strategizing where he had his best shot of getting in continued to wear away at Miles. Meanwhile, he continued juggling his ongoing school assignments with preparations and travel for forensic competitions. When he won the first extemporaneous tournament on the national speech and debate circuit at

Wake Forest over Labor Day weekend, he called Alan from Winston-Salem to share the news.

"That's great, buddy," Alan praised him. "I can't wait to see your trophy when you get home."

A month later, Miles brought the Yale tournament trophy to Alan's hospital room. With great effort, Alan lifted an unsteady hand to touch the shining surface, but he lacked the strength to hold it.

Chapter Fifty | False Pretenses

Compared to most mornings, Alan had been having a relatively good one. Most days he struggled for the energy to talk, but today he'd spent nearly as much time coherent as out of it. As noon approached, though, he grew increasingly tired, and I felt certain he would sleep through my early afternoon cafeteria dash.

Not only that, but in a rare convergence of good luck, empty elevators opened immediately and carried me straight to my designated stop. The only other cafeteria patron checked out as I hurried inside; my transaction was completed as if by automation, and I was back on Alan's floor in only about ten or fifteen minutes—a personal record.

I nearly smacked my face into Alan's door. I'd left it open as usual, as much to speed my exit and entry as to let him have a view beyond a closed door, if he woke while I was gone. At first, I thought nothing of it. Sometimes doctors or nurses came at unexpected times and closed his door for patient privacy.

I sidestepped to the nurses' station and asked, "Why is Dr. Saffran's door closed?"

"I think his partners are in there with him."

Oh, boy.

As I turned the door handle, voices within the room hushed all at once. I widened the opening, and the white-coated men surrounding Alan's bed turned toward me, like a flock of startled birds taking flight. The one standing closest to the head of the bed shoved a sheaf of papers behind his back as they all stammered variations of "Oh, Pam, hello."

I couldn't remember ever seeing Alan's partners all together in one place outside their office during work hours—or looking so upset. It was unnerving, and after my phone call with James, I was shocked they'd all come to visit.

"Wow. Hey, guys. Thank you for coming to see Alan. We weren't expecting you."

After twenty years of practicing together, you've been ignoring him and treating him like crap while he's been sick.

I couldn't see Alan's face behind the men huddled around him; I didn't know whether he was awake. If he were, I knew he wouldn't approve.

Besides, I should be glad for Alan's sake that they've come.

One of the men nodded acknowledgment of my words, his eyes on the floor. Another looked from the foot of the bed toward Alan's face. The pair standing at either side of his shoulders looked across the bed at each other.

This is weird.

"Is everything OK?"

Several broke the awkward silence at the same time. I barely understood what they said.

"We wanted to pay our respects."

"Just visiting."

"A business matter, wanted Alan's opinion."

"Miss him at the office."

These were smart men. It was downright odd hearing them stumble over one another's words. Then, as if by an invisible cue, the group stepped toward the doorway. One lingered by Alan's side a little longer—I could see my husband's heavily medicated, sleeping face once they dispersed—and he touched Alan's shoulder in a compassionate gesture before muttering, "See ya, Alan."

And then, with a few admonitions of "Take care, Pam," Alan's work partners single-filed out of the room, leaving me feeling like I'd interrupted something I didn't understand, but should.

Later, I wondered whether they'd learned my routine enough to anticipate I'd be gone during those brief moments, but it would be months before I guessed at the contents of the quickly concealed papers and the insidious reason for their visit.

* * *

One night in late September, Miles came downstairs wearing only a pair of shorts before dinner.

"Mom, the school is really putting pressure on me to figure out where to apply early."

He laid three logo-bearing shirts on our dining room table: Princeton, Harvard, and Yale. "I am not putting on a T-shirt again until I decide where I'm gonna go. My counselor said I have to give them my decision tomorrow. Everybody else has their essays and everything turned in. I'm the only one they're waiting for."

"Miles, I can see why you're upset, but go put on a shirt before we eat."

I didn't like it, but I understood the rationale behind the pressure they were putting on him. Only the best got in.

He came back downstairs still in shorts, but now wearing a royal blue sweater. I tried to bite my tongue, but didn't bite hard enough.

"Are you kidding? It's still almost ninety degrees outside. You're going to give yourself heatstroke."

"I don't care, Mom. I have to decide tonight, but I really need Dad's advice."

This is insanity.

Sweat was already beading up on Miles' forehead.

"Tell you what, Miles. After dinner, we'll go down and see Dad at the hospital."

It felt like stepping into a sauna as we entered the garage. On the way to the hospital, I worried over the sweat streaming down the side of Miles's face.

I didn't get my son's "no T-shirt without a decision" stance, but I understood why he wanted his father's advice. Alan had risen from the depths of an impoverished childhood through education. Alan had proved in his own life the adage he often quoted, that "education is the great equalizer."

Alan's whole life was a testament to education opening doors for everything a person wanted and needed. His primary priority in life was the education of his children—and they all knew it. So, it was no wonder Miles wanted his dad's input.

The lights were off in Alan's hospital room. In the corner, his Uncle Sy and Aunt Roberta sat quietly, lingering to spend as much time with Alan as they could before their scheduled flight back to Dallas in a few more hours.

I approached the side of the bed first, gently waking him.

"Honey, hey."

When Alan's eyes finally opened, Miles joined me at his side and Alan's face lit up. Relief flooded through me as I realized we'd caught him in a window of lucidity.

"Miles, buddy. How are you doing? How's your schoolwork? Are you keeping up the good grades?"

Miles leaned over the bed.

"Dad, I really need your advice. I need to know where to apply early. The college counselors at Trinity are putting all this pressure on us to figure this out, and I'm out of time. I need to know what you think."

Alan looked at our son and smiled.

"You know, buddy, that's a very important decision. Where you go to college and who you marry are probably going to be the two most important decisions you make in your life. And I think you should go…"

Alan's mouth opened as if he were drawing in a labored breath to form his next words, but in the middle of speaking, he fell asleep.

I dared not glance at Miles, but I looked at Sy. Sy looked at me. Our eyes filled with tears. Roberta openly cried.

I shook my husband's shoulder.

"Alan. Alan. Wake up. Honey, you've got to tell Miles what you were going to say."

I tried to wake him, but I couldn't. I just couldn't. Whether from exhaustion or the heavy sedation or both, his eyes refused to open again.

At my side, Miles's eyes grew wider, then blinked rapidly. Wordlessly, his face and shoulders begged, "What the hell am I gonna do now?"

I put my arm around him. "We're gonna figure this out, Miles. We *will* figure this out."

With tearful farewells to Sy and Roberta, we left the hospital. It was nearly ten o'clock at night when we got into our parked car. Miles was crying. I was crying.

"Mom, the school said I have to make this decision by tomorrow. What am I going to do?"

"We're gonna call your Aunt Maryann."

I dialed my sister, and reassured my son while waiting for her to pick up.

"We're gonna sit right here in the car until you guys decide where you'll apply early."

As my son composed himself, I told my sister why we called. "Maryann, we need your help. Miles has to figure out his best shot for which school to get in with early admission. And he has to figure it out tonight."

For two hours, we sat in that parking lot—until midnight—with my sister on speaker phone and my son on his laptop. They talked over school statistics and Miles's experiences while competing in debates on their campuses. We were the only car still parked on the third level. I jumped when a security guard tapped on my window.

"Is everything OK, ma'am?"

Other than the heart attack you just gave me?

"We're fine, we're fine, thank you."

We didn't leave the parking lot until Miles decided he'd apply early to Yale.

Chapter Fifty-One | Learning Judaism

I'd always marveled at the juxtaposition of faith and science Alan embodied. Near the time we became engaged, when we'd first spoken of permanently joining our lives together, Alan and I discussed religion and its role in our lives.

He was never pushy—in fact, he was the exact opposite—but he implied that he wanted to raise his kids Jewish, and was I going to be OK with that? He made it clear he wanted his children raised with the same Jewish traditions that formed the framework of his own ethical compass.

"I wouldn't ask you to convert," he assured me. A cloud passed over his face as he added, "That didn't work out so well with my first wife."

A brief silence fell between us. Since he'd told me about her on our first date, Alan had seldom spoken of the hurt he'd endured in that miserable experience. As if to shake off the unpleasant memory, he shook his head and looked back at me.

"But when I marry again, I'd like a rabbi. Is that all right? To have a rabbi marry us?"

"Absolutely. If that's what you want, that's fine with me."

"It's important that any children we have be raised Jewish. Would you be able to respect that?"

"Of course." How could I not admire the traditions and observances that shaped this amazing man?

"Alan, I may have been raised in a WASP-y household, but my parents taught me to respect others' beliefs. I admire the way your family honors generations of traditions. Only I won't know how to cook kosher meals."

A gentle grin lit up his face.

"That won't be a problem. My family isn't Orthodox, although my mom kept a kosher kitchen when my brother and I were little. But she hasn't in ages. That's the last thing you need to worry about."

I understood going into our marriage that we would observe the Jewish holidays. My first encounter with his parents was when I traveled with Alan to New York to observe the High Holidays just a few months after we met. Some of Alan's family expressed their doubt about his involvement with a non-Jewish woman, but they soon welcomed me as I showed my willingness to embrace their heritage.

Between us, there was never a question of whether we would observe the Jewish holidays. There was no question. I wasn't allowed to question it. And I was fine with that.

It was the least I could do.

So, we observed all the holidays together. Always. It was very important to him.

In the early years, of course, I knew very little of what or how or even when to observe them. I didn't know that many people to commemorate them with, either. We were just starting to know people as a couple. At the beginning, it was always people Alan had met as patients or who had invited us over.

But as we became more social and the kids entered school, it was up to me to find where we were going for breaking the fast and things like that. Alan expected me to make the plans. One year, I even hosted a Hanukkah party.

Other than the holidays, Alan didn't flaunt to the world he was Jewish. Nor did he impose his practices on our children when they came along. But he lived it. During Yom Kippur, for example, Alan himself fasted and stayed home from work. The kids' education, however, was too important to him, so they went to school, and he didn't expect them to fast, young as they were.

Alan was such a consistently good, ethical person that sometimes I wanted to rebel against it.

*   *   *

As willing as I was to honor Alan's Jewish traditions, it wasn't easy for me to forsake the Protestant holiday celebrations of my childhood. I sometimes straddled the fence between the cultures we grew up in. In our early years, we battled over Christmas.

My father was raised as a Christian Scientist and my mother as Protestant. Dorrie especially loved everything about the spirit of Christmas, so I'd grown up with decorations on every floor of our house, with elaborate parties and ornately wrapped presents under huge Christmas trees. As willing as I was to honor Alan's Jewish heritage, I wanted our kids to experience the anticipation and fun of opening their own Christmas gifts.

But Christmas was a big deal to Alan. It wasn't that he disliked it—he *hated* Christmas. He thought it was a hypocritical holiday for merchants to get wealthy, and Alan never approved of hypocrisy in any form.

So, I went behind his back.

Every other year, Alan was the on-call partner during Christmas, even though there were several other doctors in his medical practice; so, we had to remain local during the kids' winter school break. In December 2003, when Ella was a baby and Nat and Miles were an impressionable five and seven, we stayed at the Hard Rock Hotel in Orlando, close enough for Alan to commute.

Whenever we vacationed together, my mom always booked adjoining rooms on the concierge level so she could help with the kids and so we could have drinks and food 24/7. This year was no exception—but we had another, conspiratorial reason for the adjoining suites this time.

Since Alan left for the hospital before the children awoke each morning, I took advantage of his time away. Earlier, Dorrie and I purchased an adorable, completely decorated Christmas tree from the Festival of Trees at the Orlando Museum of Art. It had Clifford, the Big Red Dog, on the top with dog bone ornaments.

"It's about reading," I told my mother as I bought it. "As committed to education as Alan is, how could he object to that?"

"So, you're going to show it to him?" she asked, looking at me with a wry smile.

"Are you kidding? Don't you dare say a word."

The tree was small enough to fit inside Dorrie's hotel closet, but large enough that we needed a dolly to move it. She wheeled it out of her closet into our room every morning after Alan went to work. In the late afternoon or evening, when Alan called to say he was on his way back, I'd tell Mom to put the tree back in her closet.

Along with the tree, of course, we hid all the children's Christmas presents in Mom's closet. After Alan had gone to work, I even had the hotel Santa come in and wake the kids up Christmas morning!

Chapter Fifty-Two | Desperate Times

When I look back now on our—my—decision to pursue dendritic cell therapy, I can't stop myself from wondering, "Could there have been another avenue?"

I can only answer with another doubt-riddled question: "Probably?"

Would we have had the same end result? Long-term, I believe that yes, we would have had the same crappy outcome.

That's what Alan thought.

Back at the beginning, when we went to MD Anderson in Houston to see what they had to offer, we could have opted to move there, where they already had a dendritic cell therapy program in place. We could have lived there; but Alan wasn't going to do that. He eschewed disrupting our kids' lives any more than his illness had already done. He didn't want them leaving their school, their friends, their home.

So, he turned down that trial. He still thought dendritic cells were the way for him, but it was his decision to pursue the trial in Florida, rather than in Texas.

He saw his cancer as a death sentence. That even the most effective of trials might only prolong the outcome, and that other pursuits were frivolous. Alan understood the science about his disease.

But as much as I respected him for it, when I said I'd try anything to save my husband, I meant it. We'd already tried everything he could think of, and Alan had undergone procedure after procedure. Yet day by day, he slipped farther from the man he was, the man I loved, the man we needed.

We had to keep trying. I had to. It's cliché, but true, that desperate times call for desperate measures—and I was desperate to save my husband.

Even after starting and then withdrawing from the dendritic trial, when it would take a miracle to save him, I never gave up searching for a treatment to cure Alan.

So, I went looking for a miracle, and it didn't matter to me what form it might take.

That's how I wound up with a faith healer.

One night in the middle of September's fourth week, my tennis teammate,

Suzi, sat alongside me in Alan's room, a rare moment when she was the only other visitor. I gazed at Alan, willing him to get better, yet he remained still and silent, his posture a terrifying precursor of what was likely to come. Looking at his inert form, my heart lurched for my husband.

"I don't know what to do anymore, Suzi. I've tried everything. I'm desperate to save him. I'd swing a chicken over his head if someone said it would work."

She leaned toward me, speaking softly as if to avoid disturbing Alan.

"Pam, there's someone visiting from out of town who has created miracles for people. Would you be willing to see if this man could pray over Alan for complete healing?"

"Absolutely, Suzi. Get him over here."

I knew Alan wouldn't approve; but if the idea bothered him that much, he could just sit up and tell me so.

Oh, Alan, please do.

Suzi pulled her phone from her pocket and stepped into the hallway to make the call.

It seemed like the next thing I knew, a crowd of people filled the doorway. Four more women from Suzi's church spilled into the room. All of them were Alan's patients, including two who were also my tennis teammates. My eyes drifted right past them to gape up at the man accompanying them.

At six foot four, he towered over everyone in the room. Stringy hair, slicked back but frizzy at the ends, framed the wrinkles that shaped and covered his face—a face that looked like it had lived many, many lives. He stepped toward me, and in a booming voice, introduced himself using only one name.

"I believe God can supernaturally heal anybody. I have witnessed many miracles. Now stand in an unbroken circle around the patient and hold hands, while I begin the prayer."

Dumbfounded, I felt my hands clasped by the women around me as we drew tightly around Alan's bed.

"Now close your eyes," the man bellowed.

As soon as I'd complied, he began to chant prayers, his voice rising and falling in what sounded like gibberish to me. If he used any real words, they were in a language I didn't understand.

I peeked through my eyelashes.

At the foot of Alan's bed, the man gyrated and danced. All around me, the women surrounding Alan's hospital bed swayed back and forth to the rhythm of the man's outcries. Suddenly, a few words coalesced into intelligibility. "Cancer, rise out of Alan! Rise. Be gone!"

"Amen! Amen!" the women echoed. "Bring it out! Come on, cancer. Heal Alan, Lord. In the name of Jesus."

My god, Alan would totally kill me if he saw this happening.

My husband was so Jewish—and here I'd invited this unlikely man to try to heal him.

The prayers grew louder and louder. I felt like I was on a reality show.

An oncology nurse rapped sharply on the door, then turned the knob and peered inside. Her eyes darted back and forth over the group before focusing on me.

"Could you please keep it quiet?"

Chagrined, but still willing to do anything that might benefit Alan, I excused myself from the circle and stood as tall as I could.

"We are performing a religious ritual right now on my husband, Dr. Saffran. So, if you would be so kind, could you please give us some privacy? We may be a little loud."

The nurse rolled her eyes at me as she backed out the door, probably questioning the propriety of such a ritual inside a Seventh-day Adventist hospital.

I closed the door and blocked it with a chair, then returned to my place in the circle.

"Sorry about that. Please continue."

The women retook my hands, and the man waited until I closed my eyes again—temporarily, at least—before he resumed his prayers. We women swayed back and forth like teenagers at a concert, as this visiting preacher man moved about the room.

But in my desperation to cure Alan, I followed along. And I held my peace, even as I watched and swayed, my arms tugged back and forth by the women at my sides. For twenty minutes the healer ranted while we swayed and echoed the few intelligible phrases we could mimic.

Then the rhythm changed, quieted, settled. We all stood in silence—waiting for what, I didn't know—for a full five minutes.

OK, *now I know Alan really would kill me if he could see this. He would totally kill me. But I don't care. I had to try.*

I would have tried anything.

*   *   *

As Alan became more gravely ill, his doctors ordered heavy, sedating medications. Weeks earlier we'd already hired a private nurse to stay with him overnight, both at home (when he was still well enough to be there) and now that he was again hospitalized.

The on-duty nurses in the oncology unit at Florida Hospital were caring and committed, but the nature of their jobs meant they also had other patients who needed their attention. It seemed the staff, though dedicated to alleviating Alan's pain in whatever ways they could, nevertheless focused more of their energies on other patients—the ones they thought they could still save—than on my husband.

Alan's private nurse wasn't the only one attending him overnight. We'd also taken to having a family member or close friend stay with him. Even through the hours of the night, Alan had someone there to hold his hand, talk to him, be present with him.

During daytime visiting hours, in spite of his strong sedation, Alan never lacked company. Often, as many chairs surrounded Alan's bed as there were medical devices along the walls. People even sat on upended trash cans. I sometimes wondered whether both hospitals where Alan had been admitted sent out a memo: "Attention, all personnel who have ever worked with Dr. Alan Saffran, former chief of ENT. He's very ill. Please stop in and tell him and his family how much you admire and respect him."

Every day brought another colleague who sat beside Alan and reminisced over shared experiences. Strangers approached me by saying something that usually went like this: "Excuse me, Mrs. Saffran, but I'd like to tell you about the time Dr. Saffran..."

And every night brought another loved one to visit and sit with him through the long hours.

One night in late September, Maryann sat beside Alan's bed, making work notes as he slept. Suddenly he spoke without preamble, his words pushing thickly through his sedation.

"Dr. Saffran here. What can I do for you? How can I help you?"

That's Alan, I thought, when Maryann told me about it the next morning. Even in his semiconscious, drugged haze, Alan was trying to help someone else feel better.

Chapter Fifty-Three | Coming to Terms

I never consciously accepted that Alan's cancer could be fatal. That he claimed to know, right from the start, that it would be–and told me so–didn't matter. Yes, I knew he was an incredible diagnostician for his patients, as he had been for me throughout our relationship, and for our kids–and now, it seemed, for himself as well. He tried to prepare me for each next phase of his physical decline, and I marveled at his week-to-week prescience.

But I would not, could not believe Alan when it came to his horrible prognosis outcome. It was beyond comprehension that any disease process could have taken over his body so rapidly–in just six months.

It was the one prognosis I couldn't allow myself to trust that he got right. I thought I could save him. There had to be a way.

From the time I was little, my mother taught me there was a solution to every problem. In my adolescent years living and training with my tennis mentor Nick Bollettieri, he'd taught me to beat every opponent by working hard and playing smart. I'd lived by that philosophy ever since. If one game plan didn't turn out, I shifted to plan B. If B didn't work, I implemented plan C. There was always a way to win, if I just worked hard enough at it–always.

In hindsight, I realized that everybody else around Alan and me–his colleagues and his doctors, our friends and family–understood and accepted (to one degree or another) that pancreatic cancer would kill him.

Meanwhile, my husband remained patient with my refusal to understand or accept the course of his disease as inevitable. For my sake, as much as (if not more than) his, he'd gone along with all my attempts to save him.

I really thought there was a way, that something had to work. In twenty years together, there wasn't anything we hadn't been able to tackle as a team. As long as we worked together–pairing Alan's brilliant mind with my drive and determination–we could beat the monstrous tumors out of his body. We'd gotten him started on chemotherapy right away, and it worked (for a time). As soon as it lost its efficacy, we'd switched to another. I'd fought the goddamned United States Food and Drug Administration–twice–and won Alan's right to benefit from the dendritic cell treatment trials when such access was unheard of.

Of course, we were going to beat this. We had to. I had to. My heart wouldn't let my mind comprehend an outcome in which he was going to die.

But my Alan wasn't speaking anymore. Alan accepted he was dying long before I did. It started when he just could not recover from the gallbladder surgery. He knew it was too hard to fight all those tumors.

And now the sedative-induced coma was the only way to spare him from the tumor-riddled agony of organs shutting down.

He was present in body only; a body hardly recognizable as the hale, fit, handsome man who'd walked the same hallways on the other side of patient care just six months ago.

Now, with my husband's essence fading even in our presence, I began to realize I may have been wrong.

Even when our friend Frank Pohl took me shopping for funeral arrangements, I'd gone through the motions as if only to nod a long-term acknowledgment of everyone's mortality. Not because I expected Alan to die before me. Not before his fifty-fourth birthday. Not before the end of the year. Not really.

*   *   *

As I had so many times, I sat beside Alan's bed while he inhaled oxygen through a pair of tubes.

My mind and body had been in go-go-go mode for so long, that for once, I sat, letting the rhythmic beeps and whirs of monitoring equipment lull me into an unthinking trance. When my phone buzzed inside my purse, I fumbled as fast as I could to find and silence it. I was so used to encouraging Alan's rest, that even though a fire alarm and a parade of ambulances couldn't have roused him from sedation, I nevertheless wanted to shush the buzzing.

"Mrs. Saffran," the voice on the other end said, "Dr. Saffran's third dendritic cell treatment is ready for him to begin. We can schedule his leukapheresis for tomorrow."

I looked over at my husband's anemic, jaundiced, distended, sedated body. Whatever they had pouring through his IV, it was something ten times more powerful than morphine. But he was already catheterized and hooked up to other tubes—connected, I thought, to more than he'd want if he were conscious enough to say something about it.

I couldn't ask him, though. He wasn't responding anymore.

From the moment Alan first told me about the dendritic cell therapy, I'd been certain it held the key to destroying his cancer. If his own immune system could be taught to fight the malignant cells, he could beat this. We could beat this. Sarah Thayer, Omar Kayaleh, Mark Roh, Robert Wolff, all these incredible medical minds had agreed it was a good shot to take, an audible whisper in the dark to make.

And we'd taken it. We'd made it happen. I'd never really believed Alan was going to die of this, not with me fighting tooth and nail for him. But looking at him now, I couldn't make his body go through another leukapheresis ordeal.

I said no.

I was finally starting to realize that we might be coming to the end.

Chapter Fifty-Four | Coming Full Circle

Alan and I had been married about a year when the Orange County Public Schools' Project III grant money ran out, so my job as a school psychologist ended. Before long, I began working for what was then called Hospice of Central Florida.

My responsibilities involved overseeing twelve different nursing homes—including one my mother would later reside in—working with patients who had been given six months or less to live and counseling their families. Some passed so soon after qualifying, I hardly got to know them at all. Others had already been on hospice for two years when I was hired, but they were still kicking, fighting the odds at every turn.

Most of my patients were older, slowly coming to the end of long, full lives. A few were younger, diagnosed with rapid killers.

I knew the clinical textbook explanations of death and dying backward and forward, but I'd never really experienced personal death close to me. Even when Alan's father died before we married, I'd not known him well yet, and had seen only the aftereffects.

While at hospice, I saw the full spectrum of people's attitudes toward death.

Some said, "No, the doctors are wrong. He doesn't have brain cancer. He's not going to die, so we don't need any counseling."

Others would seek me out, asking, "What can we do to make her transition more peaceful?"

Before I worked for hospice, I had always envisioned death as being violent. People don't want to die. And within the families, those who would agree to meet with me at all bared their souls while their loved ones died. In some cases, there would be fireworks, as family members fought over money, who loved whom, just about everything.

But one man's death changed my perspective. He was about eighty-five and I didn't know him well, but I was with him when the priest was called in to give a final blessing. The man's wife was there, his kids, and his grandkids, too. It was the first time I ever saw someone take their last breath, and I was moved by how beautiful and peaceful it was, a very natural thing.

Friends used to ask me, "How can you work at that job where everyone is going to die? How can you be so happy there?"

I answered easily.

"I was always taught that life is a gift. It's a present that someday has to be returned. I can help them look at life as the gift it is, and I can help them and their families when that present is returned."

So, the day the hospital hospice workers first contacted me about Alan, I couldn't wrap my mind around the irony. I couldn't help thinking that I had come full circle, as those memories from two decades earlier rushed through my head.

*　　*　　*

With the help of my friend, Samantha O'Lenick, I brought Dorrie to see Alan at the end.

Sam called me one day to check in with how things were progressing with Alan, and to ask how the rest of the family was faring. She is the director of corporate communications and community partnerships for all of Florida Hospital, and was aware of our unending family health emergencies.

"Pam, we've got to take Dorrie to say goodbye to Alan," she said, but that was easier said than done. Mom had only been awake enough to become increasingly aware of her surroundings for about a month—after she'd been comatose for about four. She could no longer walk, and required skilled nursing care as she recovered from her multiple surgeries.

Fortunately, Sam knew someone at a major transportation company in town who agreed to help us transport Dorrie from the nursing care center to see Alan at Florida Hospital.

We wheeled Dorrie into his crowded room. Dorrie never hesitated to speak her mind, but she'd usually offered her opinions with at least a shade of diplomacy. This time, she spoke with unfiltered frankness.

"My god, he's so yellow."

She was right, of course; but in her state, I hadn't expected her observation to be so spot-on.

Before I could agree aloud, she turned to me and said, "Pam, life is just not fair, is it? Life is just so unfair."

Then, without preamble, she raised her voice and announced with a winning smile, "I want everybody to come down to the cafeteria and put lunch on my tab."

We all looked at one another, too stunned to know how to respond.

Just like that, Dorrie thought she was at one of the country clubs she'd frequented during her eighty years, and she was ready to put on a party.

Chapter Fifty-Five | September 28, 2013

Part of me was still hoping for a miracle. For something, some way to keep that gift with us a little longer. But now the Florida Hospital social worker had assigned grief counselors to meet with our family. From a professional standpoint, I understood. From my personal perspective, I didn't want to acknowledge it.

Yet here I was, watching my children smiling and creating handprint paintings with their father at the behest of the insightful grief counselors.

The kids had already melted under the attentions of the therapy dog they'd been introduced to a week earlier. We all missed Hershey and our other pets, and the dog let them luxuriate in unconditional love.

From the sidelines, I saw how much the therapists' attentions helped my kids, but never could I have imagined myself on this side of bereavement therapy. Besides the counselors working with my children, the hospice workers had come to Alan's hospital room to help me prepare for his death.

As they spoke about their services, I interrupted, already knowing much of what they might offer.

"Can we move him into a hospice facility? Wouldn't he be more comfortable there, with a homier setting, than here in the sterile hospital?"

Compassion was written across their faces as one answered, "I'm sorry. He's too fragile."

I didn't want to believe them. Couldn't believe them, even now.

"So, are you saying we can't move him?"

"No, we can't. He'd die in transit. The best we can do is make sure you're all as comfortable here as you can be while we wait."

And wait is what we did.

Alan's body was shutting down, and all I could do—all anyone could do—was stay at his side, watching and waiting, hoping the medication that kept him unresponsive also kept him from feeling any pain.

One of his doctors said to me, "Maybe he'll die soon," which made me angry, even when I realized his gruffly pronounced words implied "so he'll be out of pain."

For hours and hours each day, I sat in the room at Florida Hospital, just watching him. Watching his heart rate, watching the monitors. And every night I went home, hoping and praying he'd still be there by morning.

Maryann came from Boston again and slept in the chair next to Alan's bed, holding his hand through a couple of nights. The next night, Alan's cousin, Jason Saffran, came in from Los Angeles to sit with him, keeping watch and holding his hand.

When I hurried into the hospital room a few minutes before eight o'clock the next morning, I didn't have to ask Jason or Alan's nurse the same question I usually asked each morning. Their faces, and Alan's monitors, told me the night hadn't gone well.

"Jason," I said, my voice sounding half absent, "I need you to go be with the boys now. Hurry. Please."

Jason dashed for the elevator, and I turned my attention back to my husband, willing his body to stabilize. Willing his monitors to normalize.

I glanced at the equipment surrounding Alan's bloated body, then gaped at the numbers. His monitors were all over the place. His blood pressure showed 140/100, then fell to 60/40, then shot up to 120/90, then plunged again to 40/20, before it shot up again.

This is awful. So awful.

Alan's BP was crashing. He was crashing.

An hour after I'd arrived, I called home.

"Jason, get the boys, wake them up, and bring them here immediately."

I'd been watching these monitors for ten days, staring at them. When I saw how they were fluctuating, I knew. I'd never seen anybody dying like that, but I just knew. My gut told me Alan wasn't going to make it much longer.

This was it.

I hung up with Jason, took a shuddering breath, and fumbled trying to dial my friend Hollis while blinking hard to see the screen. Ella wasn't at home. She'd gone to a sleepover at Hollis's house because Park Maitland was having a schoolwide garage sale that day.

C'mon, c'mon, pick up.

"Hollis, I think it's time."

I looked again from Alan's face to the wildly fluctuating readouts.

"I need you to wake up Ella and ask her if she wants to be with her dad when he dies."

She was only ten, too young to face such a question, but I knew we had only one chance for this. And it had to be her choice.

"No," she said, "I don't want to be there."

I didn't blame her; neither did I.

So, Ella stayed with Hollis, and I paced the room. For twenty minutes, my feet swept over the floor as I watched my dear, suffering husband, hoping our sons would make it in time for one final goodbye.

Luckily, they did.

They joined Alan's mother, Cia, and Jason. At first, we congregated in the small lounge right across the hallway from Alan's room. Then, in turn, we each entered Alan's room, spoke briefly, and stepped back into the hallway lounge.

But Miles, Nat, and I quickly returned and held Alan's hand, staying not just by his side but in close physical contact as we waited while his breathing slowed.

I had read about it before, and when I worked for hospice, co-workers had forewarned me of a final, rasping gasp at the end.

Oh, dear god, what if it's like that for Alan? What will hearing that do to my boys?

But now Alan drew his dying breaths exactly as I should have expected. He was so elegant, so quiet—the same way he lived. There was no drama, no distress. In the end, it was quick. As we still held his hands, he took a final breath.

It was very peaceful for him.

Thank god.

But it was violent for me—internally—as my world realigned.

The boys and I sat with Alan's unmoving body for half an hour. In the lounge outside, Jason tried to comfort Alan's mother. I heard Dolores sob, but my own grief for Alan was too deep, and my need to be with my sons too great, for me to reach out to her.

Miles and Nat left the room, and Cia joined me. For fifteen minutes, I sat holding Alan's hand. The nurses tried to respect my privacy, but they kept checking back in. I didn't know whether it was out of concern, or whether they were in a hurry to remove his body to make way for another patient, one whose life they might still save.

Cia put her arms around me as we stood to leave. I took one look back, and said as much to the universe as to Cia, "My poor children. To lose such an incredible man. Such a wise father."

*   *   *

Before my eyes opened the next morning, I remembered—and I wished I hadn't awakened, but I knew sleep wouldn't return.

I was tired, so tired.

For six months, my first thought every morning had been, What can I do today to save Alan? Each day was such a battle that waking up hurt. It actually, really, did hurt. But in spite of the pain, I swung my feet onto the ground and I never stopped. Not until the very end.

The whole pattern of my life, from adolescence up until now, was to fight hard and win. I was used to winning, and together we'd won so many early battles in the war against my husband's cancer. Ultimately, none of those wins mattered.

So now, hurting as I was in every pore and neuron, I forced my legs to the side of the bed. For myself, I had no reason to rise; but for my kids, I had to.

And I had business to take care of.

As I'd learned when Alan's father died, there's no embalming in the Jewish religion, so everything for Alan's burial had to be expedited. There was no time to wait until I felt up to it—it had to be done today. As we prepared for his funeral and honored Jewish mourning customs, I relied on Alan's family more than ever.

Alan's uncles, Arthur and Sy, took me to the only Jewish funeral home in town that someone recommended to us, Beth Shalom Memorial Chapel. The kind man there, Samuel Goldstein, talked me through the logistics of transporting and interring Alan's body in the grave that Frank Pohl had helped me choose such a lifetime ago. Sy and Arthur supported me through all the questions and paperwork.

As I signed the final form, I told my husband's dear uncles what I'd been thinking as I inked my name. "I want to see Alan's body."

They looked at me and at each other, worried.

"Are you sure?"

"I want to see him one last time."

A few moments later, I stepped into the large room where he lay. I barely recognized him—he was so yellow with jaundice. I leaned over him, kissing his forehead, feeling the shock of cold—like stone—against my lips. I shivered at the chill of his skin, hardened like concrete.

I inhaled deeply, wanting one more whiff of the smell of him. I'd always loved Alan's sweet, clean smell. As a surgeon, he was religious about morning showers and high levels of hygiene. He never used aftershave or cologne, only plain Dial soap and T-Gel shampoo for his dandruff.

I inhaled again and let out a single half-laugh, half-sob, remembering when we were barely married. He tolerated the girly shampoos I had cluttering our shower, but he wouldn't touch them. I once bought him a different brand of bar soap—Irish Spring, or something like that—and he didn't like it at all. He said something like, "Hey, Pam, do you think you could buy more Dial the next time you're at the store?"

That was his mild way of reproaching me. That was Alan.

I needed to do this. To know he's not living anymore. I'll never forget this.

I straightened up and stared at his body one last time, but I didn't want to let the cancer define who he was or how I remembered him. Instead, I willed myself to see him the way he looked when he was vibrant and healthy.

I kissed him again and walked away.

I still had a funeral to plan—but nowhere to hold it.

Chapter Fifty-Six | An Angel in Our Corner

We hadn't meant to walk away from our membership at the Congregation of Reform Judaism (CRJ) synagogue where we'd belonged for so many years, but we'd allowed it to lapse for a resting season. Neither of us had renounced Alan's Judaic heritage—far from it. The temple had been the perfect place for our family, where I supported Alan's Jewish religious observation. But of late, we'd been so engulfed by adherence that I'd burned out.

"I just need a break," I told Alan in the weeks while I recovered from Nat's bar mitzvah. "You haven't been the one spending the last umpteen years—since Miles was in third grade—in nonstop preparation."

"That many years?"

"That's when I started dragging Miles to Hebrew school."

"Yes," he chuckled, "I remember how hard he fought you, and I guess Nat did, too."

"Exactly." I almost smiled, remembering how dramatic Miles was about it.

Sometimes I drove him and sometimes Dorrie did. From the backseat we'd hear, "Am I going to throw myself out the window of this moving car, or am I going to Hebrew school? OK, I've thought about it. I'm going to throw myself out the window now."

I sighed, half in fondness over the memory, half in exhaustion as I readied to further explain myself to Alan.

"We got Miles finished and we already had to start with Nat. But Alan, it wasn't just getting them back and forth and making them practice all that time, it was also getting them to and from their sessions with the cantor for six months, and meetings with the rabbi, and writing out their speeches. Not to mention overseeing their mitzvah projects."

I took a deep breath, half expecting Alan to stop me, but since he said nothing I continued.

"Then there was all the planning for the parties and the costs of the bands, and deejays, and dancers, and photo booths. And I had to coordinate all the guests and the relatives and getting it all together."

Alan looked into my face, still not saying anything.

"I don't mean I want to pull out forever. Of course not. But I'm beat, Alan. I need a break."

So, because we didn't belong to a temple when Alan died, and because I had never converted, my pleas to one synagogue after another to host his funeral were turned down.

I was so relieved when Rabbi Aaron Rubinger, a man I'd never met, agreed to come to my house.

"Thank you for meeting with us."

"Sharon White spoke very highly of your late husband," he said. "I've worked with her at Congregation Ohev Shalom for a while, and she insisted. She told me, 'We need to open the doors of the temple to Dr. Saffran,' and she convinced the board to approve funeral services for a non-member."

He added, "I've already heard stories from Sharon and others in the congregation who had your husband as their physician. Now, I've come to learn more about him from you, his loved ones, so I can get an even better feel of who Alan was."

As we met with the rabbi, I felt deep gratitude to the woman who'd been Alan's patient for years and who went to bat for him on our behalf. Around the room, everyone—Alan's mother and uncles, his cousins, my sisters and their families, our kids and I—answered the rabbi's questions, sharing memories and lighthearted moments.

It gave us all a blessed, much-needed positive focus at such a hollow time.

*   *   *

The day of the funeral, I got up like every other day. Showered. Dressed. Looked at the palm trees on the teal and white business card Alan handed me on June 12, 1992, the day I returned from my five-year college reunion. I fingered the edges of the card I'd kept beside my jewelry box ever since meeting the love of my life.

"This can't be real," I said, grateful my vanity mirror was covered so I wouldn't have to avoid the disbelief in my eyes. "I can't believe I have to bury my husband today."

I knew people loved Alan, but I wasn't prepared for the sight of seven hundred mourners filling the temple. As our family strode to the front, whispered voices echoed a common chorus of disbelief.

"Dr. Saffran can't be gone. He's been here for so many of us for so long. What are we going to do without him?"

My father wheeled my mother into the temple and parked her in the front with the rest of us. I couldn't help smiling, only a bit embarrassed at the thick, bright yellow socks she wore for all to see.

Finally awake from her coma, Dorrie behaved as if she knew what was happening around her, appearing to pay attention at least some of the time—especially during the video our friend Kim Kaminski put together. Dorrie's mind, though, often drifted into another world.

Part of me envied her comfortable detachment. To this day, she remembers nothing of the funeral.

The preservice chatter I'd heard was nothing compared to the near-silence that followed Frank Pohl's first words to the assembled congregation:

"'Don't forget me,' Alan said. 'Don't forget me!'"

People were stunned.

Who the hell is going to forget Alan Saffran?

No one is forgetting. But Alan, humble as he always was, worried that people might.

Our children spoke at the funeral. They were so eloquent, so together—more than I was.

Chapter Fifty-Seven | Well-Dressed Yard Workers

I'd sat shivah for Alan's father two decades earlier, but I wasn't familiar enough with the tradition to know what to do or expect. I was blessed with a bevy of dear girlfriends and neighbors who helped organize, and then did everything for me. Joan Pohl showed Cia and my friend Holly—who'd grown up as WASP-y as I had—what to do, and they helped.

They'd already covered all the mirrors in the house with blankets. By Jewish tradition, we weren't allowed to look at ourselves. We were supposed to think not about ourselves, but about the deceased, and what he did in his lifetime. Mary Roh made that easier by enlarging pictures of Alan and I together, and family photos that we put all around the house.

It's so nice to see him here, even if it is only in pictures.

Every part of our community came to the house. All the relatives. All our friends. My teammates. Alan's colleagues. Neighbors. The doorbell and phone rang, and rang, and rang again, but I never answered. Someone always did, but I didn't. I couldn't.

There were people all the time, but after four o'clock when kids came home from school and parents got off work, the house overflowed with visitors until about nine o'clock in the evening. Day in and day out, my house was packed. You couldn't even move.

My sister nudged me at one point and said, "Pam, did you know you have women in high heels outside mulching your yard?"

I followed the direction of her pointing hand and grinned as I saw my friend Julie Burrows and several other nicely dressed women distributing the contents of a mulch truck in our front yard.

"Oh my gosh. Alan and I pulled out all the weeds and things right before he got sick. We never got around to putting any plants in. I guess my front yard has been looking kind of dead ever since. I can't believe they're out there doing that."

At night, Alan's uncles Arthur and Sy led our family—and everyone else at home with us—in a small, beautiful service. It was the traditional Jewish evening prayer, the *maariv*. At twilight on the second night, we gathered just before sunset, looking out at the brilliant colors lowering into the west. Then we turned about and faced Jerusalem, watching the sun's waning light fade in the waking stars of the darkening east.

As one uncle spoke the timeless blessings, I felt the warmth of friends and family surrounding us, the peaceful lull of rhythmic recitation.

This is why Alan loved Judaism. It's just so beautiful, the whole religion. So smart, so ahead of its time.

Most of those days we spent sitting shivah passed in talking and telling stories about Alan.

Alan's best friend Jeff told my favorite story. Someone else made a comment about what a proud man Alan was, how he never wanted to show any weakness.

Jeff turned to me and said, "Pam, do you remember that time you and Alan went on a trip to an island somewhere in Maine? Way back before you were married? The place with the bicycles?"

"Chebeague? Sure. Why?"

"Did Alan ever tell you he rented a bike before that trip so he could learn how to ride one?"

My sisters chimed in with almost the same reaction as mine.

"What? No. Are you sure? He seemed to ride just fine."

Jeff nodded.

"He was embarrassed, so he didn't want to tell you. He hired someone to teach him how to ride a bike in the month before, just in case anyone wanted to ride bikes while he was there."

"Are you kidding me?"

"I'm serious. He almost didn't go. Not until he was sure he had the hang of it."

"I can't believe he didn't know how."

Jeff shrugged.

"Kids in our part of the city didn't have bikes when we were growing up. And then Alan went away to school and straight into working after. He never had the chance or the time to learn."

"Why didn't he ever tell me about that himself?"

"My guess? He was still embarrassed."

I shook my head, amazed and a little sad that Alan felt the need to keep that secret all these years. But that trip held such happy memories for me, I was glad Jeff shared it.

*   *   *

A traditional shivah is supposed to go on for seven days after burial, but we only did it for about three. The kids were in the middle of a school week, and they needed to be there. They needed the routine, and Alan would have been furious if he'd felt himself a disruption to their studies. Our kids' education meant everything to him.

Besides, by the third night I was so exhausted, I think people realized I just couldn't do it anymore. As much as the kids, I needed to find my way back into a normal routine—not that anything would ever be normal again—and I needed to distance myself from hearing the same trite phrases over and over and over again.

I couldn't believe how many people said the same unhelpful things. Clearly, they meant to console and encourage me, and I appreciated them for their failed attempts. So, I bit my tongue.

"He's in a better place."

It would be better if he were here, with us.

"Only the good die young."

If Alan's goodness killed him, I wish he hadn't been such a good man.

"He was too good for this rotten world."

Is that supposed to make me feel better about being left behind in it?

"You'll see him again someday."

But I need him now.

And "let me know if you need anything."

It sounded sincere, and I realized that before Alan died, I'd had no idea how to react to someone who had just lost their spouse. I was guilty of having said it to others countless times with the best of intentions.

But there I was, recently widowed, and the only thing I knew for sure was that I didn't know what I needed. At that point, I didn't have any idea. Even if I had, I doubt I could have mustered the strength to ask.

Chapter Fifty-Eight | Alan's Partners

In some ways, Alan was right the day he called me with his diagnosis. He was a dead man walking. But it hadn't meant we should give up.

And even though I'd failed to save him, I knew he was reassured that I would have never, ever given up on him.

I had battled alongside him for half a year, fighting for every inch of ground to keep him here. For every extra moment to have him with our kids. With me.

I'd had a mission—to save my husband.

I had failed.

Now, his last battle was finished.

After all the battles I'd won on Alan's behalf, I'd lost the war, my mission incomplete.

The despairing voice inside me cried.

There is nothing left to fight for. I'm done.

Little did I know how wrong I was.

Alan had not been dead a week, when his partners wanted me to fill out paperwork and pay the first hefty, $800-plus per month COBRA premium so our healthcare coverage wouldn't lapse.

"I need a few days. I can't do this right now. Can we please just have a month?"

But they were unyielding.

They had dropped by the house, ostensibly to pay their respects. One by one, they each made variations on the same condoling offer: "Let us know if you need anything. You know, Pam, if there's ever anything you need from us, we're here for you. Just let us know. All you have to do is ask. We're only a phone call away. Don't you worry about a thing. We're going to help you in any way we can."

I wanted to believe them, but they'd denied me the one thing I'd already asked for. In the scant handful of days since Alan's death, they'd notified me that we were no longer covered by the practice's health insurance, and I would have to go on COBRA.

We'd always had medical coverage, and with a doctor in the house, I'd never had to worry about it. Half the time when Alan brought home new insurance cards, I didn't even notice where he put them.

I couldn't begin to count the number of times friends with young kids said, "You're so lucky to be married to an ENT," often after he'd operated on their children. With all that can go wrong with kids—and their ears—as they grow up, I'd taken Alan's ever-present, watchful care over their health for granted.

And with the trauma of his death, I'd all but forgotten about the phone call I'd made on the floor outside Alan's hospital room, begging his partners to hire me as a token, even menial employee, for the chance to keep our family's health benefits uninterrupted.

I'd sent client after client their way, week after week for twenty years, while my husband put in countless hours seeing their patients when they didn't want to. So, I couldn't imagine myself calling on Alan's partners if I needed anything else.

But they didn't mind calling me.

About a week or so after they had come to the house, I got a call from one of Alan's partners.

"I hate to have to ask you this so soon, Pam, but we need you to come get Alan's things from his office."

His words knocked the wind from my lungs. I'd thought he was calling to check and see how I was doing, whether I needed anything.

Not this. Not yet.

When I didn't respond, he spoke kindly. "I'm sorry to bother you with this. I suppose it's a bit of a shock."

"Yes, it is. I hadn't thought about that yet."

"It's just that we are in dire need of using that space. Can you come in and get his things?"

Really? No one's been using his office since April, and you're in a hurry for me to clear it out now?

I couldn't understand the rush. They owned a huge, three-floor, 30,000-square-foot building with a surgery center, but they had an urgent need for me, Alan's widow, to empty out his corner office now?

"Can't it wait?"

"I'm afraid not."

I didn't want to see anyone I knew. I was physically drained and still emotionally exhausted from the funeral. I was tired of people approaching me with a mournful voice that dropped at the end of every impossible question they asked.

"How are you doing? How's everything going? Are you doing OK?"

What did they want to hear from me?

"Oh, I'm doing fabulous. My husband just died, but we're doing great."

I could tell that everyone around me was in their own pain over Alan's death, and I loved them for that; but I had my own, deeper pain. I couldn't make up for theirs.

Instead, what I'd been saying for two weeks now tasted chalky every time I said it again. "We're taking it one day at a time."

The only way to avoid more of that at Alan's old office was to go late at night—and maybe only run into the cleaning crew, who also knew Alan—or over the weekend.

"How about Saturday morning?"

He hesitated.

"If that's the earliest you can come."

"It is. I'll bring the boys to help me."

We could have let ourselves into the building. Alan always had a set of keys, which he used more times than I could count to meet and see patients there after hours and on weekends. But one of his partners insisted on meeting us. As soon as we opened the door to Alan's office, it was obvious his partners had been using it for storage.

"You can take the desk if you want it," his partner said. "Alan bought it himself."

I gaped at him. The desk was far too big to bring into our house, let alone for us to take home with us, and I was still too much in shock to fully think straight about it.

"No, you guys keep the desk."

If only I had known then how much more they meant to keep.

I did bring home Alan's chair, worn with his imprint from so many years, in spite of how seldom he actually sat there. From his desktop, I also retrieved the black-and-white picture of his grandfather, standing in an outdoor market before hand-lettered signs offering apples for sale. Alan always loved that picture.

*　　*　　*

Shortly after Alan's death, his cousin Jason said to Ella, "Let's do something fun. What do you like?"

"I love animals."

He took her out of the house, bless him, so she could step away from the sadness and the unrelenting well-meaning but wearying well-wishers.

That night, he pulled me aside.

"Pam, I'm sorry to have done this to you, but Ella really, really wants one of the dogs she saw today. I thought I'd better warn you."

The next day, she cornered me and said, "I want to go see that dog again. Mom, can we please?"

I was in a total trance, not functioning well. I hadn't even changed my clothes.

"I don't know, Ella."

How long has it been? A few days? A week? Seems like a whole lifetime ago.

Then I realized that it probably seemed like a lifetime ago to her, too.

"Mom, please. Please. I really want to go see that dog."

I looked into Ella's eyes—so much like her dad's—and asked Jason for the name of the place they'd gone.

He'd driven them to the nearest store where he could find animals—a dinky little puppy shop. As Ella dragged me inside, I cringed with revulsion.

She tugged me down one aisle and then another, stopping in front of a particular cage.

"It's that dog, right over there. I really like her."

I looked where she pointed and saw the ugliest dog I'd ever set eyes on—so ugly she was almost cute. "What is that?"

"She's a Peekapoo. Half Pekingese, half toy poodle. Isn't she cute?"

"Umm."

"Wouldn't it be great to take her home?"

"I don't know."

I looked down at my un-showered self in rumpled clothing. I didn't feel up to taking care of myself and my kids, much less an untrained dog.

"Mom, I miss Hershey, but he loves it at the Bibliowiczes' house. It wouldn't be fair to him if we brought him back."

It was true. Since we'd had to give our pets away due to Alan's compromised immunity, Hershey had become a part of their family. I wavered, remembering the comfort my animals gave me as a kid. Still, I didn't like the looks of this place.

"Ella, wouldn't you rather get a dog we can save from the pound?"

My ten-year-old daughter stepped closer to me and lowered her voice.

"Mom, look around at this place. This *is* the pound."

She had a point. These dogs were crammed into small cages behind glass.

Then one of the employees brought the ugly little cutie out to meet us.

"Mom, I love this dog."

I suspected the tiny creature was going to be a five-pound pain in the ass, but my daughter, who'd just lost her father, loved her. What else could I do?

We soon registered Teddy as a grief service dog for Ella.

Chapter Fifty-Nine | The Other Side of Grief

A few weeks after Alan died, my friend Sarah took me to breakfast. She was also a widow. Her husband grew up in Cincinnati with one of my sisters, and he died in his forties of colon cancer. He's actually buried near Alan.

He had twins in Ella's class at Park Maitland School. They were four years old when he died.

She said to me, "Pam, I'm going to tell you just one good thing about what has happened to us."

"Really? Seriously, Sarah? There's one good thing?"

"Actually, there is. We're not in the middle of a terrible divorce. We don't have angry issues with our spouses, like 'He did this' or 'He's seeing this person' or 'He cheated on me' or 'He's a liar.' We're not in a horrible disputed divorce like some of the people that we know. But the flip side of that is, we never get a break. We're on, 24/7. And those people that have ex-husbands or ex-wives, they at least get breaks. We don't get any."

And it was true, because there was no time to simply curl up in a ball and forget about the world around me. I didn't care about anything but my kids. I didn't remember to change clothes. I didn't bother to answer the phone or the door. I deleted emails from my dear tennis teammates without even opening them.

"Why bother?" was my motto.

I'd never been a morning person. Because Alan did rounds at the hospital around four in the morning, he'd return to the house by six to wake the kids for school. He was always, always, always on time.

I usually dragged my ass out of bed to the coffee pot no sooner than 7:10, still in my nightgown.

By then, Alan was flipping pancakes after walking the dog. The kids were dressed, wolfing down crispy bacon and an assortment of cereals.

For seventeen years, those were our mornings together.

Now, just trying to get my kids awake, fed, and off to school on time was a struggle. My body ached for Alan, and my eyelids felt as heavy as my feet, like his death had magnified gravity, grounding me, pulling at me, tugging me toward the center of the planet. I could hardly climb upstairs to wake Ella and the boys at 6:30 in the morning.

I knew I had to do a better job. I was already getting letters from the boys' school about them arriving late.

Dear Mrs. Saffran, your boys were late again. This is an advisory. If they're late one more time, they'll have to do detention.

You should be thankful my kids are at school. At all.

Alan would have been appalled. The boys were never late for him, but for me they always were.

I've got to strategize this.

I ransacked the house for every alarm clock I could find and set them to sound off in five-minute increments beginning at six a.m. I placed the clocks all over my bedroom; starting with the first to go off by the sofa near the window, the next on the vanity beside my jewelry box, one beside the closet, one on Alan's side of the bed, and the last—my cell phone—on my bedside table.

I have no idea how many alarms I slept through or how many times I slapped snoozes before hauling myself out of bed at 6:40. I still needed both arms to pull myself upstairs to wake the kids, but it was an earlier start to the process.

I was grateful Miles could drive Nat at that hour, because I still had to get Ella to Park Maitland, and that had made both of us red-faced.

More often than not, I'd steer into the carpool line in time to hear the final strains of "God Bless America" playing over the loudspeaker.

"Crap! You're going to miss the Pledge of Allegiance. Do I have to get out of the car and walk you in again?"

She wasn't a teenager yet, but she already had the eye roll down to an art.

"Mom, you have to sign me in *every* time I'm late."

Then her annoyance shifted to horror, as she looked for the first time at what I was wearing.

"But I don't think you can come into the school like that again."

My hair was up in what could only be described as a big hair thing, and I'd yanked a sweater on over my nightgown, to make myself appear halfway normal-looking. By the look on Ella's face, I hadn't succeeded.

She advanced several paces ahead of me as I shuffled to the office in my slippers, taking no chances on being associated with me.

That afternoon, I put a change of clothes into a bag and stowed it in my car. The next time I had to sign Ella in for a tardy arrival, I dressed first—in the car.

But that was the best I could do, because I couldn't break out of the fog. I was so indecisive over stupid things. It took me twice as long to dress, or pour a bowl of cereal, or brush my hair. Halfway through one thing, I'd start another.

The only time when things seemed clear was when I got angry. Sometimes I just lost it. A car might pull out in front of me in traffic, and I'd yell and call the other driver unflattering names. Or I'd drop a plate on the kitchen floor and suddenly hear myself screaming over a spilled sandwich.

The raging anger was such a shameful, ugly side to grieving; one I'd never known about, not even as a therapist. I had understood the theory of anger as one aspect of grieving. I'd witnessed flares of fury from clients as a therapist. But even when I had worked with hospice, my only connection with grief was professional, not personal.

From a therapist's perspective, I knew grief was born from the loss of a relationship, a connection with someone else, that when severed, turned everything selfishly, greedily inward. Now I was learning what that meant from a mourner's perspective. Alan was the one who suffered the pain and indignity of his cancer and its treatment. But finding out about his diagnosis and facing his death were the worst things that ever happened to me.

And grieving him was one of the strangest.

*   *   *

I had to put something in Alan's closet. I don't remember what it was, but opening the door, turning on the light, and walking inside felt like stepping into a sweet-smelling tomb. The scent of Alan's clean, soapy essence embraced me.

It was awful, feeling close to him only vicariously by the closeness of his shirts, suits, ties, and medical attire. He'd always made it a point to look not just professional, but nice for his patients.

I touched a few of his many, many ties, recalling how he chose ones with whimsical characters on the days when he had a lot of pediatric patients. Beneath them, his shoes were lined up, neatly polished. I realized, with a start they weren't much bigger than the ones our sons wore.

Maybe the boys will wear these someday.

When I noticed his iPad, I felt a soft smile work its way to my lips.

Alan was such a computer geek. He loved new technology. He especially loved his iPad.

I couldn't help picking it up—I was curious about the last things he had browsed. I glanced over the few emails he'd sent, and I grinned when I saw his searches for baseball statistics. I looked from the electronic device in my hand to the side of the closet with his old-fashioned baseball card collection.

He knew all the baseball players and their teams as well as he knew the anatomy of his patients' ears, noses, and throats. His memory was so incredibly accurate that when we were dating, the radio host on WMMO FM 98.9 would occasionally call our house.

"Can I talk to Alan?" he'd ask if I answered. "I'm doing a baseball trivia contest on air, and I need him to settle a question."

Then I saw what Alan had looked up on Sunday, April 7, the day before the CT scan confirmed his fatal diagnosis. He'd looked up stomach pain. Ulcers.

"Signs and symptoms of pancreatic cancer" was the final string of search terms.

But that was the day before...

The truth hit me.

He knew.

From somewhere in the back of my mind, I remembered Alan making a casual, offhand remark the day after his diagnosis.

"You know, Pam, I even looked this up."

He diagnosed himself—without telling me. Then got the scan to confirm it.

I sunk to the floor and cried.

Chapter Sixty | Invisible Wound

It was mid-October, and Miles was preparing for his extemporaneous speech at the New York City Invitational Speech and Debate tournament held at the Bronx High School of Science.

I interrupted him.

"I just found out some great news I think you're going to love."

He looked up from his notes, preoccupied but willing to listen.

"OK."

"The new president of Bronx Science graduated in your dad's class. He remembered him, and when he found out, well—he renamed the next-to-last round The Dr. Alan Saffran Semifinals."

Miles looked at me, his expression unreadable, but his voice conveyed layers of meaning. "Oh, no pressure, Mom. Thanks so much for telling me."

A few hours later, the crowded audience rose to its feet, applauding the winners. On the stage, Miles again accepted his trophy, a silver bowl so large that when he won the same event the year before, security hassled us in the airport on our flight home.

Alan remarked at the time, "We could ice skate on this thing."

I dialed Alan's number, ready to shout into the phone.

Miles won again!

Then I remembered.

Oh my god. Alan's not here. I can't call him. I can't tell him. I'm inside his old high school, our son just won this national tournament, and he'll never know.

I cried, unable to hold it in anymore.

People congratulated me through my sobs, patting me on the back and briefly hugging my shoulders. They thought I cried tears of happiness for my son—and I *was* ecstatic for Miles.

But I bawled, because I couldn't tell Alan.

Our kids—his kids—were growing, achieving, excelling, but I had nobody to share that with. I missed having Alan as my sounding board, and I needed his feedback, with the incredible wisdom he'd always shared, about how to handle situations.

My mom had always said, "Your husband can't be your best friend. That's why you have girlfriends."

But she was wrong.

Back then, I'd had so many girlfriends around me that I'd never really thought of Alan as my "best friend." He was my husband, my lover, my partner. But after he died, when I looked back on how we talked three or four times a day on the phone and every night as we went to bed, I realized he really was my best friend.

And losing him was like losing a part of myself, something no one else could see.

I realized that at the airport on the way back from the tournament. I watched a man stacking bags of chips and loading food cartons into a fridge at Starbucks. He was using only one arm; the other hung limp at the side of his uniform, small and thin. I caught his eyes as he looked up.

His expression showed surprise, as if unused to having someone smile at him. Smiling back, he whispered, "Hi."

"Hello," I said aloud, but in my head and in my eyes, I tried to say so much more.

We are so alike, you and I. Your outward handicap is obvious to everyone, that wounded appendage that leaves you with half the dexterity of those around you. My husband—my other half—has died and left me. I feel amputated, like I'm missing an appendage too, only my wound is invisible; it's on the inside, so no one notices.

Sometimes, like when I'd dialed Alan's number, I tried using that limb, only to find it gone. For the first time, I thought I had a peek into what it must be like for people wanting to use—or still feeling pain from—phantom limbs.

I'd been told by well-wishers that I would heal in time, but it offered little consolation. Like an amputee, I knew my wound would someday stop bleeding, and the scar tissue around my heart would heal, but I would never be the same again.

*   *   *

Back when Alan was still fighting for his life, Ella came to me one day.

"Mom, some of the kids at school and I are going to start a club to help raise money to fight pancreatic cancer. We're getting some of the other parents to help us with T-shirts and stuff."

"That's a nice idea, honey."

Usually I'd have been the one helping her with extracurricular projects, but at the time I had my hands full with Alan and Dorrie. When she told me her friends' parents were helping with the project, I was relieved.

I never imagined she and her fellow fifth-graders would accomplish so much.

But now, I was reading a school newsletter about what Ella and her friends had done, and I was brought to tears.

I had no idea they had approached Cindy Moon, the head of Park Maitland, for approval of their plan. Or that Ella designed the logo for the shirts they sold to raise money. Or that they'd had their Cross Out Cancer organization trademarked so people could still contribute to it online.

On October 17, Park Maitland scheduled a schoolwide Cross Out Cancer day. When we pulled up to the campus and saw the WKMG Local 6 news van, I had my first inkling the event might be larger than I'd realized.

Everywhere I looked, students, parents, and school staff wore purple Cross Out Cancer Team Saffran shirts.

I was as uplifted by the tangible support for our family as I was floored by what I learned there. Less than a month after Alan's death, so many people became involved that the organization had already raised over $12,000. One hundred percent of the funds were divided between the Florida Hospital Cancer Institute and the Pancreatic Cancer Action Network.

"Ella, you did this."

Alan would be so proud.

He was always so proud of our children—and so involved with them.

He was scrupulous about making it home for dinner so he could help the kids with their homework afterward. 'Class' was held in the kitchen. Dorrie called it the "little red schoolhouse." He helped with all their class assignments; math, science, everything. He was their go-to person for all the subjects.

Our friends would even call Alan for help with their kids' homework. It wasn't unusual for a Trinity family to phone in the evening and ask his opinion on a particular science question.

I, on the other hand, was as much help to them as chopped liver. They were doing things like calculus.

The first time I helped Ella with one of her assignments after Alan died, it didn't go well. The next day she came home and announced, "Mom, I got two right out of twenty."

We had to laugh. And laugh.

"From now on, Ella, we're Googling everything."

Chapter Sixty-One | The Runaround

I have never hesitated to handle business matters over the phone, but I dreaded making this call about Alan's life insurance policy. Steeling myself when the kids were at school in early October, I dialed the number of the company's home office.

It would be the first of many, many calls.

"I'm sorry about your husband's death," said Barbara, whose voice I would come to know well. "And we'll be sure to process your claim as quickly as possible. But first we'll need you to send us a copy of the long form death certificate."

There's more than one kind?

"How do I know whether I have the one you need?"

"Does it have a place where the doctor signed off on your husband's cause of death?"

There was no mystery about the cause of Alan's death, but I supposed it made sense for the life insurance company to require documentation. I didn't yet realize the number of hoops I'd have to jump through to prove it.

I fumbled through a stack of paperwork and pulled out the engraved certificate, hating the official declaration it made as my eyes skimmed through the document.

"No, it doesn't have that. Where do I get the one I need?"

I learned that would come from the funeral home, and it took about another ten days to get it.

"Mrs. Saffran, we have your late husband's completed death certificates ready for you now," said the caller from the funeral home. "Would you like us to mail them or would you prefer to pick them up?"

I'd prefer I didn't need them at all.

After I picked them up, I FedExed a certified copy of the required death certificate to Barbara's office.

Thank god that's over with. Now all I have to do is wait.

Little did I know how long.

There should have been no ifs, ands, or buts about my claim on Alan's policy.

But the company had questions. It was a big policy, and it soon became clear they didn't want to pay me. In a way, I didn't blame them—I'd only submitted to the insurance company the first of what we'd all expected would be many premiums for his term policy.

But it was paid in full, and the six-month waiting period had passed before Alan's diagnosis.

That didn't stop the company from stalling, trying to say he must have been ill when we signed him up.

One morning, I awoke thinking more clearly than I had since Alan's death. I remembered that our friend Jason Mendelsohn was in the insurance business.

"Jason, I'm having a hard time getting payment from Alan's policy. How do I go about this?"

The next thing I knew, we were on a conference call.

"All right, Barbara," Jason said, "Tell us what Pam needs to do next. And what will she need after that?"

Quite a lot, it turned out.

It took me at least twenty different phone conversations, but not just with the insurance company.

They wanted Alan's medical records prior to his diagnosis. It had been years since Alan's last medical exam. He hadn't had any health issues before or since; when he got something minor like a cold or even major like the flu, he just kept working through it.

I called Alan's internist and spoke with him personally before I contacted his office staff. "I just want to give you a heads-up. Alan's life insurance company will be calling you."

"Pam," he said, "we've got it covered. We know exactly how to handle this for you. You don't need to worry about a thing."

I had to coordinate with the medical records staff of Alan's three different doctors and ask them to send copies of his old records directly to the insurer.

I waited to hear back as one week, then another passed. When the insurance company contacted me again, though, it wasn't with the news I wanted. It was another request for those same records.

"But we've already sent you all of them," I told Barbara, after getting yet another notification that they couldn't process my claim until they received Alan's complete medical history before the cancer. "Yes, I know there are only three doctors listed. Because that's all he saw."

Sometimes I wanted to lob the phone over the desk.

Even with so few records, the company took its sweet time processing them.

I called for an update and was told, "We still haven't received your late husband's medical records. Perhaps you should remind the staff at his doctors' offices that we cannot proceed on your claim without them."

The trouble with that assertion was I knew the women in the medical records departments at each doctor's office—they'd all been patients of Alan's, and every one of them had been eager to help me. So, I'd call them back—again.

"Have you had a chance to send Alan's records to his life insurance company yet?"

To a person, they had.

"Oh, yes, we sent those the same day you asked for them, Mrs. Saffran."

"Did you send them with a signature required for delivery?"

"Yes, of course we did." Then they'd check Alan's file and tell me the dates.

I called Barbara back.

"You received Alan's medical records in your office on October 15. The doctors' staff said they have proof of delivery."

"Oh, yes, I see them here now. I just found them."

Once might have been an oversight. Twice a coincidence. Three times out of three doctors' records—that was too hard to believe.

Meanwhile, the insurance company continued to collect interest on the money they were supposed to have paid out within a reasonable time of receiving my claim.

As frustrated as I was, I was grateful—as grateful as I could be in regard to anything relating to my husband's death—for the timing of the policy we'd purchased.

Thank god mother was such a pushy lunatic about it.

* * *

I shivered in the cold November air. My stomach clenched, hurting as if I'd been punched.

The ballroom was full of music and children's laughter, but I was outside trying to call my neighbor, Mary Roh.

"Mary, I need you to do me a huge favor. I'm two days into chaperoning Ella's class trip in Colonial Williamsburg, and we've got another three days to go. Alan's life insurance company just called and said they're finally sending the check today. Someone has to sign for it. Can you keep an eye out for any delivery trucks?"

"Pam, there's a FedEx driver getting back into a truck in front of your house right now."

"Can you run and stop him?"

I heard a clunk, then a door slam, then nothing.

My mind raced.

I need this insurance money. I've got three kids' schooling to pay for. And property taxes are due. And COBRA payments for our health insurance. And Alan told me to get a safer car.

But every reason I cited felt like a rationalization of the unforgivable fact of what the expected funds meant: I was being paid for the death of my husband, and no amount of blood money was worth that cost.

Then I heard Mary's winded voice.

"I got it, Pam. I signed for it, and it will be waiting for you when you're back."

"I owe you, Mary."

"Not a chance. You have fun up there with Ella."

Fun?

I was doing my best to make sure Ella thought so, but it was painful being surrounded by families who hadn't just lost a spouse or parent. I grew more drained at every site we toured.

But Ella needs this.

Chapter Sixty-Two | Our Biggest Dispute

I knew—had always known—Miles learned his work ethic from Alan, and we'd seen proof of his intelligence at an early age. In fact, our son's intelligence was one of the few things Alan and I fought over.

We came from two different worlds, but we formed a balanced parenting partnership. He was soft-spoken and gentle in his approach, and I was the more assertive go-getter, always pushing the envelope. I was like the military general, and he was the military psychologist.

When we became parents, he was the good cop, I was the bad cop, and we sometimes joked that our kids were in and out of PTSD every other week.

This issue, though, of how best to educate our young son, was one of our biggest disagreements.

The genesis of our dispute started when Miles was a baby.

At first I didn't realize how unusual it was, when at nine months, he began pointing at and sounding out the alphabet board I kept for him in the back seat of the car.

"EM—mm-mm-mm. OH-oh-oh-oh. Ay—yay-yay-yay."

As Miles got older, I began noticing differences between him and his peers. While other children sat and dozed contentedly, propped in front of animated movies, Miles leaned forward with interest over anything with letters. He'd watch *Sesame Street* alphabets over and over, and his favorite bedtime toy was a plush letter A.

One night when Alan and I came home from a dinner date, our babysitter, my friend Holly's sister, said, "I know this is going to sound crazy, but before Miles fell asleep, I could almost swear I heard him through the baby monitor saying the alphabet backwards."

Later, a few months shy of Miles's third birthday, I took him to renowned psychologist Ellen Winner.

After evaluating him, she told me, "You should start him playing the piano, among other things. It would be really good for him."

That sounded reasonable, and so did her assertion that he probably needed to skip a grade at some point. It made sense to me, especially when I recalled that Alan had skipped a grade when he was young.

"But be careful of his social needs," she cautioned, "because boys mature differently."

Alan and I looked into school programs to help Miles grow academically, so when we enrolled Miles in private school, I pushed for having him skip a year.

Alan threw as close to a fit as he ever came. He seldom put his opinions above anyone else's, but on this he was adamant.

"No, Pam. I will not do that to my son. I've been there, remember?"

"You told me you were bored to tears in school before you skipped a grade."

"I was."

"Then why do you want to inflict that on Miles?"

"I don't, but there's more to school than an academic education."

That took me aback. Ever since becoming a father, he'd all but obsessed over our children's education.

"Like what?"

"I always felt really behind developmentally. The school just did it without asking me or my parents."

"But Alan, it worked out so great for you. I mean, you started college ahead of time."

"That's part of the problem. Do you have any idea what it was like to be only sixteen when I enrolled at Columbia, still living in my parents' apartment? Everybody in my classes was an adult. It wasn't good, Pam."

In the back of my mind, I remembered Dr. Winner's caution, which I hadn't shared with Alan.

Throughout Miles's kindergarten year, I kept pressing the point.

Eventually, to keep the peace at home, Alan backed down.

"Fine, Pam. You go right ahead and do what you want to do. But don't blame me if we both regret it."

When Miles finished kindergarten that year, he entered second grade at the end of summer. That first year, the change seemed a good fit for him, and he fit in with his peers well enough.

When Miles entered third grade at age seven, the difference in ages became more apparent. Some of his classmates were nine.

I hated to admit it, but Alan was right. Physically and emotionally, Miles was two years too young to fit in. The gap was just too big, so we ended up correcting it. And it was fine.

To Alan's credit, he never threw it in my face or said I told you so.

He was too good for that.

*　　*　　*

When you lose someone you love, there are so many triggers to remind you of what you've lost.

Every widow and widower I've talked to has a hard time at the grocery store. And it was no different for me.

I'd be shopping, and there was a certain type of granola Alan loved. I'd catch myself reaching for it and stop.

What the hell am I doing?

One of those trips to the grocery store was soon after he died. My kids were hungry, and all we had in the house were bagels. I had no interest in eating, but they sure did. I stood in the aisle, looking at the yogurt. Alan loved one of the new Greek yogurts that had just come out. He liked cottage cheese, and grapefruit, and all kinds of healthy things.

That's Alan, I thought. Always making the right decisions—for himself, for our family.

Alan's absence could sneak up on me anytime, anyplace.

When I'd sit in the Panera in Winter Park, I would look across the street and see all the restaurants that we used to go to on Park Avenue.

Alan loved that street. He was from New York City, but just couldn't believe he'd ended up in this little charming town with its brick streets and Spanish moss. We'd drive up and down Park Avenue, especially during the holidays when all the lights were lit. He thought it was so beautiful.

He really appreciated where he was. He really appreciated who he was and how he got there.

So many triggers.

Ella and I were in Connecticut with Nat for a speech tournament in which he was competing. The place was filled with parents, with fathers. Suddenly I thought, "Where's Alan? He should be here."

All the moments of all the things he's missing. That's what makes me so mad. So angry. He worked hard for his kids, and yet he doesn't get to enjoy any of the results.

And I'm angry not just for Alan, but at him, too, for dying.

What the hell? Why? Why? Why? You've left me and the kids! What were you thinking?

But then, my mind kicks in, and I realize he would have chewed off his right arm to stay here.

Chapter Sixty-Three | Waiting to Hear from Yale

The closer we came toward mid-December, the more we all stressed over whether Miles would get into Yale. On the fifteenth, at exactly five o'clock, acceptance notifications—and denials—would be made public to all the kids across the country who'd applied early.

Friends kept reassuring me, "You don't have to worry about Miles. Of course, he'll get in." He was as well-respected by his teachers and peers as Alan was. He'd played sports (and been to national-level competitions), and he was rated number one in the country for speech and debate.

But it was still too easy to dwell on how hard it was to get into any of the top Ivy League schools.

The odds were not in anybody's favor. Not even my son's.

And I had no idea how he'd fared in his applications and essay, which were due just days after his father died.

I never even saw an outline or rough draft.

Guilt gnawed at my insides.

Could I have made a difference by helping him?

The rational and irrational halves of my mind argued back and forth over what I should have done and what I wasn't able to do.

On some level, though, I had to accept I wasn't in any condition to do more than I did—I'd been planning a funeral. I had two other children to comfort. I held so many tasks in my overfilled hands and such heaviness in my broken heart, that helping Miles with academic goals was the least of my priorities.

But now the soul-searching had to come to an end, because Miles was going to find out at 5 p.m. if he was accepted.

Unfortunately, I was in the woods, two miles from our house with Ella looking for a lost dog. I kept checking my watch.

"I have to get home, Ella. Your brother's going to find out at five o'clock."

"I know, Mom, but we have to find Tricky."

Even though I knew only seconds had passed, I glanced at my watch again.

"Of course we do. But the Johnsons are much more likely to find him than we are."

Their small, blind, deaf, twelve-year-old dog had wandered off, with only his supposed remaining sense of smell to guide him home.

I was torn by frustration.

I had to be there with my daughter, helping her close friend and their family find their dog. They needed my help, and Ella needed to know she could count on me.

But so did my son. I had to get home. I had every hope he'd get in, but I had prepared if he didn't.

A friend had suggested I order two cakes for that night's dinner, one in Yale blue with a message of congratulations, and one in subdued hues without a message.

But I knew no cake would offer sufficient consolation if he didn't make it, so I wanted to be there—just in case.

Finally, at 4:49, someone called out, "Got him!"

I wanted to leave that minute, but Ella had to wait with her friend to give Tricky a proper welcome.

I jangled the keys and tapped my foot, trying to speed her along.

My phone buzzed at 5:02.

"Mom, I got in!"

"He made it!" I screamed, startling the other searchers. "I'll be there in two minutes," I promised my son.

I ran in the door and scooped Miles into a rib-crushing hug.

"I'm so proud of you! I'm so happy for you!"

Miles beamed as he showed me the light blue bulldog with its message shouting CONGRATULATIONS in all caps across his laptop screen.

"Your father would be so proud of you. And I'm proud of you, too. Your hard work has finally paid off!"

Finally is right. Something good has happened after all we've battled in the last year.

Later that night, I said, "Miles, now that you're in, will you tell me what you wrote your essay about?"

He grew quiet a moment.

"I'll let you read it."

I smiled—and cried—as I read. He spoke of Alan making our home a place of learning; like a "little red schoolhouse" where he "learned on the shoulders of giants."

I was so proud, and yet so sad that Alan never got to know where Miles would go to college.

*　　*　　*

It seemed like all the world around me was celebrating the Christmas season. I couldn't stand the holiday hoopla. Music, lights, decorations. The commercialism seemed more heartless than ever.

Of course it's heartless. My sweetheart is gone.

If I'd had the energy, I'd have said "Bah, humbug!" to everyone who wished me happy holidays during that bleak month.

And as December 25 approached, with the New Year looming just a week behind it, my spirits were as low as they'd been at any time since Alan's death.

I both yearned for and pushed away from the familiarity of the Christmas season. Maybe it was because this was my first widowed holiday season. Maybe it was simply because I was a widow. In spite of hearing remonstrations from well-meaning but clueless busybodies—"He wouldn't want you to be sad, dear"—I knew a sense of melancholy was natural, so soon after Alan's death.

What I couldn't have anticipated before losing Alan was how much harder it was living with that melancholy, as a widow, than I'd thought it could be.

When the twenty-fifth arrived, I checked my email more out of habit than out of expectation. To my surprise, there was a message from Alan's best friend, Jeff.

There was an image of Alan at the top of the screen, one I didn't recognize. He was sitting in one of the chairs in our bedroom. He'd unfastened the top two buttons of his white collared shirt, as if he had recently walked in the door from the office.

My heart flip-flopped and my eyes fluttered at the sight of his picture and the words in the email:

From: Jeff
Date: Wednesday, December 25, 2013, 12:57 p.m.
Subject: A Video to Share

Pam,

Hope you guys are doing all right this Christmas. I know it must be incredibly tough for you right now.

As rough as it was, I just spent the last several hours editing these videos from Alan, so you could each have yours today.

I love you guys so much and am completely beyond words anymore.

My eyes returned to the picture of Alan while my hands greedily clicked on the blue play button.

Within seconds, I blinked at a black screen and big, red writing:

August 19, 2013

To Pam

From Alan, with LOVE.

I stopped breathing.

Six weeks before he died.

The written words faded, and my husband—moving, blinking, breathing, smiling—appeared before me.

"Hi, Pam."

That voice. I hadn't heard Alan's voice in so long. I wiped my eyes quickly, not wanting a single image blurred by tears.

"I just wanted to say a few words just in case there's...in these crazy past few months...I haven't had a chance to say it.

"You have been a rock. You've been a wonderful wife for nineteen years. You've been a wonderful companion. A great friend.

"You have done everything for me since I've gotten sick. Your strength, your spirit, your ability to never give up..."

His eyes widened and his voice broke, but he grinned as it did.

"I've never..." Alan stopped and laughed.

Oh, how I'd missed his laugh.

Then he shook his head, smiling with his eyes lit up, that wonderful smile that lifted and lit his whole face.

"I've never seen anything like it," he continued.

Then his expression changed. It became not sad, but serious. For the first time, his eyes faced me directly, held me as if he were speaking with me, merely an arm's length away instead of from the other side of a lens and a lifetime.

"I will love you forever and with all my heart. Continue to do a great job raising the kids. Continue to be a great, caring, strong woman. We will meet up again."

He sniffed, his eyes moistened, and he looked down. Before his next words played, the light in the room around him shifted. Shadows fell at different angles.

I later wondered how long it had taken him to compose himself before he finished his message to me.

"And I love you very much, for everything that you've always done. For who you are. And for your love and kindness. You will always be with me."

A minute and a half. Ninety seconds of my husband's love from beyond.

Alan had also prepared similar messages for each of our kids—messages so private, so personal, that I haven't seen them. With Jeff's help, Alan had given us all one last holiday gift.

Chapter Sixty-Four | Turning the Screws

One of the reasons Alan updated his will the summer before he died was so his estate wouldn't go into probate. Unfortunately, when I was raw with grief and shouldn't have had to deal with it, I had to start taking care of unwanted business matters. Alan's partners forced me into probate.

The ownership documents for the medical building named me as Alan's beneficiary; his shares should have gone directly to me immediately after his death. However, his partners refused to turn them over.

As the process began, I was numb inside, but I still had papers to sign and decisions to make and bills to pay and kids to tend. I wasn't up to handling any of it, but I had to.

Maybe I should get Frank to help me get bought out of the practice and just keep my shares of the rental properties. That would be one less thing to have to handle, but I'd still get the semiannual income from the rentals to cover the kids' tuition.

Being forced into probate added another hat of responsibility for me to wear; the court appointed executor of my late husband's estate, legally designated as his personal representative. I had to pay bills out of Alan's estate in a timely manner, but some didn't arrive until two years later, after the estate was closed out.

One thing I could count on was that there would always be bills. I was still receiving doctor and hospital bills and chemo bills—$15,000 for every time he'd been treated. And all three children's semester school fees were due.

In January, I was expecting two distribution checks from the rental fees of the properties Alan and his partners owned—but only one came. Combined, they would cover the kids' education cost, as Alan and I had planned—but now I was short of funds.

I called the business manager, not bothering with small talk once he picked up.

"Donald, I've only received one of the distribution checks that I need to pay the kids' education bills—I have two at Trinity and one at Park Maitland. You know full well that's why Alan and I invested so heavily in the properties—so we could fund his kids' schooling. Why is it late?"

"I'm sorry, Pam. I can't send it."

"Alan told me, when he was on that hospital bed, to expect distribution checks on both buildings in January and again on both in July. Are you no longer renting out the properties?"

"Of course we are."

"Then aren't you receiving rental income on both properties?"

"Yes."

"Then why are you suddenly unwilling to distribute their income as you're supposed to?"

"It's out of my hands, Pam. Back in July, the partners put a moratorium on all future distributions to shareholders."

"That's ridiculous. Alan said nothing of the sort."

"It's in the documents. I'm afraid my hands are tied."

"I want a copy of those documents."

Silence.

"Donald?"

"I will have to get back to you on that. I don't think I have the authority to send you those."

"Why not?"

"I think you should talk to the group's attorney and work directly through him. Do you need his number?"

"No, Donald. I don't need it. Alan and I have known him a long time. Thank you for your help."

*   *   *

I was burning up, too angry to make another call until I'd given myself a good talking-to.

It's OK. It can be good to be filled with fire, but what counts is what you do with that fire. I need to show my kids that even though life can be cruel and unfair, we can go on.

But I had so much anger. I didn't want anybody to see that side of me, because it wasn't a pretty side. I didn't want to see anybody.

I just want to be normal.

It could become a new, different normal, or at least a normal that we could learn to live with. My boys could still play on the high school varsity tennis team, they could still enter speech tournaments and travel all over the country. Ella and I could still schedule play dates and visits to the park with her friends.

Alan's cancer was not going to win. Yes, it had already taken Alan; but I was not going to let us lose any more of who we were.

The kids knew I was fighting something, but they were so busy with their homework and after-school activities that they didn't see most of it, and I tried not to let them.

My sons were old enough to appreciate the financial change in our lives, and Ella was on the cusp of grasping it.

When the time came to apply to colleges, Miles said to me, "Mom, I can look at other places."

I knew he'd received over 300 scholarship offers to choose from, including state colleges and universities of every size from all over the country.

No. That's not what was supposed to happen.

He showed me a letter from one university.

"Mom, this is a really good honors program, and they'll give me a scholarship and a stipend."

I turned to him and I said, "You know what? No one expected your father to die, so no one expects you to go somewhere like that. I know it's a great school, but you're going to go to the best you can. If I have to scrub toilets, that's what I'm going to do."

The whole reason we had kids was to continue on. To do better than we did. Would that mean it was always going to work? No, but Alan always wanted our kids to go further—and I wasn't going to chop them off at the legs.

It's not their fault their father died. It's nobody's fault—just a genetic mutation.

Maybe it was wrong of me to shield them, as much as I could, from what was happening. Not just with fighting Alan's partners, but when I was fighting the battle for his life. I tried to keep their lives as normal as possible so they could continue to do well in school.

That was my job.

I could have remained bitter, angry, spiteful that other wives still had their husbands and kids their fathers.

But what good would that do any of us? Living with anger the rest of our lives? What kind of life would that be? What would I be modeling to my kids about enduring hardships? That we just throw in the towel and give up? No way.

Chapter Sixty-Five | Putting Up Obstacles

Since I had gotten nowhere with the business manager at Alan's practice, my next step was to call the practice's longtime attorney, David. While I was on hold, I realized I hadn't seen him come to the house or offer any condolences after the funeral, even though Alan worked with him for years as president of the medical practice that hired David.

With a theatrical greeting, he interrupted my thoughts, drawing out my name like a breath of air.

"Paaam Saafffrraaan."

His voice echoed.

Really? He's got me on speaker? I wonder who else is there.

His next words perplexed me even more.

"I just came back from Switzerland. The fondue is wonderful there. My daughter's doing a year-long study abroad. What a program."

No "how are you, how are the kids, what a loss"—no acknowledgment of Alan, or me, whatsoever.

"That's, uh, great that you went to Switzerland, David. I'm happy for you. But hey, I was just wondering, where are the corporate documents?"

"Why? Why do you want the corporate documents?" There was nothing casual or open in his tone now. "I'm afraid I can't share them with you."

"David, I need to have those. I'm the court-appointed executor of Alan's estate."

"Well, I don't have any way to verify that. You could just be saying it. I would need to see proof before I could show you anything."

I couldn't believe what I was hearing.

"David, how long have you been employed by our medical group?"

I'd seen Alan going over the practice's expense reports. I knew the partnership kept him on a $30,000 retainer; I'd seen his name at the bottom of the page every year, and every year I'd thought the same thing—what a waste of money.

"I'm employed by the medical practice, not you."

I forced myself not to lose my temper.

"How long have you worked for Alan's medical practice, then?"

"Over fifteen years."

"And weren't your wife and children patients of Alan's?"

His "yes" sounded grudging.

"So why wouldn't I, as his wife, be the court-appointed executor of his estate?"

"Well, I, how do I know that? Without proof of your legal standing as Alan's representative, I can't show you anything."

I was fuming by now, and barely kept my voice civil.

"You'll have the documents on your desk in thirty minutes."

I got in the car, drove to his office in downtown Orlando, and handed the documents to his paralegal.

He never took or returned any of my calls after that day.

That night, when Frank Pohl called to check in with us, as he and his wife did every night, I gave him an honest answer when he asked how I was doing.

"It's not going well, Frank. I think I'm going to have a problem."

"What do you mean? What's going on?"

I told Frank about the partnership's attorney being unwilling to give me the documents I needed. "I think I need to hire an asshole attorney."

He laughed at first.

"Well, I don't know any, because I can't stand them."

"Don't you have someone in your firm who's a strong litigator?"

"Of course I do. And I think I know just the one to help you. We have a partner I hired about ten years ago. She put herself through law school as a single mom with two babies in diapers by playing online poker."

"I'll take her."

*   *   *

Several months after Alan's death, well-meaning friends kept telling me, "You have to get support. You have to get grief counseling."

I'd *been* a hospice counselor, so I knew the importance of processing grief in healthy ways—and how to do it. I also knew having that knowledge wasn't enough. As much to satisfy my friends' suggestions as to help myself, I considered various options and soon settled on one that sounded intriguing.

The night I walked into a meeting of one support group, forty-five women sat in a huge circle. It was both empowering and disheartening to see so many other women like me.

The reality was awful. One—and only one—newly widowed woman spoke the entire hour, crying about her husband and his tragic construction accident only two weeks prior. Still deeply in shock, she shared raw pain that was too much for me.

I'm supposed to be doing this for myself? This is agony. What am I doing here? I've left kids at home who need me there with them.

I never went back.

So, I started looking for a therapist who dealt with grief. The grief counselors in the hospital had been helpful, and I hoped to find someone similar.

When I finally found someone with recommendations I respected, I scheduled an appointment, this time including the kids.

I could tell right away I'd made a mistake.

"So, you're Dr. Saffran's family," the therapist said, as we chose seats inside her office. "I'm so happy to meet you and work with you. I'm so sorry about his death. Do you know how much I appreciated your husband? Fifteen years ago, he saved my son's life. Did he ever tell you about that? I think it's such a tragedy that such a talented doctor died so young."

For the first twenty minutes of our fifty-minute session, she went on and on and on. I didn't want to color my kids' experience, but their body language spoke volumes.

Well, this is a great waste of time. Now we're all feeling even worse.

I wasn't about to put my kids (or myself) through anything like that again. I decided when the time was right for any of us to revisit the idea of grief counseling, I'd shift my search to a city far enough away to find a counselor Alan hadn't treated as a patient.

Chapter Sixty-Six | Turning the Tables

On Frank's recommendation, I contacted attorney Teresa Phillips. She was a perfect fit to help me fight what increasingly felt like a 'good old boy' mentality inside Alan's practice.

At every turn, they'd stonewalled my requests for copies of corporate documents. Meanwhile, Teresa reviewed the original corporate files Alan had kept in our bedroom closet, and she set up a face-to-face appointment with his partners.

The day of that appointment, Teresa and I agreed to meet first at the law office and then arrive together in her car. In her arms, she carried two of the biggest binders I'd ever seen. They must have each been at least six inches thick.

"What on earth are those?"

"These are the corporate documents I've compiled. One copy is ours and the other is for them. It has all the operating terms for the different corporations owned by the partnership—for the medical practice and each of the buildings they own and rent out."

When we got to the structure that Alan and I had watched being built from the ground up, Teresa and I rode the elevator to the third floor where his practice had been. Inside the waiting room, Alan's reception staff greeted me warmly.

"The doctors," we were told, "would be with us shortly."

I looked around the waiting room where I'd been millions of times before, smiling at the toys around us. Most brought back sweet memories; Alan and I donated them from our home over the years as our children outgrew them.

Only one of the men who approached us was Alan's fellow physician in the practice. Michael had the longest-running connection with Alan (going all the way back to med school). We'd been at one another's weddings, our children had birthday parties together, and our family vacationed with his when our kids were little. For a long time, we'd been associates—and I thought friends.

He'd taken over as president of the practice during Alan's illness. Alongside him stood David, the lawyer who no longer took my calls, and Donald, the practice's business manager.

Michael smiled broadly.

"Why don't we just go ahead and meet here?"

"I think we need to sit down and go over a few things."

"Then sit."

"Michael, we're not doing any such thing. This is a waiting room. We're going to actually go to a conference room and hold this meeting."

Teresa backed me up.

"Doctor, I believe these matters would be better handled in private."

I took Teresa by the arm and tugged her along as I stepped around him.

I still own enough of this building to sit at the table I helped my husband pick out without holding a business discussion in the lobby.

We walked down the hallway I'd traversed countless times over twenty years, the hallway leading toward the corner office I'd cleared of Alan's things so soon after his funeral. We paused at the conference room doorway, but it was so filled with files and other paperwork and storage that we bypassed it.

"This will do," one of the men said, indicating the employees' lunch break kitchen area. The round table looked barely large enough for four, but someone pulled up an extra chair, and the men sat together in a curved row. They chatted lightly among themselves.

As Teresa and I walked toward the chairs on the other side, I noticed the table wobbled under their elbows. One checked his watch, another yawned, and the third said, "This won't take very long, will it? Because I have other things to attend to."

In a sweet voice, Teresa said, "Here you go." Then she slammed the binder onto the table right in front of them.

They looked shocked as the table shook. With their attention fully on her, Teresa slammed the second binder onto our side of the table.

Her action broke their mood.

"All right, gentlemen. Let's get started."

Too soon, though, they recovered their cavalier attitude.

As Teresa outlined their obligation to pay my share of the rental income, they all crossed arms and leaned farther back in their chairs, distancing themselves from both speaker and subject and shaking their heads.

Instead of acknowledging her points, they addressed me with increasingly condescending comments.

"Oh, we can fix this. We really don't need to have our attorneys involved. We'll work it out."

"You just need to continue to stay as a shareholder. Let us handle the business side of things, Pam."

"You shouldn't be so worried about this."

"I wasn't worried until you failed to fulfill your obligation to distribute the full rental income," I said.

David said, "We can't make that distribution right now. The building's falling apart. We have so many repairs. The doors themselves are a mess."

"Yes, we already saw that you recently spent over ten thousand dollars on landscaping. We don't care about your repairs. I want out. Buy me out."

"Why would you demand that kind of money, Pam? You don't think we can pay that, do you?"

They had every excuse in the books. They didn't have enough money, they couldn't do this or that, they had too many upcoming expenses.

Teresa was quiet at first, but as their refusals grew increasingly heated—and insulting—she grew proportionally more protective of me.

As she argued on my behalf, I bit my tongue so many times I could taste blood.

After an hour and a half, we reached the tipping point.

"Losing Alan's income is a devastating loss for the practice," one of them said. "We've never had a partner die before. You can't imagine how difficult this has been for us, Pam."

"Difficult for *you*?" I wanted to say more, none of it printable, but Teresa, standing up, placed a hand on my shoulder.

"We're done here," she said, facing them. "You'll get a copy of our court filing."

The minute we stepped outside, I let loose.

"Can you believe that asshole wanted to keep us in the toy room? Here I am, f---ing grieving the man they called their partner, and I'm having to fight them for a fair buyout?"

"I've seen it all. And that was about the worst I've seen," Teresa responded. "At least now they know they'll have to answer to the court if they don't respond to us."

When we got back inside the car, Teresa turned to me and said, "This is going to be a battle, and it isn't going to be easy."

I'd figured that myself. They hadn't been willing to budge in any way.

I turned to face Teresa. "You know what? As far as I'm concerned, they've just shot themselves in the foot. They want to fight me over whether they'll distribute the rent money? Fine, they can fight about it. That's all I wanted when I walked into that room."

Just that damn check.

"But you know what? After what they just tried to pull, that's not going to be all they're going to have to fight me for."

"What do you have in mind?"

"If they'd just sent me the damn distribution check on time, I wouldn't be here, you wouldn't be here, and I'd be willing to let them get away with a token buyout of my shares down the road. I'd have worked with them on a payment plan or installments or whatever. And walked away."

I threw my arms out to the side, then shoved one pointing hand toward the building.

"But if they want war, they've got it. I happen to know they haven't had those properties appraised in years. If they're going to wave a white flag about what's fair value, let's get the property appraiser and the court in on the conversation. And while we're getting that rental distribution reinstated, we're going to tell *them* what's fair value. They're going to buy me out, and they're going to be fair about it, even if we have to get the court to *make* them."

When I pulled onto the street, I didn't look back. It was the last meeting I ever had with Alan's former partners. I never returned, and from then on, any contact was between our lawyers.

*   *   *

As June approached, there were constant reminders of Father's Day.

I hated it.

We'd always made a big deal about Father's Day for Alan. The kids ran into our room in the morning and climbed onto him, showering him with hugs and gifts they'd made him. It wasn't easy for them to figure out what he wanted—he never asked for anything, not even when pressed—but they tried. One year Ella, who knew her father liked washing his own car, assembled car wax and a sponge as her gift.

And every year we took Alan to a fancy restaurant, like the Grand Bohemian. After, we'd end the day by seeing a play or movie with the kids.

Our first Father's Day without Alan was atypical in more ways than the obvious. Miles and Nat were in Kansas City, competing at a national speech and debate tournament. Ella and I stayed in Florida with my dear friend, Cia, who'd returned to offer her support through what she rightly suspected would be a difficult weekend for us.

That morning, we made the hour drive to the beach in my Suburban; the one with so much wear and tear, Alan wanted me to trade it in for a new vehicle. Before we started out, Ella said, "Mom, are you sure we can make it all the way there and back?"

"Of course we will."

We brought four Mylar balloons—purple, in honor of pancreatic cancer—and in the back seat on our way to Daytona Beach, Ella used a Sharpie to write on each one: "To my dad in heaven."

We stood at the water's edge and released them, one by one, into the sea breeze. The wind whipped our hair and the balloons rose in a frenzy of shining purple. We watched, until at last, they appeared no larger than specks against the cloudless sky.

Eventually we piled back into the SUV, but it wouldn't move.

"C'mon, Pam, what's the problem?" Cia asked.

"I'm trying, but I think we're stuck. We can't leave."

"Um, Mom?"

"Honey, I'm trying to figure this out."

I pressed the gas down harder.

"Mom! Look back here!"

I glanced into the rearview mirror and yanked my foot from the gas. Behind us, clouds of sand slowed and fell as the wheels stopped spinning. Cia burst out laughing.

I called AAA, but I was told tow trucks aren't allowed on the beach because they also might get stuck.

"What are we going to do, Mom? How are we going to get home?"

I couldn't let Ella down. Not on this day, of all days. I left her with Cia and approached other beachgoers and passersby.

"Excuse me, could you please help us? Will you help me, please?"

Most walked right on by without acknowledgment, while others politely declined.

Eventually, two well-built guys in muscle shirts drove up and offered to help. They had enough rope in their pickup truck to pull my Suburban free.

"I cannot thank you enough. You're lifesavers," I told them, as they drove away.

By the time we were on the road, Cia was again laughing so hard tears streamed down her face.

Chapter Sixty-Seven | Caught in the Act

I got an excited phone call from Teresa to meet her at her office. When I arrived, she had brightly flagged documents placed in neat piles beside a foot-thick file. The records she had been poring over were the ones I had requested as Alan's executor. They hadn't arrived until close of business on the last day before the court would compel them to comply.

"The business manager was partly right in what he told you about the partnership deciding no one would receive rental income on the buildings for the unforeseen future. They documented that vote."

I slumped.

"Then why did you sound so positive on the phone?"

"Oh, I'm not done yet." Teresa smiled as she picked up another folder. "We've got the agenda and the minutes from that meeting they held on August 27, the one they didn't inform Alan or you about."

The week after his emergency gallbladder surgery. He was in so much pain.

"The minutes claim those present at the meeting 'represented' all the ownership shares, but it also records that your husband was not present. It makes no mention of who allegedly represented him and his shares. However, the minutes also indicate who wasn't a partner but who *was* invited and present—one of the partnership's building tenants."

She showed me the name, and I nodded.

"The business manager. The one Alan said was getting a huge discount on his rent in addition to receiving a salary. Plus, he uses that office space to run his other business."

"And he's not a listed owner and therefore wouldn't be entitled to a vote in the running of the practice. Interesting, especially in light of the final item of business listed in the minutes, which, incidentally, did not appear on the agenda for the meeting."

"What is it?"

"The final resolution of that board meeting states that 'all present unanimously approve a moratorium beginning July 2013 on semi-annual cash distributions.' In other words, without Alan's vote or proxy, they decided at the end of August to retroactively stop rental distributions on at least one of the medical buildings."

"Can they do that?"

"Not according to the original, unamended operating agreement."

She indicated a thick folder of pages, also rainbow-flecked by sticky notes, but picked up a smaller set of pages and handed them across the desk.

"Now, you've got to see this document." Her eyes sparked as she handed it to me, and her fierce grin looked triumphant. "It's telling."

I glanced at the all-caps title of the document: FIRST AMENDMENT TO THE OPERATING AGREEMENT.

My initial reaction was bemusement.

Bit of an overkill on that.

I scanned over the legalese, but I wasn't sure I understood correctly what I read.

"I'm sorry, Teresa. Can you just explain what this means?"

"In lay terms, it's an amendment to how the company ownership was to be run."

"What kind of changes did they make?"

"We'll get to that in a minute. There are a couple of other points I want to show you. First, take note of the date, and then turn to the back page listing all the required signatures."

On the second line of the document, I found "dated as of _____ __, 2013."

Flipping through the other pages, I confirmed what was on the first page.

"There is no date. The lines are blank."

"Exactly. And the signatures?"

On the final page, I saw the names, positions, and signatures of every member of the company board. Every signature, that is, but Alan's.

I fingered the typewritten letters beneath it—Alan J. Saffran, M.D.—then looked up at Teresa.

She nodded.

"The primary change they wanted to make," she said, taking the pages back and scanning to somewhere on the second sheet, "was this: 'Upon the withdrawal'—which an earlier paragraph defines to include death or transference to a surviving spouse—'of an owner or partner, the beneficiary or shareholder loses all rights to vote.'"

"So, they didn't need Alan's vote for the moratorium?"

"Oh, but they did. We've got them, Pam. The minutes from the meeting they held back in August—without inviting Alan or you as his proxy—clearly state they discussed making such a change. But at that time, they were legally bound to involve all the members."

"So, they were trying to cut us off from having a say."

"About the moratorium on payments, about anything. And this document proves they *knew* they needed Alan's signature to make it binding, even though they held the meeting without informing him."

I gasped, as an assault of memory flashed before me.

Alan's hospital room. Styrofoam food containers in my hands. The partners huddled around his bed like vultures, startled by my entry. Papers shuffled away from sight. Eyes that wouldn't meet mine as they slinked away.

It was almost beyond comprehension. I knew Teresa was just the messenger, but my voice rose in frustration.

"Alan gave his best years to building up that practice. He was its president until he got sick. He was loyal to the practice and loyal to them—and they tried to do this to us, to him, while he was terminally ill?"

Anger made my hands shake, but it only fueled my resolve.

"I need you to do whatever it takes to make them honor the agreement they had with Alan. Whatever it takes."

And that's what Teresa did.

I won! I got Alan's ownership share of the buildings and received a fair buyout.

*   *   *

Before Alan died, life held color. Afterward, everything was gray.

All I could think about was keeping my kids together.

Nothing else mattered anymore. The yard, the house, the laundry. I'd barely tended to those kinds of details while I was fighting for my husband's life. Much less after I'd lost it.

I felt disconnected. The invisible thread that tethered me to Alan flailed about, seeking its ground, but finding nothing to hold.

I couldn't remember when things happened. And I wore Alan's death like a hat.

Right after he died, I blurted it out to everybody.

It was totally normal, this exclamation of grief.

If you were the checkout person at Walgreens or the grocery store, or the friend I ran into on the street, I would share it with you. Whether it was someone I played tennis with, whether I was at the school for parent's night ... it didn't matter who you were. Whoever I was talking to, that person was going to know right away what I had been through—like it or not.

Ella would tell me, "Mom, not everybody needs to know what happened."

Sometimes my kids would say, "Stop playing the victim card."

And I'd say, "That's really mean. I'm not playing the victim card."

But I think at some point, maybe I was, at least at the beginning. Because I just felt so bad. So awful.

I just couldn't believe that something so horrible happened to us.

We had such great kids.

Why?

Why would there be such a tragedy, when everything had been so perfect?

When I look back on it now, I realize how much I did talk about Alan. Now I'm much more at peace with it. It's totally different. The grief is incorporated into who I am, but it's like a pie.

At the very beginning, the biggest slice was Alan's death. But now, the slices are more divided, more balanced: my health, my kids, what happened to Alan. Now it's more holistic. More about living a good life.

Before it was, "Life is unfair."

Now it is, "Life is unfair, but it's still good. It doesn't end in a period anymore. It's followed by a comma."

Chapter Sixty-Eight | It's a Mitzvah

Despite the promise I made to Alan to replace the aging Suburban, I didn't dare spend the money because of the kids' ongoing and future education costs. Even with his life insurance payment and my successful settlement with his partners, I still hesitated. The car itself, however, was beginning to threaten its own retirement by emitting increasingly disturbing sounds.

Maybe I'll price a couple of used ones.

I took Ella with me to a dealership with four-wheel drive vehicles like I'd always wanted. "Now remember, I'm just looking today. I probably won't buy anything."

As we pulled onto a street near the dealership, Ella said, "Mom, you can't park anywhere near there."

I understood what she meant. Every time I decelerated, the Yukon made a horrible, screeching *EEEEE* sound. Every time I picked her up in the carpool line at Park Maitland, she covered her ears.

I parked a couple of blocks away so the salespeople wouldn't see—or hear—how badly I needed to do business with them.

I forced myself to keep a poker face while I looked around the showroom. The young employee whose turn it was to help the next customer was nearly as shiny as the cars around us. I described the features I wanted.

"Mrs. Saffran, we do have a used car like the one you're interested in. It's being detailed right now. If you and your daughter would like to help yourselves to the offerings in our valued customer lounge while you wait, I'll page you over the speaker as soon as it's ready."

"Sounds good to me," Ella said, taking me by the hand and tugging me in the direction of the lounge.

In one area they were giving massages, and there was an ice cream bar in another. I'd never seen so many different coffees outside a Starbucks.

"Mom, this place is fabulous."

"I know. I think I'm going to buy a car."

We'd barely finished our ice cream when we heard, "Pam Saffran, your car is ready to test drive. Please come to the lobby at your convenience."

As I crossed the showroom to the lobby, a woman came running from an office doorway. "Pam Saffran?" she called out, looking back and forth and hollering my name. "Pam Saffran? Is there a Pam Saffran here?"

Taken aback, I nodded. "I'm Pam Saffran."

"Could you please come into my office?"

"I'm supposed to go on a test drive."

"The test drive can wait." When I looked from her to the lobby, she added, "Don't worry about it. I'm their boss. I'll let them know."

I looked at Ella, who shrugged, and we stepped into an office the size of a small restaurant. She gestured us toward comfortable cushioned chairs.

"Please take a seat. I want to talk to you about something."

"OK."

She sat across from us and told us her name. The plaque on her desk identified her as the general manager.

This woman's the big cheese here.

"Are you related to Dr. Alan Saffran?"

"Yes, he was my husband."

"Mrs. Saffran, let me just tell you a story. I have worked very hard to get to where I am, but your husband allowed that to happen. It's because of him you're sitting here in the general manager's office today."

Ella and I leaned forward. Since Alan's death, I'd heard countless people tell me how much they loved and admired him, but I'd never heard something like this before.

"I don't understand."

"The rest of the people out on the floor are men, but I'm in charge. Do you have any idea how hard it is to advance as a woman in this business?"

"I can only imagine."

"When I first started here, I had to work my way through the ranks of this 'good old boy' business of selling cars. Just keeping my position required that I put in extra hours. I couldn't leave, even if I needed to."

"I'm sorry, I don't understand."

"My sons were tiny back then, and one had really bad ear infections."

"So that's how you met my husband, at his office?"

"Initially, but after that your husband would bring his medical bag and come to my office to examine my child so I didn't have to leave work. I cannot even tell you how many times he did that."

Her eyes welled.

"Because of your husband, I am sitting where I am today."

I was shocked.

"You see any car out there that you like, Mrs. Saffran?"

Then she promised to discount a five-figure amount from whichever I chose.

"Really?"

"Any car you like."

"Yes!" Ella and I fist-bumped.

She had me coax my piece of crap car onto the lot to trade it in, and she said, "We're also going to give you ten for your trade-in."

"Ten dollars?"

"No, ten thousand."

I couldn't believe anyone, even one of Alan's grateful patients, would give me anything for that old heap—let alone ten thousand dollars!

Before we left her office, I'd signed the papers for my new car for far less than I'd expected to pay for a used one.

Thanks for the great deal, Alan.

*   *   *

One of the biggest things that happens after you lose your husband is you begin to doubt yourself. You become almost insecure, in a lot of ways. You question your decisions and your choices. You don't have your springboard or your rock anymore, so you kind of feel like you're floating without any ground beneath you.

I read all these articles that warned against making a major decision—don't sell your house within the first year, don't buy this or that. Good advice, but what about the small things in life? You know, does my car need to be tuned up right now? Do the kids need clothes for school? Do I need to get a tutor? Is Ella going to be OK in math?

As a trained therapist, I tried talking myself out of those self-doubts.

I'd tell a client, "You have to give yourself a break. You have to be easy on yourself. It's not your fault."

You think your life is going down a certain path. And all of a sudden that path changes course, and you have to be willing to shift to that new course, or you're going to be left behind.

It took a while to figure that out for myself. The first couple of months after Alan died, I really beat myself up. I was in a dark place. I was going through the motions of everyday living, but I wasn't really living. I was just getting by.

"OK, Pam. You can get through the next hour. And then, you can get through tomorrow afternoon."

And then, slowly, every once in a while, I'd actually find myself laughing at something, and the joy started returning.

Will it ever be the same? My god, no. We're never going to be the same. I'm never going to be the same. I will have a huge void. But it doesn't mean that I can't be happy again.

And I do find myself forgetting about what I went through and what Alan went through, and the pain when I think that my kids don't have a father.

Then I realize there is a lot to life. When I look at the pictures of Alan, I feel like he's with me. Like he's right there on my shoulder or by my side. I can feel him. I don't know what that is.

One night, I was looking for note cards for Ella to use to study for a French test.

I went to look in the hallway where we keep a lot of school supplies, and I found a notebook kept by the nurse that was with Alan at the end. It was dated 9-22-13.

"Alan walked to the bathroom. Refused to brush teeth. Gave him a sponge bath. 2:15 a.m. Alan used the commode next to the bed. Flushed the pan."

It was like a hit again, almost exactly two years later, and I went in the other room and started crying, looking at these notes that brought back his memory so vividly.

"What the hell was yesterday's date? The twenty-first?" And those notes were dated on the twenty-second.

I was crying and crying while Ella was studying her French. I wiped my tears away and came back in.

"You know what, Ella? I'm sorry, but I can't find any note cards."

I went to put the notebook back—and there was a whole new stack of note cards there. Where had they come from?

I think Alan was trying to talk to me.

Chapter Sixty-Nine | Turning the Corner

About a year after Alan died, I started thinking, "I need to go back to who I was."

I knew I needed to do that, but my mind wasn't there yet.

I was still angry. Mad at everybody and everything. I hated when people told me:

"There's got to be a reason."

"You'll find that reason one day."

"He's in a better place."

At the end of 2014, on New Year's Eve—my second without Alan—it seemed even worse, looking at whole families, where kids had their fathers and spouses had each other.

I sat alone on the sofa, thinking, "I can't go on like this. I can't live in this kind of misery."

Then the ball dropped at Times Square, and all of a sudden it was like a veil lifted. It was the weirdest, physical thing.

Everything shifted—my perspective, my outlook, my vision. I felt like I could finally see again.

I heard myself say, "I can live. I can do this. It's going to be extremely hard, and I'm going to be exhausted half the time, but I can do this."

I woke up the next day feeling like a person again.

I didn't know what that was. Maybe it was God. Or Alan.

But it was something. When that shade lifted, I was at peace.

And it was around that time that my friend Cia and I jumped into the business of flipping houses.

Our plan was straightforward enough. Cia found a shell of a house in Cincinnati and would oversee everything with the contractors; I would provide the capital, and once the house sold, we'd split the profits fifty-fifty.

From the moment we first discussed the undertaking, I saw it as a creative way to pay some of my family's looming bills. With Alan gone, I'd had to try new strategies for paying our kids' education bills—the education Alan always wanted them to have. He sacrificed so much of his life, working hard, long hours so they could have the best education, never dreaming he wouldn't be here to finish what we'd mapped out together.

Now, I had a new plan to follow with Cia: To buy, remodel, and resell this first house. I found myself transformed as much as the property. Our project gave me something to do that was separate from my life with Alan. It was a chance to try new things I hadn't done with him. I was doing this creative, productive new project; not as my late husband's wife, but as myself.

It was exciting, but I was certainly not in my comfort zone. I'd already learned that being widowed means being catapulted into a very uncomfortable place for a very long time, and some of the realities of house flipping were just as uncomfortable.

It was a big undertaking for two women with no experience in the business. By the time we finished, we realized we should have started where we lived in Florida, not where we had lived in Ohio. We also went through a couple of shysters before we found a general contractor with the skills—and ethics—to get the work done.

It took us over a year to remodel that first house (and it seemed to take even longer to sell), but in that year, we learned more than we could have imagined when we began.

And in that year, I started reconstructing my life.

*　　*　　*

My tennis teammates were constantly checking on me, letting me know they were thinking of me, and even though I didn't respond to their messages, they'd still ask, "Are you up to it now? Would you like to play?"

But I hadn't played since the day of Alan's diagnosis. I couldn't even look at my tennis racket in the back corner of my closet. At some point in the months of his illness, I'd draped a sweater over it like a curtain.

I couldn't think about tennis. I didn't want anything to do with it, not even when my teammates were so diligent about reaching out to me.

If I bothered to respond at all, I'd send back a terse "no."

Sometimes they'd email. For a full year after Alan died, I ignored them entirely. I wouldn't even read the subject lines before I deleted them.

Eventually, some days I'd at least take a quick look—"We need another player for next week's match against ..."—before deleting.

And eventually I responded, but only to decline.

"No, I'm not ready."

When I caught myself showing enough interest to read them all the way through, I wondered: Am I *beginning to come back to myself? Am I ready?*

When I not only read, but thought about their messages, I knew I was on my way to returning.

Maybe I should play sometime. Maybe I could.

Chapter Seventy | Rebirth

As we approached the second Father's Day after Alan's death, my thoughts kept drifting to one of the first widows I'd ever met with as a hospice counselor.

All these years later, I remembered her lovely, dignified elegance. The day after her husband died, we did a grief exercise where we released a balloon into the air, sending it toward heaven.

We watched it lift, bob, and dance in unseen air currents. When she broke the silence, she said beautiful things about her husband. As the balloon climbed higher, she said how much she loved him, how he was so good to her, how she thanked him for thirty-five years of marriage.

That's what I want to do with the kids this year.

This time, we were better prepared when the middle of June approached than we were the year before.

We had a fun family dinner on Alan's beloved Park Avenue in Winter Park, laughing and enjoying being together for the day. Finally, I said, "OK kids, it's time to go visit Dad's grave."

I got the balloons out of the car and started blowing them up. Before I'd tied the first one, Miles cracked up.

"What's so funny?"

He was laughing so hard he couldn't answer, and the sound was contagious. Before long, Nat and Ella joined in. By the time Miles found his voice, I was laughing too hard to blow up the next balloon.

"Mom, these things aren't going to float anywhere—they need helium."

Still laughing along with the others, I looked at my son, then at the empty balloon in my hand.

"It's the thought that counts, so help me blow these things up."

We went through the motions of expanding and tying them, thinking our wishes for Alan, and threw them into the air.

Every balloon exploded in a loud POP as soon as it hit the prickly grass.

We laughed till we cried.

It felt wonderful.

AFTERWORD

For two years after Alan's death, Dorrie did much better. She's the ultimate fighter. She's a force, and she raised a force.

She created a miniature business at the care center here, where she'd recuperated. Inside the Gardens at DePugh, Dorrie had the staff convert a janitor's closet into a store, and she ran it, keeping track of all sales herself and charging yesterday's prices for today's snacks—like Diet Coke for twenty-five cents.

In October 2015, we moved her to a nursing home in Boston to be closer to my sisters. In March 2017, she took a turn for the worse. My dear Dorrie is now under hospice care.

EPILOGUE

Eighteen months after Alan died, I found myself on a plane to Boston to comfort my sister Maryann. Her husband Mort had died suddenly in his sleep at only sixty-one.

I remembered all the things people said to me when I was widowed. Their comments were well-meant, but they usually didn't help, and often left me angry and upset.

Maryann had been so incredibly supportive and helpful to my family and me during our time of need, so I wanted to offer her the benefit of my experience. I wanted to tell her something that would make sense. This is what I wrote to her during the flight.

> Dear Maryann,
>
> Remember when your kids were young and you counted everything in months? I remember being with Alan at a friend's house when Miles was a toddler and overhearing, "He started sitting up at four months, can you believe it?" or "She smiled at me at three months. Isn't she advanced?"
>
> Well, when one is grieving, time seems to be measured in the same way. It's been eighteen months since Alan died, and we are just starting to get used to our new normal.
>
> You are going to go through a rollercoaster of emotions. You're going to be OK one minute, and the next, crying uncontrollably for no apparent reason. Your bad days are going to outnumber your good days at first, and you are going to be angry. I mean really angry. Angry at God, angry at the sight of couples, angry at whole families.
>
> It's like you'll have a grenade inside of you that explodes every time you see a family with a mother, father, and their kids.
>
> But no one will see this. Because while you look strong on the outside, inside you are crumbling.
>
> You're going to feel you have been cheated. No more planning where you will retire together, no more planning what to do for the kids' next spring break. It's all gone, simply vanished.
>
> What will be left are the wonderful memories you shared with one another and with his children. His DNA in beautiful life forms.

These incredible children the two of you made together are now your sole responsibility. Cherish them, because they are going to guide you and will be the lifeline that pulls you from your river of despair.

Welcome to the club no one wants to be in. Welcome, widow sister.

ACKNOWLEDGMENTS

I have been trying for nearly three years to write this book. It was so hard in the beginning, and it was never easy at the end. Sometimes, I didn't want to revisit my pain. Other times, I couldn't escape it. But I can honestly say now that I am proud of the journey I've taken, and I am so thankful for the people who have helped me bring my story to life.

At every turn, my three beautiful, wonderful children—Miles, Nathaniel, and Ella—gave me the strength to put one foot in front of the other. They have been my encouragement and inspiration from the beginning.

Uncle Arthur and Aunt Marlene have been my rock and given me and my children endless support. They sat beside me in my darkest hours and through their gentle encouragement guided me to the light.

I'm so grateful to my big sisters. Maryann and Caroline gave me unfailing support, kept me grounded, and made me laugh at times when all I wanted to do was cry.

Also, my father, Jay Thompson, and his significant other Geri, for being there when I couldn't be everywhere at the same time.

To the Saffrans—Uncle Sy, Aunt Roberta, Grandma Dolores, Uncle Bruce, and Aunt Elaine—many, many thanks for your support.

Thank you to Alan's cousins Michelle, Jill, Jenny, Mindy, and Jason for keeping me and the kids close in our time of need.

I can't thank enough my priceless friends Cia, the Rohs, Samantha Kearns O'Lenick, the Pohls, the Shader Smiths, the Mendelsohns, the Bibliowiczes, the Hills, and my tennis teammates for their support.

My editor, Alex Beasley, was incredible. I was in such good hands. His faith in me, his friendship, and, above all, his deft command of the language made this possible.

Hannah Forman and Miki Hickel guided me along the process of publishing this book and added the finishing touches.

Endless thanks to Judy Watson Tracy, whose photography made me and my book look better than I could have ever hoped!

Above all, I want to thank my beloved husband, Alan. Every day I could hear him whispering encouragement in my ear. He inspires me to be a better person, to embrace life, never take things for granted, and to continue to live in his honor. Alan...you will never be forgotten. Your legacy lives on in your kids and the beautiful memories we had together. There is not a day that goes by that I don't ask myself, "What would Alan do?"

ABOUT THE AUTHOR

Pam Saffran grew up in Cincinnati in a house alive with the laughter and mischief of four young girls. While her father, Jay, wanted Pam and her sisters to be good at many pursuits, her mother, Dorrie, had a different approach. She insisted that her daughters pursue their strengths. For Pam, that was tennis.

Every summer, starting when she was eleven, Pam attended the famed Nick Bollettieri tennis camp in Florida. The training paid off. Pam was a two-time All-American in women's tennis at Skidmore College in New York and named New York State Female Athlete of The Year. In 2007, Pam was inducted into the Skidmore Hall of Fame.

Pam has a bachelor's degree in psychology from Skidmore and a master's in counseling from Rollins College's Graduate School of Counseling in Winter Park, Florida. She is a Licensed Mental Health Counselor in Florida and recognized by the National Board for Certified Counselors.

Pam, fifty-one, lives in Winter Park–near Orlando–where she is raising her three children as a solo parent. Her two sons are away at college. Miles, the oldest, is a junior at Yale. His brother, Nat, is a freshman at Columbia University. He's a pre-med student, following in Alan's footsteps. Her daughter, Ella, is in middle school. The family's Peekapoo, Teddy, has the run of the house.

CONTACT INFORMATION

Website: http://pamsaffran.com

Facebook: https://www.facebook.com/ListeningforEchoes/

Twitter: https://twitter.com/pamsaff

HELP & RESOURCES

PANCREATIC CANCER SUPPORT & RESEARCH

Pancreatic Cancer Action Network
https://www.pancan.org

American Cancer Society
https://www.cancer.org/cancer/pancreatic-cancer.html

National Pancreatic Cancer Foundation
http://www.npcf.us

GRIEF SUPPORT

GreifNet.org
http://www.griefnet.org

Hello Grief (for children, teens, and adults)
http://www.hellogrief.org

Hospice Foundation of America (HFA)
https://hospicefoundation.org

National Widowers' Organization
http://www.nationalwidowers.org

BRAIN ANEURYSM SUPPORT

Brain Aneurysm Foundation
http://www.bafound.org

Brain Aneurysm Support Community
http://www.bafsupport.org